INDEX

Jan-July 2018

Current Affairs Roundup 2019

for All Competitive Exams

Events | People
Ideas | Issues

Covers :
• Timeline-National/ International
• Bills, Acts, Policies, Schemes & Summits
• Economy/ Banking/ Environment
updates

- **Corporate Office :** 45, 2nd Floor, Maharishi Dayanand Marg, Corner Market, Malviya Nagar, New Delhi-110017
  Tel. : 011-49842349 / 49842350

Access Code : Scratch the label gently

INSTRUCTIONS

1. Go to **www.educoreonline.com/register.htm**
2. Enter your details along with your 16 digit Access Code.
3. Click Register and you would be successfully redirected to the Login Page.
   Note: If you are already registered with us, you just have to login **(http://www.educoreonline.com/login.htm)** and enter your new 16 Character Unique Code under your Account Section.
4. Login with your registered email ID and password.
5. You can now view you free e-books under your Library.
6. You can read your e-books either Online or Offline. To read the e-books offline, simply download our Educore App and download the e-books inside the app. Educore App is available for Windows Desktop, iOS and Android.
   Note: You need to be connected to the Internet to run the interactive tests.
7. You are also welcome to visit our store **www.educoreonline.com** for your future purchases.
8. Contact us at **support@educoreonline.com** for any further assistance.

For further information about books from DISHA,

Log on to **www.dishapublication.com** or email to **info@dishapublication.com**

AT A GLANCE 2018

	Social	Economy	Polity
NATIONAL			
April	MS Dhoni conferred with Padma Bhushan; Kerala lifts Santosh Trophy beating WB	RBI directs banks to stop services to businesses dealing in virtual currencies RBI directs bBanks to stop services to businesses dealing in virtual currencies	All BJP ministers in J & K resign over Kathua rape case
	Delhi becomes the first Indian city to introduce BS-VI; 65th National Film Awards held	CCEA approves restructured National Bamboo Mission	Congress-led opposition presses charges for CJI impeachment; rejected by Rajya Sabha chairman
	Vinod Khanna post-humously honoured with Dadasaheb Phalke Award	CSIR wins National Intellectual Property (IP) Award 2018	Sitaram Yechury re-elected as CPI(M) general secretary
	Gujarati poet Sitanshu Yashaschandra chosen for 2017 Saraswati Samman	RBI eases External borrowing norms to enable cheaper funds	Sikkim's Pawan Chamling becomes India's longest-serving chief minister
May	Chennai Super Kings Wins IPL 2018 against Sunrisers Hyderabad	Union Cabinet approves ordinance to amend Insolvency and Bankruptcy Code	Karnatka Assembly elections 2018; BJP emerges single largest party, Congress second
	Samagra Shiksha scheme for school education from pre-school to senior secondary levels launched	India ranked the 6th wealthiest country in the world - The AfrAsia Bank Global Wealth Migration Review	JD (S)'s Kumaraswamy becomes Chief Minister of Karnatka

	Zojila tunnel project in Leh inaugurated by PM; Nipah Virus outbreak causes 14 deaths in Kerala	TCS becomes first company to achieve 7 lakh crore market capitalisation mile-stone	UP government asks ex-CMs to vacate bungalows in 15 days
	Gender discrimination kills 239000 girls each year in India: Lancet study	Core industries register 4.7% growth in April 2018	By-elections 2018: 4 Lok Sabha, 10 Assembly seats go for polls
June	Farmers' organisations begin 10-day 'gaon bandh'	Insolvency and Bank-ruptcy Code (Amend-ment) Ordinance, 2018 Promulgated	RLD wins Kairana bypoll, SP Noorpur assembly seat, RJD wrested Jokihat assembly seat; BJP wins Palghar
	Reservations in Promotions: Centre gets go ahead from SC	RBI hikes Repo Rate to 6.25%; Rs. 8500 Crore Bailout Package for Sugar Industry Approved	AAP-LG standoff: Delhi CM Arvind Kejriwal ends dharna at Raj Niwas
	Pradhan Mantri Awas Yojana (Urban): Govt approves construction of 1.5 lakh affordable houses .... currentaffairs. gktoday.in/page/12 © GKToday	RBI allows Urban Co-operative Banks to become Small Finance Banks	Madras HC appoints third judge to decide on AIADMK MLAs' disquali-fication after split verdict
	PM promises farmers income doubling by 2022	RBI revises housing loan limits under Priority Sector Lending	Mehbooba Mufti resigns after BJP pulls out of alliance with PDP in Jammu & Kashmir; Governor's rule in J&K

	Social	Economy	Polity
INTERNATIONAL			
April	Prof. Robert Langlands gets the Abel Prize	Redenomination of Venezuelan currency announced	Abdel Fattah el-sisir re-elected as the Egyptian president
	The XXI Commonwealth Games inaugurated in Gold Coast, Australia	Free trade bloc for Africa launched by AfCFTA	Martin Vizcarra sworn in as Peru's president; Win Myint elected as Myanmar's president
	India ranks 138th in World Press Freedom Index 2018; Mary Kom wins gold at CW Games 2018	India becomes world's sixth largest economy: IMF	Abiye Ahmed elected as Prime Minister of Ethiopia; Turkey hosts critical summit on Syria with Russia and Iran
	India-China Informal Summit held in Wuhan	Fitch retains India's sovereign rating at 'BBB-' with 'stable' outlook	Kim Jong-un & Moon Jae-in shake hands at the truce village of Panmunjom
May	Polish author Olga Tokarczuk wins Man Booker International prize 2018	Walmart buys 77 percent stake in Flipkart	Venezuelan President Nicolas Maduro re-elected Venezuelan President Nicolas Maduro re-elected
	Forbes World's Most Powerful People list 2018: PM Modi ranked 9th, Xi Jinping tops	India tops list of fastest growing economies for coming decade: Harvard study	Vladimir Putin sworn in as Russian President for fourth time; US opens new embassy in Jerusalem
	Trump announces US withdrawal from Iran nuclear deal	India's economy is projected to grow 7.6% in 2018-19: UN WESP	Mahathir Mohamad sworn in as Malaysia's seventh Prime Minister
	India is fifth largest military spender in the world: SIPRI	5th India-CLMV Busi-ness Conclave held at Phnom Penh, Cambodia	Ex-Chief Justice Nasirul Mulk named as care-taker PM of Pakistan

June	India's Current Maternal Mortality Ratio is 130 per 10000 live births in 2016	Pradhan Mantri Gram Sadak Yojana: Govt inks $500 million loan agreement with World Bank	India, Japan, US: Malabar Exercise 2018 to be held off coast of Guam in Philippine Sea
	Friendship Medal: China awards its first highest state honour to Russian President Vladimir Putin	India mulls new group of 8-10 countries in WTO	Trump and Kim Arrive in Singapore for Historic 'denuclearisation' Summit Meeting
	Global Peace Index 2018: India ranks 136th Iceland tops	FDI in India rises to US $61.96 billion in 2017-18: DIPP	Pedro Sanchez sworn in as Spain's Prime Minister
	The 2018 FIFA World Cup taking place in Russia	WB approved Water Resources and River Development Min's Rs 6000 crore scheme, 'Atal Bhujal Yojana'	United States withdraws from UN Human Rights Council due to bias against Israel

TIMELINE NATIONAL

January to June, 2018	
Ist January	India and Pakistan exchange list of nuclear sites for 27th consecutive year
2nd January	171st Araadhanai Music Festival begins in Tamil Nadu; Women & Child Development minister Maneka Gandhi inaugurates online portal NARI; Parliament passes Insolvency and Bankruptcy Code Amendment Bill, 2017; Lok Sabha passes Ancient Monuments and Archaeological Sites and Remains (Amendment) Bill, 2017;Parliament passes NABARD amendment bill,2017
3rd January	Cabinet approves establishment of new AIIMS at Bilaspur
4th January	The Cabinet Committee on Economic Affairs (CCEA) approves construction of bi-directional Zojila Tunnel in J&K
5th January	Government launches 7.75% Savings (Taxable) Bonds 2018
6th January	26th World Book Fair held in New Delhi with focus on environment
7th January	International Kite festival launched in Gujarat
9th January	Haryana becomes first state to launch High-Risk Pregnancy portal; The Pravasi Bharatiya Divas (PBD) is celebrated
10th January	The third meeting of Council of Trade Development and Promotion (CTDP) was held in New Delhi.
11th January	India misses 2017 deadline for Kala Azar elimination; The 4th International Dharma-Dhamma Conference was held at Rajgir in Nalanda district, Bihar
12th January	National Youth Festival held in New Delhi; The Union Ministry of Railways has launched Smart Freight Operation Optimisation & Real Time Information (SFOORTI) application
13th January	Fourth ASEAN-India Ministerial Meeting on Agriculture & Forestry held in Delhi

14th January	Kerala Government launches Kerala Accelerator Program for early-stage start-ups; 7th Rashtriya Sanskriti Mahotsav 2018 held in Karnataka
15th January	International Workshop on Disaster Resilient Infrastructure held in New Delhi; India ranks 30th on WEF's Global Manufacturing Index; India, Israel sign 9 agreements in space, defence, cybersecurity; India, Sri Lanka sign four agreements for collaboration in ICT sector
16th January	PM inaugurates Rajasthan's first oil refinery at Barmer; Government ends Haj subsidy
17th January	
18th January	PM Narendra Modi, Benjamin Netanyahu inaugurate iCREATE facility; Agni-5 ballistic missile successfully test-fired
19th January	India joins Australia Group export control regime; Government launches National CSR Data Portal & Corporate Data Portal
20th January	25th GST council meet held in New Delhi
21st January	Manipur Government launches health assurance scheme for poor & disabled people
23rd January	India ranked 62nd on WEF's Inclusive Development Index 2018; First International Dam Safety Conference held in Thiruvananthapuram
24th January	Tamil Nadu CM Edappadi K Palanichamy receives UNESCO Award; India, Vietnam sign two agreements
25th January	Government announces recipients of 2018 Padma awards
27th January	India-Japan Smart Grid Pilot Project inaugurated in Panipat
28th January	India, Lao PDR sign civil aviation cooperation agreement; India, Cambodia ink 4 pacts
30th January	Uttar Pradesh launches Mukhyamantri Awas Yojana Grameen; Soumitra Chatterjee presented with France's Legion d'Honneur

February 2018	
1st February	7th India Energy Congress begins in New Delhi; Finance Minister Arun Jaitley presented the Union Budget 2018-2019
2nd February	32nd Surajkund International Crafts Mela begins
3rd February	PM Modi inaugurates Assam-Global Investors Summit 2018; India won U-19 Cricket World Cup.
5th February	South Asia Region Public Procurement Conference held in New Delhi
6th February	Nuclear- capable Agni-I missile test fired successful
8th February	National Meet on Grassroot Informatics-VIVID 2018 held in New Delhi
9th February	ISRO sets up 473 Village Resource Centres for rural development through satellite technology
10th February	Renowned litterateur Chandrasekhar Rath passes away
12th February	Shikhar Dhawan becomes first Indian batsman to score century in 100th ODI
13th February	India-Russia Agriculture Business summit held in New Delhi
14th February	President Kovind inaugurates international conference 'Agricon-2018' in Kanpur
15th February	President of Iran, Hassan Rouhani was on three day visit to India from 15-17 February 2018
16th February	PM Modi inaugurates World Sustainable Development Summit in New Delhi
18th February	PM lays foundation stone of Navi Mumbai International airport
19th February	22nd edition of World Congress on Information Technology and 26th edition of Nasscom India Leadership Forum held in Hyderabad
20th February	Nuclear- capable Agni-II missile test-fired successfully; Cabinet approves six rail projects in 4 states
21st February	Odisha approves long term linkage policy for bauxite
23rd February	NITI Aayog to soon launch special cell for women entrepreneurs

24th February	India successfully test-fires nuclear capable 'Dhanush' missile
25th February	Union Government, ADB sign $ 84 million loan for expansion of water supply in Bihar
26th February	RBI launches Ombudsman Scheme for NBFCs, Sri Devi died.
27th February	Saudi Arabia allows women to enlist in military; UN Security Council adopts Russian-drafted resolution on Yemen sanctions
28th February	India ranked 47th in Inclusive Internet Index 2018
March 2018	
1st March	UIDAI launches blue coloured Baal Aadhaar; National Science Day 2018 observed across India
2nd March	Russia has called off strategic talks with the US set for this month
3rd March	Anti Tank Guided Missile NAG successfully test-fired
4th March	UDP extends support to NPP for government formation in Meghalaya
5th March	Union Cabinet approves Fugitive Economic Offenders Bill, 2018; NDA sweeps Nagaland and Tripura, split verdict in Meghalaya;
6th March	NPP's Conrad Sangma sworn-in as Chief Minister of Meghalaya
7th March	Sharp decline in child marriages in India: UNICEF
8th March	NITI Aayog launches Women Entrepreneurship Platform;
9th March	PM launches National Nutrition Mission and pan-India expansion of Beti Bachao Beti Padhao
11th March	Environment Ministry notifies rules to regulate the use of POPs
12th March	Supreme Court extends March 31 deadline for Aadhaar linking; Union Government forms Tribunal to solve Mahanadi Water Dispute
13th March	Lucknow's legendary Begum Hamida Habibullah dies at 102; The National Association of Software and Services Companies (NASSCOM) in association with Facebook launched "Design4India Studio" in Bengaluru.

14th March	Supreme Court bars foreign lawyers, law firms from practicing in India
15th March	Pune ranked first in ASICS urban governance survey, Bengaluru at bottom
16th March	Haryana Assembly passes bill proposing death penalty in rape of girls below 12 years
17th March	India's first cloned Assamese buffalo born
19th March	Lalu Prasad convicted in another fodder scam case
20th March	Karnataka Government approves 'religious minority' status for Lingayats
21st March	SC directs Centre to frame model scheme for welfare of construction workers
22nd March	All pharmacies and chemists have to report TB cases: Government; UGC grants autonomy to 60 higher educational institutions
23rd March	Investigation necessary before arresting public servant under SC/ST law: SC
24th March	HC sets aside EC disqualification of 20 AAP MLAs, asks for fresh hearing; Rajya Sabha election result: BJP 68, Congress 54, TMC 13 in the Upper House
April 2018	
1st April	Delhi becomes first city to roll-out Euro VI fuel, Odisha Formation Day, India becomes world's second largest mobile phone producer: ICA, Inauguration of World-Class tourist amenities at Konark Sun Temple coincided with Utkal Diwas the foundation day of Odisha State, Kerala defeated West Bengal and won its sixth title in the 72nd Santosh Trophy (Football).
2nd April	India ranks 37th in global startup ecosystem in 2017: Report, Mukesh Ambani is Asia's third richest, five Indians in Bloomberg Billionaires top 100 Index, Mahendra Singh Dhoni was conferred the prestigious Padma Bhushan Award by President Ram Nath Kovind
3rd April	Arun Jaitley reappointed as Leader of Rajya Sabha
4th April	India third most vulnerable country to cyber threats (ISTR)

5th April	India pips Japan, becomes second largest manufacturer of crude steel,National Maritime day, RBI directs banks to stop services to businesses dealing in virtual currencies
6th April	India ranks 9th globally in cryptojacking activities, Chhattisgarh awarded 'State of the Year'
7th April	Assam Spring Festival organised at Manas National Park, Indian tennis ace Leander Paes won Davis Cup which is his 43rd win
8th April	The Dadasaheb Phalke Excellence Award for 2018 is being awarded to Bollywood actor Anushka Sharma
9th April	8th Theatre Olympics concludes in Mumbai, SBI to invest ₹ 80 bn in hydropower project of Nepal, Four kingfisher bird species thriving in Krishna Wildlife Sanctuarya
10th April	Vice President inaugurates "Scientific Convention on World Homoeopathy Day"
11th April	Delhi's IGI Airport ranked among World's Top 20 Busiest Airports, Asian Development Bank Noted that Indian economy will grow by 7.3% in FY'18, 7.6% in FW19
12th April	ISRO launched the navigation satellite IRNSS-II, Ace shuttler Kidambi Srikanth becomes World No 1
13 April	Dharmendra to receive Raj Kapoor Lifetime Achievement award, India's Heena Sidhu won a gold medal in the 10m air pistol category at the International Shooting Competitions of Hannover (ISCH)
14th April	Kohli and Mithali voted world's best cricketers: Wisden's leading cricketers of the year
15th April	India 3rd largest solar market in world: Mercom
16th April	Vinod Khanna post-humously honoured with Dadasaheb Phalke Award
17th April	Guwahati has India's first railway station run by solar power
18th April	Smriti Irani launches GNFC's Neem project in UP
19th April	Taipei World Trade Centre opens in Delhi
20th April	First International SME Small, Medium Enterprises) Convention 2018 to be held in New Delhi

21st April	Indian women make a clean sweep at 8th South Asian Judo Championship in Nepal
22nd April	Sitaram Yechury re-elected as CPI(M) general secretary
23th April	Congress-led opposition presses charges for CJI impeachment; rejected by Rajya Sabha chairman
24th April	Mohamed Salah Crowned PFA Player Of The Year
25th April	CCEA approves restructured National Bamboo Mission
27th April	Dalmia Bharat Limited has signed a MoU with the Tourism Ministry to take up Red Fort and Gandikota Fort (Andhra Pradesh) under the 'Adopt a Heritage' project.
28th April	RBI eases External borrowing norms to enable cheaper funds
30th April	Sikkim's Pawan Chamling becomes India's longest-serving chief minister
May 2018	
1st May	Maharashtra Day and Gujarat Diwas
2nd May	Maharashtra became the first state to provide digitally-signed land record receipts, Bilateral trade between India and China resumes through Nathu La border
3rd May	India's Neeraj Goyat is WBC Asia Boxer of the Year, Pakyong airport in Sikkim to become the 100th functional airport in India
4th May	FDI Confidence Index 2018: India ranks 11th, Sachin Tendulkar, Anurag Thakur launch 'Khel Mahakumbh'
5th May	First organized census of Indus Dolphins begins in Punjab, ADB projects India's growth at 7.3% in 2018 at the 51st ADB Annual Meeting
6th May	India among top 5 defence spenders: SIPRI Report
7th May	SRO develops atomic clock for the indigenous navigation satellites
9th May	Narendra Modi Among Top 10 Most Powerful People In The World: Forbes

11th May	National Technology Day
14th May	inauguration International Children's Film Festival Of Kerala
15th May	Gender discrimination kills 239000 girls each year in India: Lancet study
17th May	BSE becomes first Indian stock exchange to get US SEC's DOSM recognition
18th May	Tripura reserves 10% police posts for women
19th May	Nipah Virus outbreak causes 14 deaths in Kerala
20th May	India ranked the 6th wealthiest country in the world - The AfrAsia Bank Global Wealth Migration Review
21st May	Bhushan Steel Acquisition By Tata Steel
23rd May	Union Cabinet approves ordinance to amend Insolvency and Bankruptcy Code, JD (S)'s Kumaraswamy becomes Chief Minister of Karnatka
24th May	Samagra Shiksha scheme for school education from pre-school to senior secondary levels launched
25th May	TCS becomes first company to achieve 7 lakh crore market capitalisation mile-stone
26th May	Narendra Modi laid the foundation stone for the 2400MW first phase of NTPC's Patratu Super Thermal Power Project in Jharkhand
27th May	Chennai Super Kings Wins IPL 2018 against Sunrisers Hyderabad , Nipah Virus outbreak causes 14 deaths in Kerala
28th May	By-elections 2018: 4 Lok Sabha, 10 Assembly seats go for polls
29th May	Cochin International Airport world's first fully solar energm) owered airport: UNEP
30th May	FB set to launch WhatsApp Pay with 4 major banks (HDFC,ICICI,AXIS & SBI) in India
31st May	Core industries register 4.7% growth in April 2018

June 2018	
1st June	Farmers' organisations begin 10-day 'gaon bandh'
3rd June	"Pradhan Mantri Awas Yojana (Urban): Govt approves construction of 1.5 lakh affordable houses
5th June	RLD wins Kairana bypoll, SP Noorpur assembly seat, RJD wrested Jokihat assembly seat; BJP wins Palghar
6th June	Reservations in Promotions: Centre gets go ahead from SC
7th June	Insolvency and Bankruptcy Code (Amendment) Ordinance, 2018 Promulgated
8th June	RBI hikes Repo Rate to 6.25%
9th June	RBI allows Urban Co-operative Banks to become Small Finance Banks
12th June	₹ 8500 Crore Bailout Package for Sugar Industry Approved
15th June	Cabinet approves withdrawal of Nalanda University (Amendment) Bill, 2013
16th June	RBI revises housing loan limits under Priority Sector Lending
16th June	India to host European Union Film Festival
17th June	TCS becomes first Company to close over ₹ 7 Trillion Market Cap
18th June	Madras HC appoints third judge to decide on AIADMK MLAs' disqualification after split verdict
18th June	Union Cabinet approves proposal for enactment of Dam Safety Bill, 2018
19th June	Mehbooba Mufti resigns after BJP pulls out of alliance with PDP in Jammu & Kashmir; Governor's rule in J&K
20th June	AAP-LG standoff: Delhi CM Arvind Kejriwal ends dharna at Raj Niwas
21st June	PM promises farmers income doubling by 2022
23rd June	PM Modi to inaugurate AIIB Annual Meeting 2018

TIMELINE INTERNATIONAL

January to June, 2018	
Ist January	Saudi Arabia, UAE introduce VAT for first time
2nd January	China develops underwater surveillance networks in Indian Ocean, South China Sea
3rd January	Six countries enter United Nations Security Council; Pakistan successfully tests Herba missile
4th January	India excludes Pakistan from SAARC initiative
5th January	US puts Pakistan on Special Watch List for severe violations of religious freedom; NASA to launch two missions — GOLD and ICON to explore the ionosphere
9th January	SpaceX has launched secret Zuma Mission for US government
12th January	China has announced to provide financial support to construct counter-terrorism base in Badakshan province of northern Afghanistan
13th January	Nepal starts receiving internet connection from China
15th January	NASA discovers farthest known galaxy in the universe "SPT0615-JD"
17th January	China builds world's biggest air purifier in Xian
18th January	10th Global Forum for Food & Agriculture held in Berlin
19th January	China launches 2 remote sensing satellites;
20th January	Mercedes-Benz first to launch locally-made BS-VI-compliant car
24th January	Paul Romer resigned from his position as the World Bank's chief
26th January	Chinese scientists for first time successfully clone monkeys
28th January	The World Leprosy Day is observed internationally
29th January	Swiss tennis player Roger Federer (World No. 2) has retained his Men's Singles title by winning 2018 Australian Open
30th January	US lifts ban on refugees from 11 "High Risk" countries
31st January	United Arab Emirates opens world's longest zip line

February 2018	
2nd February	India joins Ashgabat agreement; China launches electromagnetic satellite to study earthquake precursors
5th February	Saudi Arabia allows woman to start business without male permission
6th February	SpaceX launches "Falcon Heavy"- world most powerful rocket towards Mars
7th February	Bangladesh elects Abdul Hamid as president for seond consecutive term
9th February	Olympic winter games started at Pyeongchang in South Korea; PM Modi's 3 Nation visit to Palestine, UAE and Oman
11th February	Gevora, the world's tallest hotel, opens in Dubai; Sixth World Government Summit held in Dubai
14th February	Jacob Zuma resigned from his position as South Africa's President
16th February	Munich Security Conference begins in Germany
18th February	Tropical cyclone Kelvin hits West Australia
19th February	Pakistan approves Mandarin as one of its three official languages; Israel successfully tests Arrow-3 advanced missile defence system
20th February	India to host World Environment Day 2018; India 12th worst nation for newborns: UNICEF Report
22nd February	India successfully conducts night trial of Prithvi-II missile
23rd February	India ranks 81st in global corruption perception index
24th February	India successfully test-fires nuclear capable 'Dhanush' missile
25th February	Union Government, ADB sign $ 84 million loan for expansion of water supply in Bihar
26th February	Michael McCormack named as Australia's new Deputy Prime Minister
27th February	Saudi Arabia allows women to enlist in military
28th February	Tokyo 2020 Olympics mascots unveiled

March 2018	
1st March	World Rare Disease Day observed
2nd March	Zero Discrimination Day 2018 observed globally
3rd March	China proposes removal of 2-term limit for President
4th March	World Wildlife Day 2018 observed across the world
5th March	Oscars 2018: 'The Shape of Water' won maximum awards
6th March	Ethnic cleansing of Rohingya continue: UN; North Korea seeks to ease military tensions with South in historic meeting
7th March	Forbes' 32nd World's Billionaires List released: Jeff Bezos tops list for first time
8th March	India, Pakistan agree to release elderly, women and child prisoners
9th March	Myanmar's Aung San Suu Kyi stripped of human rights award
10th March	Oscars 2018: 'The Shape of Water' won maximum awards
11th March	India and France sign 14 MoUs during visit of French President Emmanuel
12th March	Divorced Saudi mothers can now retain custody of children
13th March	Legendary French fashion designer Hubert de Givenchy dies at 91
14th March	Renowned physicist Stephen Hawking passed away at the age of 76;
15th March	Google launches Google assistance in Hindi
16th March	Qatar donates $50 million to UN Relief agency for Palestinians
17th March	India, ADB sign $120 million loan to improve rail infrastructure
18th March	Singapore, Paris are world's costliest cities; Chennai, Bangalore among cheapest
19th March	India clinches Nidahas Trophy in last-ball thriller; Li Keqiang re-elected as Prime Minister of China for second term
20th March	Russia blocks UN Security Council meeting on human rights in Syria

21st March	Facebook CEO Mark Zuckerberg apologised for the data debacle
22nd March	India, Hong Kong sign double taxation avoidance agreement
23rd March	John R Bolton appointed as new National Security Adviser to US President Donald Trump
24th March	Global carbon emissions hit record high in 2017: IEA Report

April 2018	
1st April	US, South Korea begin "Foal Eagle drill" army drills amid diplomatic thaw, China's Tiangong-1 (English translation - "Heavenly Palace") space station is set to re-enter the Earth's atmosphere between 1st and 2nd April 2018.
2nd April	World Autism Awareness Day, Abdel Fattah el-sisir re-elected as the Egyptian president, Martin Vizcarra sworn in as Peru's president; Win Myint elected as Myanmar's president
3rd April	Turkey launches construction of first-ever nuclear plant, 7th Moscow Conference will start on 4th April
4th April	Commonwealth Games 2018 starts at Gold Coast in Australia, International Day for Mine Awareness and Assistance in Mine Action, Qatar introduces national service for women
5th April	Global Logistics Summit held in New Delhi
6th April	Qatar introduces national service for women
7th April	World Health Day,
8th April	United Arab Emirates (UAE) and Malaysia concluded joint military exercise "Desert Tiger 5"
9th April	Singapore and China signed MoU along the Belt and Road Initiative (BRI)
10th April	1200-year-old Buddha cliff carvings found in Tibet
11th April	First International conference on Water, Environment held in Kathmandu
12th April	World's first long-distance electric bus line to begin in Paris
13th April	India becomes world's sixth largest economy: IMF
14th April	India, Russia sign seven MoU at Defence expo, Bisket Jatra being celebrated in Nepal

15th April	UN launches road safety trust fund
16th April	US, Nigeria hold military summit in Abuja
17th April	World Haemophilia Day
18th April	India wins six elections to UN Economic and Social Council bodies,World Heritage Day
19th April	Red Bull's Daniel Ricciardo wins 2018 Chinese Grand Prix
20th April	Malaria Summit held in London, G-20 Finance Ministers and Central Bank Governors (FMCBG) Meeting held in Washington D.C.
21st April	Swaziland King changes his country's name to 'Kingdom of eSwatini'
22nd April	World Earth Day,Kyrgyzstan forms new government headed by president ally
23rd April	Rafael Nadal wins 31st Monte Carlo Masters Title
24th April	Iran bans banks from using cryptocurrencies
25th April	Six countries that have suspended their membership from UNASUR are Argentina, Brazil, Chile, Colombia, Paraguay and Peru
26 April	India ranks 138th in World Press Freedom Index 2018; Mary Kom wins gold at CW Games 2018
27th April	Fitch retains India's sovereign rating at 'BBB-' with 'stable' outlook, Kim Jong-un & Moon Jae-in shake hands at the truce village of Panmunjom
28th April	India-China Informal Summit held in Wuhan
29th April	Abiye Ahmed elected as Prime Minister of Ethiopia; Turkey hosts critical summit on Syria with Russia and Iran
30th April	International Buddhist Conference held in Lumbini, Nepal
May 2018	
1st May	World Labour day
2nd May	India has joined the United States and China as one of the world's five biggest military spenders

3rd May	World Press Freedom Day, World Tuna Day, China launches "APSTAR-6C" satellite to provide transmission across Asia-Pacific region
4th May	India is fifth largest military spender in the world: SIPRI, India tops list of fastest growing economies for coming decade: Harvard study
5th Day	NASA launches InSight spacecraft to Mars to study Red Planet's quakes
6th May	US opens new embassy in Jerusalem
7th May	Vladimir Putin sworn in as Russian President for fourth time
8th May	Trump announces US withdrawal from Iran nuclear deal, ,World Red Cross Day
9th May	Mahathir Mohamad sworn in as Malaysia's seventh Prime Minister
10th May	Forbes World's Most Powerful People list 2018: PM Modi ranked 9th, Xi Jinping tops
11th May	SpaceX launches most powerful Falcon 9 rocket, carrying Bangladesh's first communication satellite
12th May	World Migratory Bird Day
14th May	Walmart buys 77 percent stake in Flipkart
15th May	Chinese State-Run Bank Launches India-Dedicated Investment Fund
16th May	WHO launches 'REPLACE' to eliminate trans fat in foods by 2023
17th May	India's economy is projected to grow 7.6% in 2018-19: UN WESP
18th May	International Museum Day
19th May	71st Cannes Festival is held in Cannes
20th May	26th BASIC Ministerial meeting of Environment Ministers in Durban
21st May	Venezuelan President Nicolas Maduro re-elected Venezuelan President Nicolas Maduro re-elected
22nd May	First informal Summit between India and Russia held in the city of Sochi

23rd May	Polish author Olga Tokarczuk wins Man Booker International prize 2018,
24th May	5th India-CLMV Busi-ness Conclave held at Phnom Penh, Cambodia
25th May	International Missing Children's Day, World Thyroid Day
26th May	Columbia the first latin American nation to join NATO
27th May	Japan's women win the Uber Cup ahead of Asian Games : Bangkok
28th May	Ex-Chief Justice Nasirul Mulk named as care-taker PM of Pakistan
29th May	Azerbaijan inaugurates European gas pipeline
30th April	Facebook to offer digital literacy programme for women
31st May	World NO Tobacco day

June 2018

1st June	Pradhan Mantri Gram Sadak Yojana: Govt inks $500 million loan agreement with World Bank
2nd June	Pedro Sanchez sworn in as Spain's Prime Minister
3rd June	WB approved Water Resources and River Development Min's ₹ 6000 crore scheme, 'Atal Bhujal Yojana'
6th June	India's Current Maternal Mortality Ratio is 130 per 10000 live births in 2016
7th June	FDI in India rises to US $61.96 billion in 2017-18: DIPP
8th June	Global Peace Index 2018: India ranks 136th Iceland tops
9th June	Friendship Medal: China awards its first highest state honour to Russian President Vladimir Putin
10th June	Trump and Kim Arrive in Singapore for Historic 'denuclearisation' Summit Meeting
12th June	India mulls new group of 8-10 countries in WTO
14th June	The 2018 FIFA World Cup taking place in Russia
14th June	World Blood Donor Day
14th June	US approves sale of AH-64E Apache attack helicopters to India

15th June	India, Japan, US: Malabar Exercise 2018 to be held off coast of Guam in Philippine Sea
18th June	US President Donald Trump orders US Military to form 'Space Force'
21st June	United States withdraws from UN Human Rights Council due to bias against Israel
22nd June	World's first International Centre for Humanitarian Forensics launched in Gujarat
22nd June	World's hungry population on rise again due to conflict, climate change: UN report
23rd June	Mongolia launches construction of its first oil refinery with $1 billion Indian aid

CARRIE LAM SWORN IN AS FIRST FEMALE CHIEF EXECUTIVE OF HONG KONG

JULY 3, 2017

Carrie Lam was sworn in as the first female Chief Executive (CE) of the Hong Kong Special Administrative Region (HKSAR), an autonomous territory of China on the Pearl River Delta.

The CE of Hong Kong is the head and representative of the Hong Kong and also head of the Government of Hong Kong.

Carrie Lam took her oath to office before Chinese President Xi Jinping on the occasion marking 20th anniversary of Hong Kong's return to China from Britain. She is fifth CE of Hong Kong since it became part of China in 1997.

Prior to getting elected as CE, she was the Chief Secretary for Administration of Hong Kong SAR Government (from 2012 to 2017), the senior most rank of principal officials of Hong Kong.

RAM NATH KOVIND ELECTED AS INDIA'S 14TH PRESIDENT

JULY 20, 2017

Former governor Ram Nath Kovind was elected as India's 14th President. He will be only the second Dalit leader after K R Narayanan since Independence to occupy India's highest ceremonial post.

In the final vote count, NDA nominee Kovind received 65.6% votes translating into 702,044 Electoral College votes, while UPA candidate Meira Kumar managed to get 34.35% (367,314 votes). 522 MPs voted for Kovind, while 225 parliamentarians voted for Meira Kumar. In the last Presidential polls held in 2012, Pranab Mukherjee had defeated PA Sangma by over 69% votes.

INDIA PLACED 88TH IN MONEY HOARDING IN SWISS BANKS

JULY 4, 2017

As per analysis of the latest figures compiled by the Zurich based SNB (Swiss National Bank) as on 2016-end, India has slipped to the 88th place in terms of money parked by its citizens with Swiss banks.

The analysis shows that the money officially held by Indians with banks in Switzerland now accounts for a meager 0.04% of the total funds kept by all foreign clients in the Swiss banking system.

The latest data from the SNB comes ahead of a new framework for automatic exchange of information signed between Switzerland and India to help check the black money menace. The funds mentioned are the official figures and do not indicate the quantum of black money.

INDIA RANKED 96TH IN FIFA RANKINGS

JULY 6, 2017

As per the updated FIFA world football rankings, the Indian national football has managed to secure the 96th spot moving up four places. Earlier, India was placed at the 100th position. This is the best ranking secured by India in 21 years. India had ranked 101st in the FIFA rankings for April. The current ranking is far better off than the 173rd rank secured in March 2015. Since the beginning of the world ranking system, India has been averaging at the 134th rank. In 1996, India managed to secure the 94th spot. Till date, it remains the country's best ever FIFA ranking.

At present, Germany leads the rankings. Germany is followed by Brazil, Argentina, Portugal, and Switzerland in the rankings. Among Asian countries, Iran leads at No. 23.

HARINDER PAL SANDHU WON SOUTH AUSTRALIAN OPEN SQUASH TITLE

JULY 8, 2017

India's Harinder Pal Sandhu has defeated Rhys Dowling of Australia 11-8 12-10 11-4 to lift South Australian Open squash title. This will be Sandhu's first PSA tournament victory in Australia. South Australian Open squash title is on the Professional Squash Association (PSA) international circuit.

This victory will be Sandhu's third this season after winning two in Malaysia in May. Overall, this will be Sandhu's eight title win at the PSA level. He had also managed to reach the quarterfinals of the Asian Individual Squash Championship in Chennai in April.

INDIA WILL HOST 8TH INTERNATIONAL THEATRE OLYMPICS IN 2018

JULY 14, 2017

India for the first time will host 8th International Theatre Olympics, the greatest carnival of theatre in the world in 2018. The 51-day carnival of theatre will begin on February 17, 2018.

The mega international event will be organized by the National School of Drama (NSD) in coordination with the Union Culture Ministry.

The 2018 Theatre Olympics will showcase best of the theatre productions from around the world. Besides, it will provide India an opportunity to showcase the richness and diversity of its culture to the world. It will host about 500 shows from across the world in 15 different cities across India including Delhi, Mumbai, Bengaluru, Kolkata and Chennai.

UNESCO PUT OLD CITY OF HEBRON ON ITS HERITAGE IN DANGER LIST

JULY 7, 2017

The UNESCO World Heritage Committee acting on a proposal brought by Palestine has put the West Bank city of Hebron on its list of world heritage in danger. This has made Israel angry and has triggered a new Israeli-Palestinian spat at the international body.

NGT BANNED NYLON, SYNTHETIC MANJA

JULY 12, 2017

The National Green Tribunal (NGT) has imposed nationwide blanket ban on the use of kite strings (manja), made of nylon or any synthetic material on the grounds that it poses a threat to animals and humans.

The judgment of Tribunal came on a plea filed by animal rights body People for Ethical Treatment of Animals (PETA) and others.

INDIA'S FIRST SOLAR POWERED DEMU TRAIN LAUNCHED

JULY 14, 2017

Indian Railways has launched India's first solar powered diesel multiple unit (DEMU) broad gauge train. It is 1600 Horse Power (HP) train with all solar powered coaches.

The train will run from Sarai Rohilla in Delhi to Farukh Nagar in Haryana. It will replace an existing non-solar powered rake on the same route.

1 JULY: WORLD POPULATION DAY

JULY 11, 2017

The World Population Day is observed across the world on July 11 to attention on the urgency and importance of population issue. Observance of the day aims at increase people's awareness on various population issues such as the importance of family planning, maternal health, gender equality, poverty and human rights.

2017 theme: *"Family Planning- Empowering People, Developing Nations"*. The theme highlights importance of family planning as it allows people to attain their desired number of children and determine the spacing of pregnancies.

INDIA, US AND JAPAN NAVIES KICKED OFF 2017 MALABAR EXERCISE

JULY 10, 2017

India, Japan and United States (US) navies have kicked off 2017 MALABAR trilateral naval Exercise near Chennai in Bay of Bengal. This year it is the 21st edition of the naval exercise.

In this edition of the exercise, total of around 15 warships, two submarines and scores of fighter jets, surveillance aircraft and helicopters from three navies will take part.

ENGLAND WON 2017 ICC WOMEN'S WORLD CUP

JULY 24, 2017

England's women's cricket team won 2017 ICC World Cup title by defeating India by 9 runs at Lord's Cricket Ground in London. It was England's fourth Women's World Cup title. Besides the inaugural edition in 1973, England had won the World Cup in 1993 and 2009 as well.

In this edition of World Cup, Tammy Beaumont of England was awarded Player of the Series title. She had made most runs (410) in the tournament. Dane van Niekerk of South Africa took most wickets (15) in the tournament.

The 2017 Women's Cricket World Cup was the eleventh edition of the Cup since 1973, and the third to be held in England after 1973 and 1993 tournaments. Notably, it was India's second appearance in the Women's World Cup final, having lost to Australia in 2005.

ARVIND PANAGARIYA RESIGNED

AUGUST 1, 2017

Arvind Panagariya (64) has resigned as Vice Chairman of NITI (National Institution for Transforming India) Aayog and announced to return to academics in US.

He resigned after his public service leave for two years from the Columbia University, where he is professor of Indian Political Economy did not receive extension. He was appointed as the as Vice Chairman of NITI Aayog in January 2015 and held cabinet minister rank.

GOVERNMENT LAUNCHED E-RAKAM PORTAL

AUGUST 2, 2017

The Union Government has launched e-Rashtriya Kisan Agri Mandi (e-RaKAM) portal to provide a platform for farmers to sell agricultural produce.

e-RaKAM is a first of its kind initiative that leverages technology to connect farmers from the smallest villages to the biggest markets of the world through internet.

7 AUGUST: NATIONAL HANDLOOM DAY

AUGUST 7, 2017

The National Handloom Day is being observed every year on 7 August to honour the handloom weavers in the country and also carter an impetus to India's handloom industry. This year it was third edition of the National Handloom Day after it was instituted in 2015.

The celebration of the day seeks to highlight the contribution of handloom to the socioeconomic development of the country and promote handlooms to increase income of weavers and also enhance their pride.

INDIA RANKED 43RD IN GLOBAL RETIREMENT INDEX

AUGUST 9, 2017

India has been ranked at 43rd position in 2017 Global Retirement Index (GRI) published by French asset management company Natixis Global.

The index ranks 43 countries on the basis of four factors viz. the material means to live comfortably in retirement (Material Well-being); access to quality health services (Health); access to quality financial services to help preserve savings value and maximize income (Finances) and a clean and safe environment (Quality of Life).

75TH ANNIVERSARY OF QUIT INDIA MOVEMENT

AUGUST 9, 2017

The 75th anniversary of the Quit India Movement was observed across the country. This year's theme was *"Sankalp se Siddhi- the attainment through resolve"*.

Prime Minister Narendra Modi in his recent Mann Ki Baat programme had called for launching the mega campaign Sankalp Se Siddhi. The campaign pledges to build new India by 2022. It calls on everyone to pledge together towards Clean India, Poverty–free India, Corruption-free India, Terrorism-free India, Communalism-free India, Casteism-free India.

15TH BIMSTEC MINISTERIAL MEETING IN KATHMANDU

AUGUST 11, 2017

The 15th edition of Bay of Bengal Initiative for Multi-Sectoral Technical and Economic Cooperation (BIMSTEC) ministerial meeting was held in Kathmandu, Nepal.

The two-day meet was inaugurated by Prime Minister of Nepal Sher Bahadur Deuba and will be chaired by Deputy Prime Minister and Minister for Foreign Affairs Krishna Bahadur Mahara. India was represented by External Affairs Minister Sushma Swaraj.

MELBOURNE TOPPED IN 2017 EIU LIVEABILITY INDEX

AUGUST 17, 2017

According to the 2017 Global Liveability Report compiled by the Economist Intelligence Unit (EIU), Australian city Melbourne is the most liveable city in the world.

The EIU Liveability index scores 140 major cities of the world on the scale ranging from 0 (least liveable city) to 100 (most liveable city) based on healthcare, education, stability, culture, environment and infrastructure parameters. No Indian city was ranked in the top ten or bottom ten.

INDIA, NEPAL SIGNED 8 MOUS

AUGUST 24, 2017

India and Nepal have signed eight Memorandum of Understanding (MoUs) in various fields including Housing grant, prevention of drugs, and post-earthquake reconstruction packages in health and education sectors.

The agreements were inked after delegation level talks between Prime Minister Narendra Modi and his visiting Nepalese counterpart Sher Bahadur Deuba in New Delhi. The two leaders also jointly inaugurated the Kataiya-Kusaha and Raxaul-Parwanipur cross border Transmission lines.

INDIA-ASEAN YOUTH SUMMIT

AUGUST 14, 2017

The India-ASEAN Youth Summit began in Bhopal, Madhya Pradesh to commemorate 25th anniversary of Association of Southeast Asian Nations (ASEAN)–India dialogue partnership in the ongoing year.

The first of its kind event was organised by Union Foreign Ministry, Union Sports Ministry, Madhya Pradesh government and India Foundation.

ODISHA LAUNCHED ROOFTOP SOLAR PROJECT

AUGUST 24, 2017

Odisha Government has launched a grid-connected rooftop solar programme through net-metering system at the State Secretariat in capital city of Bhubaneswar.

The programme aims at harnessing renewable solar capacity through people's participation to further strengthen the grid and reduce power losses and benefit the public. It will also help state to targets in addressing the climate change action plan.

DIPAK MISRA SWORN IN AS CHIEF JUSTICE OF INDIA

AUGUST 28, 2017

Justice Dipak Misra (64) sworn in as the 45th Chief Justice of India (CJI). He was administered the oath of office by President Ram Nath Kovind at the Rashtrapati Bhawan.

He succeeds Chief Justice J S Khehar. He will have tenure of 14 months and will demit office in October 2018. He is third person from Odisha to be appointed the CJI, after Justices Ranganath Misra and G B Pattanaik.

SINDHU WON SILVER MEDAL 2017 WORLD BADMINTON CHAMPIONSHIP

AUGUST 28, 2017

Indian ace shuttler and 2017 Rio Olympic silver medallist PV Sindhu won the silver medal in 2017 World Badminton Championship held at Glasgow, Scotland (United Kingdom).

In the final match, Sindhu lost to Japan's Nozomi Okuhara by 19-21, 22-20, 20-22 score. Earlier, in Saina Nehwal had won bronze medal. This is for first time; Indian shutters have won two medals in the Championship.

It was overall Sindhu's third medal at the World Championships as she earlier had won bronze medals in 2013 and 2014 editions.

GOVERNMENT CLEARED 100% STRATEGIC SALE OF CEL

AUGUST 30, 2017

The Union Government (Department of Investment and Public Asset Management) has approved a 100% disinvestment through strategic sale along with transfer of management control of Central Electronics Ltd. (CEL).

CEL was incorporated as CPSE in 1974 under the administrative control of Ministry of Science and Technology. It is wholly owned by the government and has a net worth of ₹ 50.34 crore as on March 2017.

The government is planning to engage an advisor from a consulting firm, investment banker or financial institution or merchant banker for providing advisory services and managing the disinvestment process.

GUJARAT STATE, GCMMF DAIRIES SIGNED MOU

SEPTEMBER 8, 2017

The Women & Child Welfare Department of the Gujarat Government, Gujarat Milk Marketing Federation (GCMMF) and three leading dairies have signed a joint MOU to save Anganwadi children from malnutrition.

INDIA'S FIRST ADVANCED HOMOEOPATHY VIROLOGY LAB INAUGURATED

SEPTEMBER 13, 2017

The laboratory is established at a cost of Rs. 8 crore is the only one in India for conducting basic and fundamental research in Homoeopathy for viral diseases like influenza, Japanese encephalitis, dengue, chikungunya and swine flu. New drugs and technologies would also be developed at the laboratory to combat emerging challenges of viral diseases.

INDIA, JAPAN SIGNED MOU FOR EXPANSION OF BIOTECH LABORATORY

SEPTEMBER 14, 2017

India and Japan have signed a MoU for the expansion of an international laboratory set up for a collaborative research in the area of biotechnology. The agreement was signed after the delegation-level talks between visiting Japanese Prime Minister Shinzo Abe and Indian Prime Minister Narendra Modi.

GOOGLE'S DIGITAL PAYMENT APP 'TEZ' LAUNCHED

SEPTEMBER 18, 2017

Finance Minister Arun Jaitley launched Google's Unified Payments Interface (UPI)-based digital payment service called 'Tez'. The new digital payments app is expected to make a major change in the digital payments landscape in India. It would support several local languages including Hindi, Bengali, Gujarati, Kannada, Marathi, Tamil and Telugu.

INDIA REFUSED TO SIGN BALI DECLARATION OVER ROHINGYA ISSUE

SEPTEMBER 8, 2017

India reiterated its stance that the purpose of convening the Parliamentary forum was to arrive at mutual consensus for implementation of sustainable development goal, which requires inclusive and broad-based development processes.

UNION CABINET APPROVED OF 1 PER CENT DEARNESS ALLOWANCE

SEPTEMBER 13, 2017

The Cabinet gave its approval for release of additional 1 per cent Dearness Allowance (DA) to Central Government employees and Dearness Relief (DR) to pensioners with effect from 1 July 2017. The release of the additional 1 per cent instalment of DA over the existing rate of 4 per cent of the Basic Pay or Pension has been done to compensate for price rise.

HUMAN CAPITAL REPORT 2017

SEPTEMBER 14, 2017

The Index provides a means of measuring the quantifiable elements of the world's talent potential so that greater attention can be focused on delivering it. The Global Human Capital Index aims to provide a holistic assessment of a country's human capital—both current and expected—across its population. The Global Human Capital Index 2017 ranks 130 countries on how well they are developing and deploying their human capital potential.

ZSI RELEASED FIRST COMPENDIUM OF ANIMAL DIVERSITY

SEPTEMBER 13, 2017

The compendium is the first consolidated and updated information of the faunal diversity of the Sundarbans. It lists over 2600 species, including the new species described from the mangrove ecosystem as well as threats faced by them due to climate change. It catalogues the entire faunal diversity of Sundarban Biosphere Reserve covering 9630 square kilometres spread over 19 blocks in South 24 Parganas and North 24 Parganas of West Bengal.

'WOOD IS GOOD' CAMPAIGN LAUNCHED

SEPTEMBER 14, 2017

Union Minister of Environment, Forest and Climate Change, Harsh Vardhan launched the 'Wood is Good' campaign to promote wood as a climate-friendly resource and substitute to materials like steel and plastic, as it is a renewable resource, having zero carbon footprint, unlike other materials that leave carbon footprint in their production.

GATEWAY AWARDS 2017

SEPTEMBER 14, 2017

Jawaharlal Nehru Port Container Terminal (JNPCT) was awarded "Container Terminal of the Year" Award at the Gateway Awards 2017 that was held in Mumbai. The terminal owned by the Jawaharlal Nehru Port won the award for its proactive strategies to ease congestion, smooth delivery of containers and revamping of infrastructure to support trade amidst adverse conditions.

NATIONAL HINDI DIWAS 2017

SEPTEMBER 14, 2017

The day marks the adaptation of Hindi language as the official language of India by the Constituent Assembly of India on 14 September 1949. The decision of using Hindi as official language was ratified by Indian Constitution via amendment 343 which stated that all government communications will be penned in Hindi (Devanagari Script). This amendment came into effect on 26 January 1950.

INDIAN RAILWAYS PERMITTED M-AADHAAR AS ID PROOF

SEPTEMBER 14, 2017

The Ministry of Railways has decided to allow m-Aadhaar, a digital version of the Aadhaar card, as proof of identity for travellers in any reserved class.

The m-Aadhaar is a mobile app launched by the Unique Identification Authority of India (UIDAI) on which a person can download his/her Aadhaar card. It can, however, be downloaded only on the mobile number to which Aadhaar has been linked.

GOA WILL HOST 36TH NATIONAL GAMES

SEPTEMBER 14, 2017

The Indian Olympic Association (IOA) formally awarded the rights to host the 36th National Games to Goa. The National Games of India comprises various disciplines in which sportsmen from the different states of India participate against each other. The National Games were formerly known as the Indian Olympic Games. The first Modern National Games on the lines of the Olympics were held in 1985 in New Delhi.

Y C MODI APPOINTED AS DG OF NIA

SEPTEMBER 18, 2017

Y C Modi is an IPS officer of the 1979 batch of the Haryana cadre. He had also been part of a Supreme Court-appointed Special Investigation Team (SIT) that probed 2002 Gujarat riots case. He has also served as the Additional Director General of Police in Shillong, and Additional Director in the Central Bureau of Investigation (CBI).

GSTN REOPENED WINDOW FOR COMPOSITION SCHEME

SEPTEMBER 18, 2017

The facility for composition scheme was opened for taxpayers with a turnover of up to ₹ 75 lakh. These taxpayers will be allowed to be a part of the scheme, which offers easy compliance for business as returns are to be filed only quarterly, till 30 September 2017. The scheme was reopened to facilitate about 75 lakh registered businesses which opted for the scheme but failed to be a part of the scheme till 16 August 2017.

TRIPURA BECAME FIRST STATE TO SET UP DISTRICT FAMILY WELFARE COMMITTEES

SEPTEMBER 19, 2017

The district family welfare committees have been set up to deal with the issue of fake and biased complaints by women against their husbands, in-laws and husband's relatives. The decision to set up the committees came following an order of the Supreme Court to form such committees in all states.

UDAAN SCHEME IN J& K

SEPTEMBER 21, 2017

The Union Cabinet chaired by the Prime Minister Narendra Modi on 20 September 2017 approved Home Ministry's proposal for extension of the time period of the "Special Industry Initiative for J&K" - Udaan scheme till 31 December 2018 without any modification and cost escalation.

HIMACHAL PRADESH BECAME FIRST STATE TO LAUNCH ELECTRIC BUS SERVICE

SEPTEMBER 22, 2017

The Himachal Pradesh government has launched first-of-its-kind electric bus service in the ecologically fragile 51km-long stretch between Manali and Rohtang Pass. The move was made amidst concern over increasing environmental degradation in the Rohtang Pass area due to plying of diesel taxis.

50 NATIONS SIGNED TREATY ON THE PROHIBITION OF NUCLEAR WEAPONS

SEPTEMBER 22, 2017

Brazil was the first country to sign the ban, followed by nations from Algeria to Venezuela. Fifty states as different as Indonesia and Ireland had put their names to the treaty; others can sign later if they like. Guyana, Thailand and the Vatican also have already ratified the treaty, which needs 50 ratifications to take effect among the nations that back it.

NIGERIAN LAWYER ZANNAH MUSTAPHA WON 2017 UNHCR NANSEN REFUGEE AWARD

SEPTEMBER 22, 2017

Zannah Mustapha had negotiated and helped secure the release of more than 100 schoolgirls from Chibok kidnapped by the Boko Haram militant group. He will be bestowed with the prestigious Nansen Refugee Award at a ceremony taking place in Geneva on 2 October 2017.The The United Nations High Commissioner for Refugees (UNHCR) called him "a champion for the rights of displaced children growing up amid violence in North East Nigeria".

INS KALVARI DELIVERED TO INDIAN NAVY

SEPTEMBER 22, 2017

INS Kalvari, the first of the six Scorpene-class submarines was delivered to the Indian Navy by Mazagon Dock Limited (MDL). The submarine will soon be commissioned into the Indian Navy. The development marks a major milestone in Indian Navy's submarine programme as the vessel is expected to bolster India's maritime prowess.

PT. DEEN DAYAL UPADHAYAY VIGYAN GRAM SANKUL PARIYOJANA LAUNCHED

SEPTEMBER 25, 2017

The Project will experiment and Endeavour to formulate and implement appropriate Science and Technology (S&T) interventions for sustainable development through cluster approach in Uttarakhand. The project has been inspired by teachings and ideals of Pt. Deen Dayal Upadhayay whose birth centenary falls in the year 2017.

ROYANA SINGH APPOINTED AS FIRST WOMAN CHIEF PROCTOR OF BHU

SEPTEMBER 29, 2017

The Banaras Hindu University has appointed Royana Singh as the first woman Chief Proctor of the institution. The appointment was approved by Vice Chancellor Girish Chandra Tripathi. Prior to this appointment, Royana served as an assistant professor at the Institute of Medical Science (Anatomy Department).

WORLD RABIES DAY OBSERVED

SEPTEMBER 28, 2017

The day's theme sets the goal of reaching zero human deaths from canine rabies by the year 2030. At the global conference on rabies elimination in 2015, a common goal of zero human deaths from canine rabies by 2030 was agreed by the World Health Organization, World Organisation for Animal Health, UN Food and Agriculture Organization and GARC.

INDIA JUMPED TO 14TH RANK AS BEST COUNTRY FOR EXPATS: HSBC SURVEY

SEPTEMBER 29, 2017

India jumped up the global rankings by 12 places to take the 14th position in terms of best country for expats to work in and live says a HSBC survey. The ranking is a part of HSBCs latest expat explorer survey that covered 27,587 expats from 159 countries and territories in March and April this year.

2 OCTOBER: INTERNATIONAL DAY OF NON-VIOLENCE

OCTOBER 2, 2017

The International Day of Non-violence is celebrated every year on 2 October throughout world on the birth anniversary of Mahatma Gandhi, leader of Indian independence movement and also pioneer of philosophy of non-violence (ahimsa).

Observance of this day seeks to promote principles of non-violence through education and public awareness and is observed by all countries of the UN. In India, this day is celebrated as Gandhi Jayanti.

31 OCTOBER: RASHTRIYA EKTA DIWAS

OCTOBER 31, 2017

Rashtriya Ekta Diwas (National Unity Day) is observed every year across India on 31 October to commemorate birth anniversary of Sardar Vallabhai Patel who had played important role in unifying the country.

Observance of day provides an opportunity to re-affirm inherent strength and resilience of our nation to withstand actual and potential threats to unity, integrity and security of our country.

GOVERNMENT LAUNCHED SECURE HIMALAYA PROJECT

OCTOBER 3, 2017

The Union Government had launched **SECURE Himalaya,** a six-year project to ensure conservation of locally and globally significant biodiversity, land and forest resources in high Himalayan ecosystem spread over four states viz. Himachal Pradesh, Jammu and Kashmir, Uttarakhand and Sikkim.

INDIA TOPPED LIST OF POLLUTION-LINKED DEATHS: STUDY

OCTOBER 20, 2017

According to new study published in medical journal The Lancet, India has topped list of countries with pollution-related deaths in 2015.

In India, 2.51 million people died prematurely in 2015 due to diseases linked to air, water and other forms of pollution. Of the 2.51 million deaths in India, 1.81 million were related to air pollution, 0.64 million to water pollution, 0.17 million to occupational exposure and 95,000 linked to lead pollution

RAJNISH KUMAR APPOINTED AS NEW CHAIRMAN OF SBI

OCTOBER 5, 2017

The Appointments Committee of the Cabinet (ACC) has appointed Rajnish Kumar (59) as the new chairman of State Bank of India (SBI). His name was recommended by Vinod Rai-led Bank Board Bureau.

Rajnish Kumar will be 25th chairman of the country's largest lender and succeeds Arundhati Bhattacharya who retired from the service.

GLOBAL PASSPORT POWER RANK 2017: INDIA RANKED 75

OCTOBER 26, 2017

India's passport was ranked 75th among 94 countries in recently released Global Passport Power Rank 2017. India was ranked three notches better than its previous ranking.

According to this index, Singapore has world's most powerful passport, making it first Asian country to top it. Singapore is followed by Germany, Sweden and South Korea.

PARYATAN PARV TO BOOST TOURISM

OCTOBER 5, 2017

The Union Ministry of Tourism in collaboration with Other Union Ministries and State Governments has launched nationwide 'Paryatan Parv' to showcase cultural diversity of country and reinforce the principle of 'Tourism for All'. Its objective is to draw focus on the benefits of tourism.

It was inaugurated at Humayun's Tomb and will be held across the country from the 5th to 25th October 2017.

CBDT SIGNED 2 MORE APAS WITH TAXPAYERS

OCTOBER 7, 2017

The Central Board of Direct Taxes (CBDT) has signed two more advance pricing agreements (APAs) in September 2017 with Indian taxpayers in order to reduce litigation by providing certainty in transfer pricing.

The two signed APAs pertain to automobile and healthcare consulting sectors. They include provision of IT enabled services (ITES), provision of software development services and provision of engineering design services.

BUREAU OF INDIAN STANDARDS ACT 2016 COMES INTO EFFECT

OCTOBER 14, 2017

Ministry of Consumer Affairs, Food and Public Distribution has brought into effect new Bureau of Indian standards (BIS) Act 2016 which was notified in March 2016.

The Act replaced Bureau of Indian Standards Act, 1986. It aims to help in ease of doing business in country, enhance 'Make In India' campaign and ensure availability of quality products and services to the consumers.

MCX LAUNCHED INDIA'S FIRST COMMODITY OPTIONS IN GOLD

OCTOBER 18, 20171 Comment

Largest commodity bourse Multi-Commodity Exchange of India Ltd (MCX) launched India's first commodity options in gold. It was launched by Union Finance Minister Arun Jaitley.

The gold futures contract will have bi-monthly duration. The option will also have the existing gold kilo futures contract as its underlie.

APEDA WILL PROMOTE NE PRODUCTS IN BANGLADESH AND MYANMAR

OCTOBER 21, 2017

The Agricultural and Processed Food Products Export Development Authority (APEDA) has taken up a programme for promotion of north eastern products in Bangladesh and Myanmar. In this regard, it has proposed to organize promotional programmes in Bangladesh and Myanmar in association with the High Commission of India in Dhaka and its Embassy in Yangon.

The export of APEDA scheduled products to Bangladesh during 2016-17 was of US $396.44 million.

SOUTH ASIA'S FIRST RO-RO FERRY SERVICE LAUNCHED

OCTOBER 23, 2017

Prime Minister Narendra Modi inaugurated first phase of Ro-Ro (roll-on, roll-off) ferry service between Ghogha in Bhavnagar district and Dahej in Bharuch district in the Gulf of Cambay, Gujarat. It is South Asia's first world class Ro-Ro ferry service.

WORLD'S LARGEST COMBUSTION RESEARCH CENTRE INAUGURATED

OCTOBER 14, 2017

National Centre for Combustion Research and Development (NCCRD) was inaugurated at Indian Institute of Technology (IIT), Madras in Tamil Nadu. It is world's largest combustion research centre and one of best diagnostic centers in the country to understand combustion

INDIA RANKED 8TH IN 2017 VALUABLE NATION BRAND LIST

OCTOBER 10, 2017

According to Brand Finance's recently released Nation Brands 2017 report, India was ranked 8th out of 100 countries on a list of most valuable nation brands. This year India slipped by one spot compared to 7th rank in 2016 and ceded its previous spot to Canada.

INDIAN HANDICRAFTS AND GIFTS-DELHI FAIR INAUGURATED

OCTOBER 12, 2017

The 44th edition of Indian Handicrafts and Gifts (IHGF)-Delhi Fair was held at India Expo Centre and Mart on outskirts of Delhi in Greater Noida. It was organized by Export Promotion Council for Handicrafts (EPCH) and was inaugurated by Union Textiles Minister Smriti Irani.

MITRA SHAKTI 2017: INDIA-SRI LANKA JOINT MILITARY EXERCISE

OCTOBER 13, 2017

The 5th India-Sri Lanka joint training exercise "Mitra Shakti 2017" was held Aundh Military Station in Pune, Maharshtra. The two weeks exercise (October 13 and 25) is based on Counter Terrorist Operations (CTO) and Infantry company from both countries are participating in it.

INDIAN NAVY APPROVED NEW MISSION-BASED DEPLOYMENT PLAN

OCTOBER 26, 2017

Indian Navy has approved new mission-based deployment plan for deploying mission-ready ships and aircraft along critical sea lanes of communications and choke points in Indian Ocean Region (IOR).

It was discussed in the ongoing naval commanders' conference. Besides, new transition cycle for ships from maintenance periods to operational deployments was also approved.

SAARCLAW CONFERENCE HELD

OCTOBER 28, 2017

The 14th South Asian Association for Regional Co-operation in Law (SAARCLAW) Conference was held in Colombo, capital city of Sri Lanka along with 11th SAARC Chief Justices Conference.

The three-day conference was inaugurated by Sri Lankan Prime Minister Ranil Wickremesinghe and saw participation from South Asia's top Judges, legal practitioners and academics.

INDIA TOPPED LIST OF NEW TB CASES IN 2016: WHO REPORT

OCTOBER 31, 2017

According to the Global TB Report 2017 released by World Health Organization (WHO), India has topped list of seven countries, accounting for 64% of the over 10 million new tuberculosis (TB) cases worldwide in year 2016. India was followed by Indonesia, China, Philippines, Pakistan, Nigeria and South Africa.

NIRBHAY SUB-SONIC CRUISE MISSILE SUCCESSFULLY FLIGHT TESTED

NOVEMBER 7, 2017

Defense Research and Development Organization (DRDO) successfully conducted flight test of its indigenously designed and developed long range sub-sonic cruise missile 'Nirbhay' from test range at Chandipur, Odisha.

It was the fifth experimental test of Nirbhay missile system. It achieved all mission objectives completely from lift-off till the final splash, boosting the confidence of all scientists associated with the trial.

TYRANNOMYRMEX ALII: NEW ANT SPECIES DISCOVERED IN THE WESTERN GHATS

NOVEMBER 8, 2017

Researchers have discovered new species of ant in the Periyar Tiger Reserve, Kerala in Western Ghats, as one of the world's 'hottest hotspots' of biological diversity. It has been named Tyrannomyrmex alii (or T. alii), after eminent myrmecologist Musthak Ali, who is regarded as the India's 'ant man'.

INDIA RE-ELECTED MEMBER OF UNESCO'S EXECUTIVE BOARD

NOVEMBER 10, 2017

India was re-elected as member of executive board of United Nations educational, scientific and cultural organization (UNESCO). Executive board is UNESCO's top decision-making body. The election was held at 39th session of General Conference of UNESCO in Paris, France.

INDIA ASKS UN TO DECLARE 2018 AS INTERNATIONAL YEAR OF MILLETS

NOVEMBER 24, 2017

India has sent proposal to the United Nations (UN) for declaring the year 2018 as 'International Year of Millets'. If the proposal is agreed, it will raise awareness about millets among consumers, policy makers, industry and Research and Development (R&D) sector.

APEC SUMMIT HELD IN VIETNAM

NOVEMBER 13, 2017

The Asia-Pacific Economic Cooperation (APEC) summit was held in Da Nang, Vietnam. The theme of summit was 'Creating New Dynamism, Fostering a Shared Future'.

Leaders of 21 Pacific Rim countries attended this meeting. This was second time Vietnam hosted APEC summit, having hosted the event previously in 2006. Next year's APEC summit will be held in Papua New Guinea.

CHINA SUCCESSFULLY LAUNCHED REMOTE SENSING SATELLITES

NOVEMBER 26, 2017

China has successfully launched remote sensing satellites designed to conduct electromagnetic probes and other experiments.

The satellites whose numbers were not specified yet were launched on board of Long March-2C rocket from Xichang Satellite Launch Center in southwestern Sichuan province.

CCEA APPROVED CONTINUATION OF FOUR PROGRAMMES

NOVEMBER 17, 2017

The Cabinet Committee on Economic Affairs (CCEA) has approved four sub-schemes under Umbrella Scheme Integrated Child Development Services (ICDS). These four schemes include anganwadi services, programme for adolescent girls called Sabla, Child Protection Services and National Creche Scheme.

GIRISH KARNAD CONFERRED WITH 2017 TATA LITERATURE LIVE LIFETIME ACHIEVEMENT AWARD

NOVEMBER 20, 2017

Actor-playwright Girish Karnad (79) was conferred with 2017 Tata Literature Live Lifetime Achievement Award for his outstanding contribution in field of theatre at the eighth edition of the Tata Literature festival held in Mumbai, Maharashtra.

GOVERNMENT WILL INITIATE SAFE CITY PLAN FOR WOMEN IN EIGHT CITIES

NOVEMBER 23, 2017

Government will soon initiate a comprehensive 'safe city' plan for women in eight cities for women in eight metropolitan cities of the country. It will be implemented in Delhi, Mumbai, Kolkata, Ahmadabad, Chennai, Lucknow, Bengaluru and Hyderabad. Decision in this regard was taken Steering Committee meeting under chairmanship of Union Home Secretary

MIRABAI CHANU WON GOLD AT WORLD WEIGHTLIFTING CHAMPIONSHIPS

NOVEMBER 30, 2017

India's Saikhom Mirabai Chanu won gold medal at World Weightlifting Championships held in Anaheim, United States. She achieved this feat by lifting new world record of 194kg – 85kg snatch and 109kg clean-and-jerk in the 48 kg weight category. Thailand's Sukcharoen Thunya won silver medal with total lift of 193, while Segura Ana Iris won bronze medal with 182kg lift.

HORNBILL FESTIVAL INAUGURATED

DECEMBER 2, 2017

President Ram Nath Kovind inaugurated 18th edition of the Hornbill Festival at the Naga Heritage Village in Kisama, Nagaland. The festival coincided with 54th statehood day of Nagaland.

Hornbill Festival also called as the 'Festival of Festivals' in Nagaland is tourism promotional extravaganza to revive, protect and preserve the richness and uniqueness of Naga heritage.

ADIVASI MAHOTSAV 2017: TRIBAL FESTIVAL ORGANIZED

DECEMBER 11, 2017

The Aadivasi Mahotsav 2017 was held in Raipur, Chhattisgarh to display the rich and diverse tribal traditions of the central state. It was inaugurated by Union Tribal Affairs Minister Jual Oram and Chhattisgarh Chief Minister Dr Raman Singh.

VIGILANT ACE: SOUTH KOREA, US LAUNCHED LARGEST AIR EXERCISE

DECEMBER 4, 2017

South Korea and United States have launched Vigilant Ace, their largest-ever joint aerial drills. The exercise comes after North Korea tested Hwasong-15, its most advanced and powerful Inter Continental Ballistic Missile (ICBM) as part of its weapons programme.

UNGA ADOPTS RESOLUTION REJECTING US DECLARATION OF JERUSALEM

DECEMBER 22, 2017

The United Nations General Assembly (UNGA) has overwhelmingly adopted resolution declaring United States of America (USA) recognition of Jerusalem as Israel's capital as 'null and void'.

The resolution was moved by Turkey and Yemen and was adopted with 128 countries voting in favour including major political powers such as India, Japan Britain, France, Germany and 9 against it, while 35 abstained.

UP FIRST STATE TO ENDORSE TRIPLE TALAQ DRAFT BILL

DECEMBER 7, 2017

Uttar Pradesh became first state to endorse Union Government's draft law — Muslim Women (Protection of Rights on Marriage) Act that makes practice of instant "triple talaq" or talaq-e-biddat a cognisable and non-bailable criminal offence. The draft law was endorsed by the state cabinet meeting chaired by Chief Minister Yogi Adityanath.

INDIA ADMITTED INTO WASSENAAR ARRANGEMENT

DECEMBER 8, 2017

Elite export control regime Wassenaar Arrangement (WA) has decided to admit India as its new member. The decision was taken at two-day plenary meeting of grouping in Vienna, Austria. India will be Arrangement's 42nd participating state.

ICAN RECEIVES 2017 NOBEL PEACE PRIZE

DECEMBER 11, 2017

The Geneva-based International Campaign to Abolish Nuclear Weapons (ICAN) received the 2017 Nobel Peace Prize at ceremony held in Oslo, Norway. The award was received by Beatrice Fihn, leader of ICAN and Hiroshima nuclear bombing survivor Setsuko Thurlow.

ICAN, a coalition of 468 grassroots non-governmental groups has been in forefront of pushing for end to use of nuclear weapons through United Nations Treaty on the Prohibition of Nuclear Weapons adopted by 122 nations in July 2017.

GANGA GRAM PROJECT LAUNCHED

DECEMBER 23, 2017

The Union Ministry of Drinking Water & Sanitation has formally launched 'Ganga Gram' project at the Ganga Gram Swachata Sammelan held in New Delhi.

The project was launched under the clean Ganga mission-Namami Gange Programme for holistic sanitation development in villages on the banks of River Ganga.

VISWANATHAN ANAND WON WORLD CHESS TITLE 2017

DECEMBER 29, 2017

Chess grandmaster Viswanathan Anand (48) won World Rapid Chess Championship Title 2017 held in Riyadh, Saudi Arabia. In the final tie-breaker mini-match, Anand defeated Russia's Vladimir Fedoseev by 2-0 score to reclaim title he had won in 2003.

Earlier he defeated world champion Magnus Carlsen of Norway and went on to finish on top with 10.5 Points at the end of 15th and final round. But, he had tied with Vladimir Fedoseev and Ian Nepomniachtchi, both of Russia, who also had scored same number of points, a tie-breaker was required to decide the winner.

EVENTS

NATIONAL

GOVT ANNOUNCES 'MUHAFIZ' FOR WORKERS

DATE: 6th January, 2018

OBJECTIVE: To bring welfare programmes for the unorganized sector of the society

The Jammu and Kashmir government is set to launch a major welfare initiative for workers in the unorganised sector to provide them institutionalized socio economic security. Under the scheme, named "Muhafiz" (Guardian), around three lakh workers registered with the Jammu and Kashmir Building and Other Construction Workers' Welfare Board (JKBOCWWB) would be covered under accidental, life and disability insurance. The scheme also envisages extending a micro credit facility to the workers and facilitating their registration through online and other modes. The total premium involved for these workers in the first instance would be about Rs 5 crore. The JKBOCWWB would be starting the credit facility with a limit of Rs 10,000 and the counter guarantee, which would be deposited by the board with the J&K Bank, would be about Rs 30 crore. The board in the past three years has provided financial assistance of around Rs 275 crore to such workers under various components, including education, marriage, chronic diseases. Resources for socio-economic welfare of the workers would be generated through a cess levied under the Building and Other Construction Workers (RE&CS) Cess Act.

24X7 HELPLINE TO CHECK CRIME AGAINST WOMEN

DATE: 6th January, 2018

OBJECTIVE: To provide healthy and safe environment to women

Chief Minister Jai Ram Thakur announced to launch a 24x7 "Gudiya" helpline. The rape and murder of Kotkhai girl and the death of a forest guard Hoshiyar Singh under mysterious circumstances had shamed the state. The day-to-day reporting of crime against women would be monitored by the Chief Minister office and action would be taken within 48 hours. Atal Helpline for checking corruption would also be set up as it was the BJP's resolve to provide clean and efficient governance. Stringent measures would be taken to curb drug menace in the state as well as cases of cyber crime. Gudiya is a nickname given to the 16-year-old Kotkhai victim of rape and murder during the rule of the previous Congress government.

The issue had triggered massive protests and later the Himachal Pradesh High Court had referred the case to the CBI to investigate that took place in July 2017.

ZOJILA TUNNEL IN J&K

DATE: 3rd January, 2018

OBJECTIVE: To increase connectivity in Jammu & Kashmir

The Cabinet Committee on Economic Affairs approved the 6,808-crore Zojila Tunnel project in Jammu and Kashmir that will provide year-round connectivity between Srinagar, Kargil and Leh when completed. Currently, Leh-Ladakh is cut off from the rest of India for almost six months due to heavy snowfall and threat of avalanches. The project aims to construct a 14.15-km long two-lane bidirectional single tube tunnel with a parallel 14.2-km long egress or parallel escape tunnel, excluding approaches between Baltal and Minamarg in the state. The government added that the project will be an instrument for the development of the economically backward districts in J&K.

The construction period of the project is estimated at seven years with a civil construction cost of ₹ 4,899.42 crore. The total capital cost of the project is Rs 6,808.69 crore, which includes the cost towards land acquisition, resettlement and rehabilitation and other pre-construction activities as well as the maintenance and operation cost of tunnel for four years. The project will be implemented by Ministry of Road Transport & Highways through National Highways and Infrastructure Development Corporation Limited.

This project, along with other ongoing projects such as the 6.5-km long Z-Morh tunnel at Gagangir, would ensure safe, fast and cheap connectivity between the two regions of Kashmir and Ladakh.

JNPT WINS 'SAMUDRA MANTHAN – 'CARING ORGANISATION OF THE YEAR' AWARD

DATE: 4th January, 2018

OBJECTIVE: To fuel healthy competition in the maritime sector and impart an impetus to the industry

Jawaharlal Nehru Port Trust, India's Premier Container Port has won "Samudra Manthan-Caring Organisation of the Year" award organised by Bhandarkar Shipping, which is leading publication of the maritime industry and has played the role of a business and a social catalyst. The Samudra Manthan Award is a significant initiative instituted with an objective to fuel healthy competition in the maritime sector and impart an impetus to the industry to emerge stronger to work for the benefit of trade and the economy. From the total 14 categories of Samudra Manthan award, JNPT was the winner in the "Caring Organization of the Year" category.

JNPT is India's No. 1 Container Port in terms of volume and efficiency parameters. Besides achieving operational excellence, JNPT has been implementing several measures for the benefit of its employees and their families. JNPT provides excellent facilities to their staff like medical insurance, residential township with school and other amenities, transport service, canteens, rest rooms, recreation,

CSR part also JNPT has taken many key initiatives like Mukhyamantri Aarogya Marathon, jalshivaryojana and regular free health camps.

FIVE NAMAMI GANGE PROJECTS APPROVED

DATE: 5th January, 2018

OBJECTIVE: To improve the conditions of Ghats

National Mission for Clean Ganga (NMCG) has approved five projects worth ₹ 295.01 crore. Three projects pertain to sewage management in West Bengal at an estimated cost of ₹ 278.6 crore, one relates to sewage management in Uttarakhand at an estimated cost of ₹ 4.68 crore and one project worth ₹ 11.73 crore is related to ghat improvement works in Varanasi.

With these approvals, all projects related to sewage management in high pollution load towns along river Ganga have been sanctioned. In West Bengal, sewage management works in Kamarhati and Baranagar Municipalities (60 MLD STP, de-silting of sewer lines etc.) In Uttarakhand, approval was given to one project for laying of sewer lines in some of the uncovered areas in Haridwar at an estimated cost of ₹ 4.68 crore. In Varanasi, a project worth ₹ 11.73 crore for repair and retrofitting of various ghats was approved. This project aims to strengthen the poor condition of ghats through bolder pitching and stone steps to ensure improved life of ghats apart from avoiding risk and inconvenience to the visitors and pilgrims.

26TH WORLD BOOK FAIR

DATE: 6th January, 2018

OBJECTIVE: To increase awareness of environment issues like climate change, global warming, and water pollution

The 26th edition of annual World Book Fair was held in New Delhi. It was organized by National Book Trust (NBT), under Ministry of Human Resource Development in association with India Trade Promotion Organisation. The theme for the year is 'Environment and Climate Change'. It focuses on environment issues like climate change, global warming, and water pollution. European Union was Guest of Honour country for this year's book fair.

The annual book fair saw participation of around 800 publishers from across the country in different languages. The event's theme Pavilion had international rights exhibition of nearly 500 titles published in English, Hindi, and other Indian languages. The fair also witnessed panel discussions, talks, workshops, children's activities, screening of short films, special photo exhibits as well as cultural and musical performances.

NARI & E-SAMVAD PORTALS LAUNCHED

DATE: 2nd January, 2018

OBJECTIVE: To empower women by providing information on all govt. schemes

Union Minister for women and child development Maneka Gandhi launched a web portal, NARI, which will provide information on all government schemes for women. The NARI portal carries details on 350 different schemes for women which will be updated from time to time. The schemes are divided into seven different categories — education, health, employment, housing and shelter, addressing violence, decision making and social support.

Gandhi also unveiled a website for NGOs called e-SAMVAD, an interactive portal allowing NGOs to contact the ministry and share their feedback, suggestions, grievances and their best practices. Although the government in an order in April 2016 made it mandatory for all mobile phone manufactures to provide a panic button feature in cellphones from January 2017, its implementation has been delayed. The move aims at improving security for women by providing them a tool to alert the local police.

INTERNATIONAL

PAKISTAN ON US 'SPECIAL WATCH LIST'

DATE: 4th January, 2018

In a fresh move, the US has put Pakistan on its 'special watch list' for 'severe violations of religious freedom'. Around ten other nations have been listed as 'Countries of Particular Concern' by the US. The United States Secretary of State annually designates governments, which have undertaken or allowed measures to violate religious freedom, as 'Countries of Particular Concern' observing the International Religious Freedom Act of 1998. The United States Commission on International Religious Freedom has been demanding the designation of Pakistan as a CPC since 2002, arguing that the government of Pakistan continues "to perpetrate and tolerate systematic, ongoing, and egregious religious freedom violations. Religiously discriminatory constitutional provisions and legislation, such as the country's blasphemy and anti-Ahmadiyya laws, continue to result in prosecutions and imprisonments".

VISHWA HINDI DIVAS

DATE: 10th January, 2018

OBJECTIVE: To promote Hindi at the global stage

Vishwa Hindi Divas or World Hindi Day was celebrated on 10th January. To mark the occasion, Ministry of External Affairs (MEA) through its missions/posts abroad and the Department of Official Language (Rajbhasha) conducted special events to spread the greatness of the language. Vishwa Hindi Divas is celebrated to promote Hindi at the global platform.

The first World Hindi Day was celebrated in 2006. The celebration has its own importance this year as India's effort to make Hindi an official language at the United Nations is currently in headlines.

Hindi is one of the most spoken languages in the world. The number of Hindi speakers is more than 400 million, including 300 million native speakers. Hindi as a language is spoken in more than 20 countries around the globe and is being taught in more than 100 Universities of the world.

Hindi is spoken by the large Indian diaspora related with Indian Hindi Belt. A substantially large diaspora lives in countries like the USA, UK, UAE, Trinidad and Tobago, Guyana, Surinam, South Africa, Fiji and Mauritius, where it is natively spoken at home and among their own Hindustani-speaking communities.

31 SATELLITES LAUNCHED BY ISRO

DATE: 11th January, 2018

OBJECTIVE: For topographic mapping, vegetation monitoring and studying clouds

The first space mission of Indian Space Research Organisation (ISRO) in 2018 started on 11th January 2018 by beginning of 28-hour countdown to launch 31 satellites from Satish Dhawan Space Centre (SDSC), SHAR, Sriharikota (Andhra Pradesh).

The launch is unique as it is carrying 28 satellites from 6 foreign countries along with India's 3 satellites. India is launching its Cartosat-2 Series Satellite for earth observation along with one Microsatellite and one Nanosatellite. Out of 28 foreign satellites 3 are Microsatellites while 25 are Nanosatellites from six countries Canada, Finland, France, Republic of Korea, United Kingdom and United States of America.

These satellites will be launched through the PSLV-C40 rocket. ISRO scientists are hopeful for a successful launch in the New Year aftermath of failed delivery of India's eighth navigation satellite in the earth's lower orbit in August 2017.

The International customer satellites are being launched as part of the commercial arrangements between Antrix Corporation Limited (Antrix), a Government of India company under Department of Space (DOS), the commercial arm of ISRO and the International customers.

INDIA IMPROVES GLOBAL TALENT COMPETITIVENESS RANKING TO 81ST

DATE: 25th January, 2018

AGENDA/ISSUE: According to Global Talent Competitiveness Index (GTCI), India ranks to 81st which marks an improvement as compared to 92nd rank in 2017. The index was released on the first day of World Economic Forum Annual Meeting in Davos, Switzerland. GTCI is an annual study that measures and ranks countries and cities on its ability to grow, attract and retain talent. It is produced by global business school INSEAD in partnership with Adecco Group and Tata Communications.

In its list, Switzerland is at top followed by Singapore and US. European countries dominate top ranks, with 15 out of the top 25 places. Developed, high-income countries are still the global talent champions while Zurich, Stockholm and Oslo take the top spots in the GTI cities ranking.

India was at 5th position among the five BRICS countries in 2017. China has moved up to 43rd now, Russia to 53rd, South Africa to 63rd and Brazil to 73rd position.

Global Talent Competitiveness Index report of 2018 has been titled 'Diversities for competitiveness' and focuses on role of diversity in forming talent policies and innovation strategies.

Although India's ranking has improved this year, the report has warned that it faces the serious risk of worsening brain drain.

HP CM LAUNCHES ZERO BUDGET NATURAL FARMING PROJECT

DATE: 29th January, 2018

OBJECTIVE: To increase agriculture produce and the income of farmers

Himachal Pradesh Government launches Zero Budget Natural Farming (ZBNF) project to increase the income of farmers. ZBNF is set of natural farming methods where cost of growing and harvesting plants is zero. It is a farming practice that believes in natural growth of crops without adding any fertilizers and pesticides or any other foreign elements. The inputs used for seed treatments and other inoculations are locally available in form of cow dung and cow urine.

In Zero Budget system farmers need not purchase fertilizers and pesticides in order to ensure the healthy growth of crops. It requires almost no monetary investment and envisages use of 'Jeevamrutha' and 'Beejamrutha'. The main aim of ZBNF is to eliminate use of chemical pesticides and uses biological pesticides and promote of good agronomic practices. Farmers use low cost of inputs such as earthworms, cow dung, urine, plants, human excreta and such biological fertilizers for crop protection.

US LIFTS BAN ON REFUGEES FROM 11 'HIGH-RISK' COUNTRIES

DATE: 30th January, 2018

The Trump administration announces that it will resume accepting refugees from 11 "high risk" nations, but says those seeking to enter the United States will come under much tougher scrutiny than in the past. Applicants from 11 countries unnamed but understood to include 10 Muslim-majority nations plus North Korea, will face tougher "risk-based" assessments to be accepted. The new measures taken by administration will include additional interviews of applicants' family members, and close scrutiny of potential ties to organized crime.

The Trump administration has refused to identify the 11 nations, hit with a ban in October. But refugee groups say they comprise Egypt, Iran, Iraq, Libya, Mali, North Korea, Somalia, South Sudan, Sudan, Syria and Yemen.

Donald Trump has pursued a much tougher stance on immigrants and refugees from all countries since becoming president one year ago.

Annual refugee admissions have been slashed by more than half to a maximum of 45,000 in fiscal 2018, which end on Sep 31.

ISSUES

SC REVOKES ORDER ON PLAYING OF NATIONAL ANTHEM IN CINEMA HALLS

DATE: 9th January, 2018

Supreme Court revokes its interim order on mandatory playing of <u>national anthem</u> before movie screenings in <u>cinema halls</u> after multiple instances of vigilante patriotism. In its earlier order, the court ordered all cinema halls to play the anthem before screening a film. The Supreme Court has modified this and has now made it optional for cinema halls to play the national anthem before every show. The court observed that playing of the anthem was directive, but showing respect was mandatory. Accordingly, if the anthem is played, patrons in the hall are bound to show respect by standing up. The court clarified that the exception granted to disabled persons from standing up during the anthem shall remain in force on all occasions.

The current modification will be in place till the Union government takes a final decision. This will be based on the recommendations of a 12-member high-profile inter-ministerial committee. The committee was set up following the court's earlier order. The ministerial panel will also examine whether any amendments are necessary to the Prevention of Insult to National Honour Act of 1971. The 1971 Act deals with national anthem, related mandates and punishments thereof for any violations.

EVENTS

NEPAL ENDS INDIA'S MONOPOLY ON INTERNET

DATE: 13th January, 2018

Nepal ends India's monopoly on internet access by opening a new optical fibre link across the Himalayan Mountains to China. Nepal was totally dependent on India for access to the worldwide web through connections at Biratnagar, Bhairahawa and Birgunj, for which it pays a substantial sum as fees and royalties. Besides state-run Indian firms, Nepal has been acquiring bandwidth from private players such as Tata and Airtel and BSNL.

Nepal Telecom (NT), the government-owned telecom service provider, has now acquired bandwidth from China Telecom Global Limited, with its head office in Hong Kong. NT signed an agreement with the Chinese company in December 2016 to acquire bandwidth.

The Chinese optical fibre link enters Nepal at Rasuwa, 175 km north of the capital Kathmandu. A successful test of the link was conducted last week before it became operational. This will add new dynamics to Nepal-China ties.

RIFT BETWEEN CJI & SUPREME COURT JUDGES

DATE: 12th January, 2018

AGENDA/ISSUE: Four Supreme Court judges J. Chelameswar, Ranjan Gogoi, MB Lokur and Kurian Joseph take the unprecedented step of publicly criticising Chief Justice of India Dipak Misra.

During their press conference on Friday they claimed that The Administration of The Country's Highest Court was not in Order and the judges also warned that democracy would not survive in the country unless the institution is preserved.

The conference that highlighted the growing rift between senior justices and the Chief Justice of India, Dipak Misra, was held at Justice Chelameswar's residence in New Delhi.

Two top organisations of the legal fraternity emphasised on the need to resolve the matter internally. While the Bar Council deputed a seven-member team to meet all the judges individually. The SC Bar Association held an emergency meeting during which they adopted two resolutions, one of which was to "restore the credibility" of the Supreme Court. Agreeing with the Bar Council that the matter should be resolved internally, the association said the Chief Justice of India "should call a full court meeting of all judges and solve this issue".

GOVERNMENT ENDS HAJ SUBSIDY

DATE: 16th January, 2018

OBJECTIVE: The money saved to be used for education and welfare of girls from minority communities

To empower minorities with dignity, Union Minister for Minority Affairs Mukhtar Abbas Naqvi announced the decision of the Govt. about phasing out subsidies for the annual Haj pilgrimage. The Centre's decision followed a 2012 Supreme Court order asking that subsidies for the Haj be phased out by 2022 and the money saved (around Rs. 450 crore annually) be diverted to more welfare-oriented activities. Haj subsidy will be used for educational empowerment and welfare of girls from minority communities. The policy aims at rationalising distribution of the Haj quota between the Haj Committee of India and private tour operators in the ratio of 70:30 for the next five years. It also stresses on breaking the cartel of contractors with a transparent bidding process.

After Saudi Arabia hiked India's pilgrim quota by 5,000 earlier this year, the highest number of pilgrims is likely to go for Haj pilgrimage in 2018. Now, a total of 1.75 lakh Indian citizens can go for Haj.

NO KHAP CAN QUESTION IN MARRIAGES OF ADULTS: SC

DATE: 16th January, 2018

The Supreme Court says that every adult has right to marry anyone and nobody including parents, Khap panchayats or similar associations can question their choice of spouse. It also ruled that any kind of attack and interference on such adults opting for marriage, especially inter-caste marriage as 'absolutely illegal.

There have been a number of cases in which young couples have been killed in the name of family honour for indulging in inter-caste or intra-clan (gotra) marriages.

Khaps, caste or community organisations representing a clan or a group of related clans frequently make pronouncements on social issues and have often landed in controversies owing to their diktats.

The court has also warned Centre that if it doesn't take any action towards banning the Khap Panchayats and their illegal activities, then the court will have to step in to do the same.

OFFICE OF PROFIT AND DISQUALIFICATION

DATE: 21st January, 2018

AGENDA/ISSUE: President Ram Nath Kovind on the recommendation of Election Commission of India (ECI) disqualifies 20 Aam Aadmi Party (AAP) MLAs from Delhi, citing that they held offices of profit. In 2016, the ECI had issued show cause notices to 27 AAP MLAs from Delhi who held offices as parliamentary secretaries, after petition was filed seeking their disqualification.

Office of profit is a position in government which cannot be held by Member of Legislative Assembly (MLA) or Member of Parliament (MP). The post can yield salaries, perquisites and other benefits. It has not been defined in Constitution or Representation of the People Act, 1951. According to Articles 102(1)(a) and 191(1)(a) of Constitution, legislators (MP or MLA) can be barred from holding office of profit under Central Government or state government as it can put them in position to gain financial benefit. They can be disqualified in case they are of unsound mind, undischarged insolvent and not being Indian citizen or for acquiring citizenship of another country.

IDEAS

UIDAI INTRODUCES VIRTUAL ID

DATE: 10thJanuary, 2018

AGENDA/ISSUE: To address privacy concerns

TARGET/APPLICATION: The Unique Identification Authority of India (UIDAI) introduces a new concept of 'Virtual ID' which Aadhaar-card holder can generate from its website and give for various purposes including SIM verification and others instead of sharing the actual 12-digit biometric ID. This ID would be a random 16-digit number, together with biometrics of the user would give any authorized agency like a mobile company, limited details like name, address and photograph, which are enough for any verification.

UIDAI has also introduced the concept of 'limited KYC' under which it will only provide need-based or limited details of a user to an authorized agency that is providing a particular service.

The Virtual ID will be a temporary and revocable 16-digit random number mapped to a person's Aadhaar number and the Aadhaar-issuing body will start accepting it from 1 March, 2018. From 1 June, 2018 it will be compulsory for all agencies that undertake authentication to accept the Virtual ID from their users.

NITI AAYOG LAUNCHES FIRST COURSE UNDER GIAN

DATE: 16th January, 2018

OBJECTIVE: To address the challenges of urbanization

The NITI Aayog launches the first course on Sustainable Urban planning using remote sensing and Geographic Information System (GIS) at IIT Kanpur's outreach centre in Noida. This course is being conducted under the Global Initiative on Academic Network (GIAN) Program of the Ministry of Human Resource Development and supported by NITI Aayog and Ministry of Housing and Urban Affairs.

Professor Rajiv Sinha from the Department of Earth Sciences at IIT Kanpur and Dr. Patrice Carbonneau from the Department of Geography, University of Durham, UK, coordinate the course. This course aims to give participants state-of-the-art remote sensing and GIS skills which will allow them to rise to the challenge of managing the rapidly changing urban environment of Indian cities. Focus will be on issues such as water resource management, water pollution and strategic emplacements for water treatment facilities. Participants from several Government departments such as ISRO, AP Remote Sensing Application Centre, National Mission on Clean Ganga and students from different engineering colleges and universities across the country are attending the course.

MAHARASHTRA BECOMES THE FIRST STATE TO INITIATE PUBLIC CLOUD

DATE: 17th January, 2018

Maharashtra has come out with a public cloud policy virtually mandating its departments to shift their data storage onto the cloud, creating a USD 2- billion opportunity for the industry. The government had formed a four-member committee to draft a policy framework on cloud usage two months ago. This policy will result in additional private sector investments as government is one of the biggest creators and consumers of data. Government departments currently have their own data storage facilities which can be done better and cheaper by private sector vendors. In the next 20 days, five to six top cloud service providers like Amazon or Microsoft will be empanelled. Under the framework, government will make it mandatory for the data to be stored within the country and the broad idea is to use public cloud in cases wherever the Right to Information Act is applicable, and then go in for enhanced security features for private and sensitive data which will also be stored on the cloud.

AUTOMATIC COASTAL WARNING DURING DISASTERS

DATE: 19th January, 2018

OBJECTIVE: To establish Early Warning Dissemination System (EWDS) in coastal areas

Odisha is the first State in India to have developed an automatic public address system that can be activated along its entire coast. The State government is all set to commission the ambitious Early Warning Dissemination System (EWDS) that would enable loud sirens go off simultaneously from towers at 122 locations by July. Odisha can warn the vast population residing along its 480-km long coast by pressing a single button from a control room in the State capital in the event of the occurrence of natural disasters like a tsunami or a cyclone. The 122 locations include tourist destinations, fish landing centres and coastal habitations.

The sound emanating from the towers can be heard in localities up to a radius of 1.5 km. The new system will also enable authorities to alert people in smaller pockets, depending on the severity of the disaster. At present, the meteorological prediction has improved considerably and authorities handling disasters are able to know the intensity of cyclones two to three days in advance.

The EWDS comprises of technologies like Satellite-Based Mobile Data Voice Terminals (SBMDVT), Digital Mobile Radio (DMR), Mass Messaging System (MMS) and Universal Communication Interface (UCI) for inter-operability among different communication technologies.

The project, at an estimated cost of Rs. 82 crore is being implemented with assistance from the World Bank, will have towers in 22 blocks under six coastal districts.

INDIA'S FIRST FLOATING MARKET

DATE: 25th January, 2018

Kolkata is now witnessing to a floating market, the first of its kind across any metro. The 400 meters long and 60 meters wide market is located on lake at Patuli in South Kolkata. Patuli has been transformed into the floating market similar to the one in Thailand. It was open to the public from 25th January. The market will host at least 114 boats, each one accommodating two shops.

Shops will sell regular or daily-use items like vegetables, fruits, flowers, fish and meat and poultry. Shoppers will approach the boats through wooden walkways.

Special provisions have also been made to ensure that water in the lake does not stink and the aquatic life survives. The market will remain open from 6 am to 9 pm on all days, with a break in the afternoon. The Kolkata Metropolitan Development Authority, the executing agency, has apparently asked shopkeepers not to throw waste into the water. Nets will be routinely used to fish out vegetable peel, fish scales and other waste from the water.

RAPID REPORTING SYSTEM FOR SCHEME FOR ADOLESCENT GIRLS (SAG)

DATE: 25th January, 2018

Ministry of Women and Child Development (MWCD), launched the Phase -1 i.e. the beneficiary module of the Rapid Reporting System (RSS) for the SAG on the occasion of National Girl Child Day (24th January). It is a web-based online monitoring for the SAG. The URL for the portal is 'sag-rrs.nic.in.' The RRS portal will facilitate monitoring of SAG and take corrective measures by ensuring faster flow of information, accurate targeting of beneficiaries and reduction of leakages. The portal has been developed by Ministry of WCD in collaboration with National Informatics Centre (NIC)

RRS is centrally sponsored scheme implemented using platform of Integrated Child Development Services (ICDS) Scheme. Anganwadi Centres (AWCs) are focal point for delivery of services. Ministry of WCD is implementing scheme in selected 508 districts across country.

It is implemented through Centre and State share in ratio of 50:50, for nutrition component 60:40 for rest of activities for State/UTs with legislation, 90:10 for NE and 3 Himalayan States and 100% for UTs without legislative assemblies.

HP LAUNCHES 'SHAKTI' APP FOR WOMEN

DATE: 28th January, 2018

OBJECTIVE: To ensure safety and protection of women

To ensure safety and protection of women, Himachal Pradesh CM launched 'Shakti App'. Through this App a woman at the time of any trouble can press the panic (which is red in colour) button of the app in mobile to seek help and even if the mobile phone is shaken hard or dropped, then too an emergency SMS will go immediately to the nearest police control room within 20 seconds.

This App is developed by the National Informatics Centre (NIC) of the Himachal Pradesh government. The objective of the launch of the app is to fight crimes against women in the state. Internet connectivity is not required for this App. The app is available both in Hindi and English language and "On shaking hard during a scuffle the app will send the location of the sender."

This App also provides for automatic video and audio recording of the incident of assault on victim's mobile handset, which can be later used as evidence against the offender. It also has the facility to recall the wrongly sent SMS to the police control room.

PEOPLE

INDU MALHOTRA

WHY IN NEWS? : Appointed as the judge of Supreme Court

In a first of its kind incident in the history of Indian judiciary, the Supreme Court collegium recommended senior advocate Indu Malhotra as the first woman lawyer to be directly appointed as a judge of the apex court. She will be one of seven women judges that the top court has had so far since independence. At present, Justice R Banumathi is the only woman judge in the apex court.

In 1989, Justice M Fathima Beevi became the first woman to be appointed as a judge of the apex court. Thereafter, Justice Sujata V Manohar, Justice Ruma Pal, Justice Gyan Sudha Misra and Justice Ranjana Prakash Desai made it to the top court as judges.

CAREER: Indu is a senior counsel practising in the Supreme Court for the past 30 years. She was the second woman to be designated as senior advocate by the apex court in 2007. Indu joined the legal profession in 1983 and was enrolled with the Bar Council of Delhi. In 1988, she qualified as an Advocate-on-Record in the Supreme Court, and secured the first position in the examination, for which she was awarded the Mukesh Goswami Memorial Prize on Law Day.

She has also served as a member of the Centre-appointed High Level Committee (HLC) in the Ministry of Law and Justice to review 'Institutionalization of Arbitration Mechanism in India'. She has authored the third edition of a commentary 'The Law and Practice of Arbitration and Conciliation, 2014' which was released in 2014.

K. SIVAN

WHY IN NEWS? : Appointed as the new chairman of ISRO

Eminent scientist K Sivan, known as the "Rocket Man" for his significant contribution in the development of cryogenic engines for India's space programme, appointed as the new Chairman of Indian Space Research Organisation (ISRO).

Currently the Director of Vikram Sarabhai Space Centre in Thiruvananthapuram which is responsible for the design and development activities for all launch vehicles, Sivan will succeed AS Kiran Kumar and has a three year term as the ISRO chief. Sivan's appointment was cleared by the Appointment Committee of Cabinet (ACC). It comes at a time when ISRO is planning to outsource construction of satellites and rockets for future launches.

CAREER: An alumnus of IIT Bombay, Sivan has contributed significantly in Polar Satellite Launch Vehicle (PSLV), Geosynchronous Satellite Launch Vehicle (GSLV) and GSLV Mk-Ill vehicle design. He has been credited for development of the PSLV rocket that launched 104 satellites in a single mission, setting a world record in February last year. Sivan also designed a software called Sitara, which ISRO uses for simulating trajectories of its rockets.

PM NARENDRA MODI

WHY IN NEWS? : Ranked number three by Gallup International survey

Prime Minister Narendra Modi has been ranked at number three among the global leaders by Gallup International survey. PM Modi is ahead of China's Xi Jinping, Russian President Vladimir Putin, British Prime Minister Theresa May, Israel's Benjamin Netanyahu amongst others. German Chancellor Angela Merkel topped the ranking followed by French president Emmanuel Macron

The respondents in the survey, which was conducted among the people across 50 countries. According to Gallup, 53,769 people were interviewed globally. In each country, a representative sample of around 1,000 men and women has interviewed either face-to-face, or via phone, or via various online mediums.

ANIL KHANNA

WHY IN NEWS? : Appointed as the chairman of the finance commission of IOA

Senior sports administrator Anil Khanna was named Chairman of the Finance Commission of the Indian Olympic Association, which also formed a four-member advisory committee.

The IOA also formed a Medical Commission and Games Technical Conduct Committee and nominated office bearers of IOA and National Sports Federations (NSFs) to the Committees.

The advisory committee comprises Tarlochan Singh, GS Mander, S Regunathan and BS Landge.

JEFF BEZOS

WHY IN NEWS? : Becomes the richest person in the world

Amazon chairman and Chief Executive Officer Jeff Bezos overtook Microsoft Co-founder Bill Gates to become the richest person in the world, according to the Bloomberg Billionaires Index. Bezos added $10.4 billion (Rs 67,481 crore) to his net worth as Amazon shares rose 13%, the most in two-and-a-half years, on the Nasdaq stock exchange.

The last time Bezos overtook Gates as the richest person in the world was in July, 2017.

NAWAB SANAULLAH ZEHRI

WHY IN NEWS? : Resigned from the position of Chief Minister of Balochistan

Accepting advice of the prime minister, colleagues and political allies, Balochistan Chief Minister Nawab Sanaullah Zehri resigned from his position ahead of a provincial assembly session that was called for voting on a no-confidence motion against him.

Former chief minister Dr Abdul Malik Baloch escorted Zehri to the Governor's House where he formally submitted his resignation to Governor Mohammad Khan Achakzai. The governor, the constitutional head of the province, instantly accepted the resignation and issued an official notification to this effect.

A R RAHMAN

WHY IN NEWS? : Named as the official brand ambassador of Sikkim

Gangtok Academy Award winning music composer AR Rahman was named the official brand ambassador of the north eastern state of Sikkim, one of the favourite destinations of tourists preferring the upper reaches.

Sikkim Chief Minister Pawan Chamling announced Rahman's name at the inauguration of the state Red Panda Winter Carnival at Paljor Stadium in Gangtok.

CAREER: Allahrakka Rahman, best known as A R Rahman's works are noted for integrating Indian classical music with electronic music, world music and traditional orchestral arrangements. Among his awards are four National Film Awards, two Academy Awards, two Grammy Awards, a BAFTA Award, a Golden Globe, fifteen Filmfare Awards and sixteen Filmfare Awards. He has been awarded the Padma Bhushan, the third highest civilian award, in 2010 by the Government of India. In 2009, Rahman was included on the Time 100 list of the world's most influential people.

MIHAI TUDOSE

WHY IN NEWS? : Resigned from the post of Prime Minister of Romania

Romanian Prime Minister Mihai Tudose has resigned after his party withdrew its support amid a power struggle with the group's chairman, who himself, is barred from political office because of a vote-rigging conviction. The ruling left-wing Social Democratic Party (PSD) withdrew its support for Tudose.

Country's development minister Paul Stanescu would serve as the interim prime minister. Tudose is the second prime minister ousted by the Social Democrats since they won Romania's December 2016 general election. Earlier in June last year, Prime Minister Sorin Grindeanu was ousted following power struggles within his party and over the country's failed anti-corruption fight.

ANANDIBEN PATEL

WHY IN NEWS? : Appointed as the Governor of Madhya Pradesh

Former Gujarat chief minister Anandiben Patel has been appointed governor of Madhya Pradesh. Patel was first woman chief minister of Gujarat and stepped down in the wake of Patidar and Dalit agitation in the state in 2016. Patel's appointment is meant to placate the Patidar community while keeping her out of state politics

BACKGROUND: Anandiben Patel (born 21 November 1941) is an Indian politician and the former Chief Minister of Gujarat. She was the first woman Chief Minister of the state. She is a member of the Bharatiya Janata Party (BJP) since 1987. She was the Cabinet Minister for Education from 2002 to 2007. She was the Cabinet Minister of Road and Building, Revenue, Urban development and Urban Housing, Disaster Management and Capital Projects in the Government of Gujarat from 2007 to 2014.

OM PRAKASH RAWAT

WHY IN NEWS? : Appointed as the chief election commissioner

Om Prakash Rawat has been appointed as the next Chief Election Commissioner. Mr Rawat, who is currently an Election Commissioner, will succeed the outgoing Achal Kumar Joti. Ashok Lavasa, a former finance secretary and an Indian Administrative Service officer of the 1980 batch, has been appointed as an Election Commissioner, to fill up the vacancy left behind by Mr Rawat in the three-member poll panel. Sunil Arora is currently the other Election Commissioner. AK Joti, who is retiring, was the Chief Election Commissioner since June 2017.

BACKGROUND: Om Prakash Rawat, a retired IAS officer of the 1977 batch, has previously served as joint secretary in the Ministry of Defence and at many other key positions in the union and Madhya Pradesh governments. He was appointed as the Election Commissioner in August 2015. He will be the 22nd Chief Election Commissioner of India.

DILIP CHENOY

WHY IN NEWS? : Appointed as the Director General of FICCI

The Federation of Indian Chambers of Commerce & Industry (FICCI) has appointed Mr. Dilip Chenoy as its Director General. Mr. Chenoy has been the Managing Director and Chief Executive Officer of the National Skill Development Corporation (NSDC), Director General of the Society of Indian Automobile Manufacturers (SIAM) and Deputy Director General of the Confederation of Indian Industry (CII).

He was awarded the Game Changer Award in 2015 and the Rashtriya Media Ratan Award in 2013. He has been a Member of the Governing Council of the Institute of Applied Manpower Research and Member of Germany-India Skills Working Group. He was recently appointed Chairman of Sant Longowal Institute of Engineering and Technology and Member, Board of Advisors, IILM.

PRIYANKA CHOPRA

WHY IN NEWS?: Named as the Global Brand Ambassador of Harman International

HARMAN International, a wholly-owned subsidiary of Samsung Electronics Co., Ltd. focused on connected technologies for automotive, consumer and enterprise markets, today announced that actress, singer, producer and philanthropist Priyanka Chopra has been named a global brand ambassador for the company's JBL and Harman Kardon® audio brands. Chopra will participate in a series of marketing initiatives including social media and brand awareness events for JBL and Harman Kardon. As ambassador of these brands, Chopra will walk the red carpet at the Clive Davis Pre-GRAMMY Gala Salute to Industry Icons with other luminaries as part of this weekend's GRAMMY celebration. HARMAN is the official sound of the GRAMMYs and a recipient of three technical awards for its JBL, AKG and Lexicon brands.

ANUSHKA SHARMA KOHLI

WHY IN NEWS? : Named as PETA's 2017 Person of the Year

Newly-wed actress Anushka Sharma, who has always worked towards the welfare of animals, has been named PETA's 2017 Person of the Year. The actress, who is a vegetarian, has got the award for her wide-reaching work for animals, from helping to protect dogs from fireworks to advocating for horses who are forced to pull carriages in Mumbai.

In 2015, Anushka Sharma was named PETA's Hottest Vegetarian Celebrity. Some of her recent efforts to protect animals include launching her cruelty-free NUSH clothing line, visiting an animal shelter and promoting its work on her social media platforms, launching a campaign called PAWsitive to raise awareness of the suffering fireworks cause to animals, and taking to Twitter to demand a ban on cruel carriage rides in Mumbai - where often-lame horses are forced to haul passengers in all weather extremes without adequate rest, food, or water. Sharma lives with her beloved adopted dog, Dude.

Past recipients of PETA's Person of the Year Award include Dr Shashi Tharoor, former Supreme Court Justice KS Radhakrishnan Panicker, and actors Kapil Sharma, Hema Malini, R Madhavan, and Jacqueline Fernandez.

RAJINDER KHANNA

WHY IN NEWS? : Appointed Deputy National Security Adviser

CAREER: The Appointments Committee of the Cabinet, headed by Prime Minister Narendra Modi, has approved the appointment of Rajinder Khanna as the Deputy NSA on re-employment and on contractual basis. He headed the Research and Analysis Wing (RAW) from December 2014 for a fixed two-year period.

The National Security Council, headed by the Prime Minister, is the top body on all internal and external security-related matters. National Security Adviser Ajit Doval is its secretary. It is for the first time when both the NSA and Deputy NSA are from intelligence agency background.

NARINDER BATRA

WHY IN NEWS? : Elected as president of Indian Olympic Association (IOA)

CAREER: International Hockey Federation Chief Narinder Batra was elected as president of Indian Olympic Association (IOA) for a four-year term by an overwhelming majority in the polls held at its Annual General Meeting.

The 60-year-old Batra secured 142 votes while his rival Anil Khanna got 13 in a two-way contest in the polls held under the supervision of a three-member Election Commission, comprising retired High Court justices. S K Mendiratta, a legal advisor to the Election Commission of India, was the returning officer.

Batra thus has become one of the few sports administrators who head an important international federation as well as a National Olympic Committee.

President: Narinder Batra

Senior Vice-President: R K Anand

Vice-President: Addille Sumariwalla, Birendra Prasad Baishya, V D Nanavati, Sudhanshu Mittal, Sunaina Kumari, K Govindraj, Kuldeep Vats, Karan Chautala.

FEBRUARY 18 ROUNDUP

NATIONAL

INDIAN NAVY LAUNCHES INS KARANJ

DATE: 1st February 2018

OBJECTIVE: To guard the Indian coastline and secure India's interests in the Indian Ocean and Indo-Pacific Region

The Indian Navy has launched the third Scorpene-class submarine, INS Karanj. It was launched at Mazagon Dock shipyard in Mumbai.

Karanj is a milestone in indigenous defence manufacturing and it is the first time that the third submarine of a series has been manufactured indigenously. Karanj is equipped with stealth features and one of the lowest noise signatures. The submarine has an overall length of 67.5 metre and a height of about 12.3 metres. The hull form, fin and hydroplanes are specifically designed to produce minimum underwater resistance.

The newly launched vessel is scheduled to undergo a series of in-harbour and at-sea trials before its commissioning into service. The launch of Karanj marked a significant departure from the manning and training philosophy that was adopted for the first two submarines.

INS Kalvari and INS Khanderi are first two Scorpene-class submarines.

PM AUTHORS BOOK FOR STUDENTS

DATE: 4th February 2018

OBJECTIVE: To infuse confidence in students and prepare them to face the examinations and life

"Exam Warriors" written by Prime Minister Narendra Modi was launched by External Affairs Minister Sushma Swaraj in New Delhi. The book is intended for students who are set to appear for examinations this year and in future. The book is a compilation of PM's address to students focused on busting stress during exams in his monthly radio programme "Mann ki Baat".

Speaking on the occasion Ms. Swaraj said that the book is most relevant one in this exam season as it aims to instill confidence in the students and prepare them to face the difficult moments during examinations and life. She also described in detail the 25 'mantras' for students given by the Prime Minister in his book and urged them to read the book.

Union Human Resources Development Minister Prakash Javadekar was also present on the occasion.

Exam Warriors is written in a fun and interactive style, with illustrations, activities and yoga exercises. It is published by Penguin Random House India.

LPG PANCHAYAT

DATE: 13th February 2018

OBJECTIVE: To provide a platform for LPG consumers to interact with each other

The LPG Panchayat was organised by Ministry of Petroleum and Natural Gas and hosted by Rashtrapati Bhavan. The aim of the panchayat is to provide a platform for LPG consumers to interact with each other, promote mutual learning and share experiences. LPG Panchayats are organised as part of the Prime Minister Ujjwala Yojana (PMUY).

Each LPG Panchayat has about 100 LPG customers coming together, near their living areas, to discuss safe and sustainable usage of LPG, its benefits and the link between clean fuel for cooking and women's empowerment. The Ministry of Petroleum and Natural Gas intends to conduct 1 lakh such Panchayats across India before March 31, 2019.

DEVELOPMENT PROJECTS AT DAMAN & DIU

DATE: 24th February 2018

OBJECTIVE: To develop the infrastructure of Daman & Diu

Various development projects worth ₹1000 crores were launched in Daman & Diu by Prime Minister Narendra Modi.

PM laid foundation stones for various projects which include beach-front development, sea-front development, lake & market redevelopment. Projects like a heliport, water pipeline, a pedestrian bridge over the Daman Ganga River, a hostel for girls and a sports complex in Daman, among others, were also inaugurated on the occasion.

He distributed certificates to the beneficiaries of Pradhan Mantri Aawas yojana, Pradhan Mantri Jeevan Jyoti Bima Yojana, Pradhan Mantri Jeevan Suraksha Yojana, Pradhan Mantri MUDRA Yojana and also distributed permits for CNG driven vehicles.

The Prime Minister also presented Badhai kit to the newly born girl child under Beti Bachao, Beti Padhao yojana. He handed over certificates to women given free driving training by Daman and Diu administration and cycle to school going girls.

The PM inaugurated Air Odisha's flight connecting Ahmedabad with Diu under the Centre's regional connectivity scheme UDAN (*Ude Desh ka Aam Naagrik*). The Indian PM also launched helicopter services between Daman and Diu which are to be operated by Pawan Hans Ltd.

DRDO CARRIES OUT TEST-FLIGHT OF RUSTOM-2

DATE: 25th February 2018

OBJECTIVE: To develop long-endurance UAV for combat & surveillance

The Defence Research and Development Organization (DRDO) successfully carried out its newly-developed Unmanned Aerial Vehicle (UAV). The test flight of UAV named Rustom-2 took place from Aeronautical Test Range (ATR) at Chalakere in Chitradurga district of Karnataka.

Rustom-2 or TAPAS-BH-201 is a medium-altitude long-endurance UAV that has been developed by India on the lines of the American Predator drones. It is also significant due to the fact that it is the first flight in user configuration with higher power engine. The development from Rustom-1 to Rustom-2 took around seven years.

The Rustom-2 is best suited for combat roles as it is capable of flying for 24 hours at stretch and can carry weapons along with surveillance equipment.

ISSUES

INDIA SLIPS 10 RANKS TO 42 ON DEMOCRACY INDEX

DATE: 1ˢᵗ February, 2018

India world's largest democracy has slipped to 42nd place on an annual Global Democracy Index amid "rise of conservative religious ideologies" and increase in vigilantism and violence against minorities as well as other dissenting voices. While Norway has again topped the list, followed by Iceland and Sweden, compiled by the Economist Intelligence Unit (EIU), India has moved down from 32ⁿᵈ place last year and remains classified among "flawed democracies". India's overall score dropped by 0.58 points from 7.81 to 7.23.

This year's report which also measured the state of media freedom around the world noted that in India, media is "partially free". Moreover, journalists are at risk from government, military and non-state actors and radical groups, and the threat of violence has a chilling effect on media coverage.

WEST BENGAL BECOMES FIRST STATE TO OPT OUT OF "MODICARE"

DATE: 15ᵗʰ February, 2018

Chief Minister Mamata Banerjee has announced to opt out of Centre's '**Modicare**' scheme, saying the Bengal government had already enrolled 50 lakh people under its own Swasthya Sathi programme. National Health Protection Scheme (NHPS) also called Ayushman Bharat Scheme dubbed 'Modicare' seeks to provide health insurance to poor and vulnerable households. NHPS provides up to ₹ 5 lakh insurance cover to each family per year in secondary and tertiary care institutions. NHPS will have 50 crore beneficiaries which will cover the population larger than combined citizenry of US, UK, Germany and France. The Centre had drawn up health plan for the scheme in which 40% of fund for the scheme has to come from state. Under it, the central government will contribute ₹ 2,000 crore to scheme out of a total cost of ₹ 5,500-6,000 crore – the remaining amount is to be paid by the state governments. National Health Protection Scheme (NHPS) was announced in Union Budget 2018-19, where as Swasthaya Sathi scheme was launched by Bengal Govt. in the year 2016. Swasthaya Sathi scheme provides paperless, cashless, smart card based, basic health cover for secondary and tertiary care up to ₹ 1.5 Lakh per annum through Insurance mode (PSU) and Critical illness like Cancer, Neuro surgeries, cardiothoracic surgeries, liver diseases, blood disorders etc. up to ₹ 5 Lakh through assurance mode.

CAUVERY VERDICT: SC REDUCES TAMIL NADU'S WATER SHARE, KARNATAKA'S INCREASED

DATE: 16th February, 2018

The Supreme Court of India reduces Tamil Nadu's share of Cauvery water by 14.75 tmcft water per year, diverting the same to Karnataka.

SC directed the Karnataka government to release 177.25 tmcft of Cauvery water to Tamil Nadu from its inter-state Biligundlu dam, which is down from the state's earlier allocation of 192 TMC water. Earlier, as described in the Cauvery Water Tribunal's order in 2007, Karnataka had a share of 270 tmcft of Cauvery water. Now it will go up to 284.75 tmcft. The judgement was delivered by a bench comprising Chief Justice Dipak Misra, Justices Amitava Roy and A M Khanwilkar. During the ruling, Justice Misra stated that the Cauvery tribunal's 2007 award of 30 tmcft water to Kerala and 7 tmcft water to Puducherry will remain unchanged. The apex court also allowed Tami Nadu to draw an additional 10 tmcft 'groundwater' from a total of 20 tmcft beneath the Cauvery basin.

The court's order on the Cauvery water allocation will continue to hold for the next 15 years.

42 INDIAN LANGUAGES HEADING TOWARDS EXTINCTION

DATE: 20th February, 2018

According to a report of the census directorate, there are 22 scheduled languages and 100 non-scheduled languages in the country which are spoken by a large number of people. As mentioned in a list prepared by UNESCO, there are around 42 languages or dialects which are spoken by less than 10,000 people in India are endangered and may be heading towards extinction. Apart from the 22 scheduled languages, there are 31 other languages in the country which were given the status of official language by various state governments and Union territories. According to the census data, there are 1,635 rationalised mother tongues, 234 identifiable mother tongues and 22 major languages in the country.

The languages or dialects which were considered endangered, include 11 from Andaman and Nicobar Islands (Great Andamanese, Jarawa, Lamongse, Luro, Muot, Onge, Pu, Sanenyo, Sentilese, Shompen and Takahanyilang), seven from Manipur (Aimol, Aka, Koiren, Lamgang, Langrong, Purum and Tarao) and four from Himachal Pradesh (Baghati, Handuri, Pangvali and Sirmaudi). Manda, Parji and Pengo (Odisha), Koraga and Kuruba (Karnataka), Gadaba and Naiki (Andhra Pradesh), Kota and Toda (Tamil Nadu), Mra and Na (Arunachal Pradesh), Tai

Nora and Tai Rong (Assam), Bangani (Uttarakhand), Birhor (Jharkhand), Nihali (Maharashtra), Ruga (Meghalaya) and Toto (West Bengal) are also in the list of endangered language.

The Central Institute of Indian Languages, Mysore, has been working for the protection and preservation of endangered languages of the country.

MALDIVES PRESIDENT DECLARES EMERGENCY

DATE: 6th February, 2018

Maldives government has declared a state of emergency as political unrest intensified after a court ordered the release and retrial of political prisoners. Azima Shakoor (Legal Affairs Minister) announces the state of emergency on state television. The latest political crisis in Maldives is the culmination of a standoff between President Abdulla Yameen and the Maldives Supreme Court, which last week ruled that nine opponents of the president had been unfairly convicted. Those opponents include exiled former president Nasheed (who in 2015 was sentenced to 13 years in prison after a trial broadly viewed as politically motivated) and Mohamed Nazim (a former defense minister who many Maldivians believe was framed). Opposition protests have gathered pace as the President continues to refuse the court's order to free the jailed dissidents.

The United Nations and several foreign governments, including the United States, have urged the Maldives to respect the court order.

BERMUDA BECOMES WORLD'S FIRST JURISDICTION TO REPEAL SAME-SEX MARRIAGE

DATE: 8th February, 2018

Just six months after legalizing same-sex marriage, Bermuda announces, it will be rolling back the law and replacing it with an alternative. The governor approves the bill reversing the right of gay couples to marry, despite a Supreme Court ruling last year authorizing same-sex marriage. The act is intended to strike a fair balance between two currently irreconcilable groups in Bermuda, by restating that marriage must be between a male and a female while at the same time recognizing and protecting the rights of same-sex couples.

Couples in a registered domestic partnership will now have "equivalent" rights to those of married heterosexual couples, including the right to make medical decisions on behalf of one's partner. The legislation will balance opposition to same-sex marriage on the socially conservative island.

TANZANIA WITHDRAWS FROM UN REFUGEE PROGRAMME

DATE: 13th February, 2018

Tanzania announces its withdrawal of United Nation's **"Comprehensive Refugee Response Framework (CRRF)"** citing security reasons and lack of funds. Tanzania considered a safe haven for refugees, particularly from conflict-hit Democratic Republic of Congo (DRC) and Burundi. Tanzania informed the United Nations High Commissioner for Refugees (UNHCR) in January that it was suspending the granting of citizenship to some Burundian refugees and that it would discourage new asylum applications. **United Nations High Commission for Refugees (UNHCR)** granting citizenship for some refugees and their applications. The main specification New York Declaration for Refugees and Migrants calls upon UNHCR to develop and initiate the application of CRRF.

WORLD LEADERS ABANDONING HUMAN RIGHTS: AMNESTY

DATE: 22nd February, 2018

According to Amnesty International's annual human rights report published on 22nd February, World leaders are undermining human rights for millions of people with regressive policies and hate-filled rhetoric, but their actions have ignited global protest movements in response. US President Donald Trump, Russian leader Vladimir Putin, and China's President Xi Jinping, leaders of Egypt, the Philippines and Venezuela were among a number of politicians who rolled out regressive policies in 2017. Amnesty's The State of the World's Human Rights report cites Trump's controversial travel ban prohibiting entrants to the US from six Muslim-majority countries, Venezuelan authorities' use of force against demonstrators and unlawful killings in the Philippines' anti-drug war as evidence of policies resulting in an international regression on human rights. The regressive approach to human rights adopted by a number of world powerful leaders has, however, inspired new waves of social activism and protest.

IDEAS

NATIONAL

GOVERNMENT TO LAUNCH KUSUM SCHEME

DATE: 3th February, 2018

OBJECTIVE: To encourage farmers for solar farming

Union Government announces a fund of ₹ 1.4 lakh-crore for the ambitious Kisan Urja Suraksha evam Utthaan Mahaabhiyan (KUSUM) scheme. The scheme will work towards promoting solar power production up to 28,250 MW to help farmers. These schemes have four components. First is to utilize the barren land by farmers. It will build 10,000 MW solar plants on barren lands for solar farming. Second component includes installation of 17.5 lakh off grid solar farm pumps. Third component is grid connected farm pumps will be solarized.

Farmers will be given a chance to earn extra income if they help produce additional power by setting up solar power project on their barren land. The energy produced by the farmers on their barren land will be bought by the state electricity distribution companies (DISCOMS). The scheme is likely to decrease the consumption of diesel in the agriculture sector. Solar farming promotes decentralized solar power production and energy efficiency along with water security to the farmers. It will lessen the burden of diesel costs on the farmers and help them earn extra income when they set up the solar power plant on their barren land.

The total central financial assistance under scheme will be for a period of 10 years and will be ₹ 48,000 crore.

MASS MARRIAGE IN UP

DATE: 4th February, 2018

OBJECTIVE: To discourage the practice of dowry

Uttar Pradesh government has come up with a mass marriage policy for poor girls under which financial assistance of ₹ 35,000 along with gifting mobile phones and household items will be given at each wedding. It will certainly discourage dowry in marriages. Social welfare department will conduct the mass marriages. The marriage programs regarding the scheme will be organized by urban local bodies like Nagar panchayat, Nagar Palika and Nagar Nigam, Kshetra panchayats, Zila panchayats, Semi-government organizations and NGOs, which will be authorized by district magistrates of respective districts. As per the scheme, the parents of the brides must be the residents of Uttar Pradesh and must belong to Below Poverty Line (BPL) families in order to avail the benefits of the scheme. There must be minimum 10 couples in the mass marriage ceremony.

GOOGLE AND NCERT JOIN HANDS TO TEACH STUDENTS DIGITAL SAFETY

DATE: 6th February, 2018

OBJECTIVE: To make children digital citizens Google and National Council of Educational Research and Training (NCERT) have signed a pact to integrate a course on 'Digital Citizenship and Safety' in information and communication technology (ICT) curriculum. The pact is signed on 'Safer Internet Day' (February 6). The course aims to bring awareness amongst the young generations of India to make Internet a safe space. The curriculum is developed by NCERT in collaboration with Google will be used to train students from class I - class XII across 1.4 million schools in India where they will learn how to become good and responsible digital citizens. The course by Google India aims to bring social, ethical and legal aspects of internet safety and usage via structured in class lesson. The curriculum is structured with four themes - being smart, being safe, being a digital citizen and being future ready to match the intellectual and curiosity needs of different age group of the children. As they advance through their classes, they will be taught more advanced topics such as privacy, device management, intellectual property and reputation management. Finally, as they become ready to graduate as digital citizens, they will be prepared with online financial literacy and cyber crime concepts so that they are future ready.

In addition, Google has also created curriculum for teachers so that they can help students learn all about digital citizenship in their classrooms.

INTERNATIONAL

CHINA SEEKS TO SCRAP TERM LIMIT FOR PRESIDENT

DATE: 25th February, 2018

China is set to change its Constitution to remove a two-term limit on the presidency, making it possible for President Xi Jinping to remain in office beyond his current term in 2023. The party's Central Committee proposed to remove from the constitution the expression that China's president and vice president shall serve no more than two consecutive terms. It will be approved at an annual meeting of parliament that will be held on March 5, 2018. If China approves this proposal, Mr Xi need not step down after 10 years in office, unlike his immediate predecessors, Mr Hu Jintao and Mr Jiang Zemin. This approval will change the country's political course, securing Xi Jinping's place as the most powerful leader after Mao Zedong, who ruled China for more than three decades beginning in 1976.

SAUDI ARABIA ALLOWS WOMEN TO ENLIST IN MILITARY

DATE: 27th February, 2018

The kingdom of Saudi Arabia now permits women to enlist in the army to enact reforms granting females more access to a wide range of previously forbidden careers. Women citizens of Saudi Arabia aged between 25 and 35 with a high school diploma can now able to apply for positions with the rank of soldier in the provinces of Riyadh, Mecca, al-Qassim and Medina. Under Saudi Arabia's guardianship system, women who apply to join the army must also have a place of residence in the same provinces as the job's location with their male guardians, usually husband, father, brother or son. The Saudi kingdom has also opened 140 positions for women at airports and border crossings. 107,000 females have applied for these posts.

PEOPLE

JACOB ZUMA

DATE: 14th February, 2018

Resigned from the post of South African President

South African President, Jacob Zuma resigned after severe pressure from his own party, the African National Congress. This comes hours before a no-confidence motion against him came in the Parliament.

Zuma announced his resignation and added that he disagreed with his party's decision. The 75-year-old leader said that violence and division within the ANC had forced him to quit. Zuma has been accused, among other things, of using government money to build a luxurious private home. Under his rule, economic growth slowed down and unemployment reached record levels. Zuma, who has ruled South Africa since the end of apartheid, was till date considered the most powerful person in the country.

The South African Police raided the Johannesburg home of a business family that is reportedly close to Zuma. The Indian-born Gupta brothers – Ajay, Atul and Rajesh – have been accused of "state capture", a term coined to describe how the family allegedly used its relationship with Zuma to influence state contracts, Cabinet appointments and secure several multimillion-dollar deals in the country.

Deputy President Cyril Ramaphosa, who took over the leadership of the ANC in December 2017, is now set to be elected by the Parliament to the highest office. Soon after Ramaphosa took over the party, analysts had pointed out he was likely to recall Zuma from presidency.

HAILEMARIAM DESALEGN

DATE: 15th February, 2018

Resigned from the post of Ethiopian Prime Minister

Ethiopian Prime Minister Hailemariam Desalegn has submitted his resignation letter after the worst anti-government protests in a quarter-century.

Ethiopia has been rocked by months of protests demanding wider freedoms that have left hundreds dead and tens of thousands detained. The government in recent weeks released more than 6,500 detained opposition figures, journalists and others after the prime minister in a surprise announcement in January said he wanted to "widen the democratic space for all."

The protests have disrupted life and business in one of Africa's fastest-growing economies.

Ethiopia's demonstrations demanding wider freedoms began in late 2015 and engulfed much of the restive Oromia and Amhara regions before spreading into other parts of the country, leading to a months-long state of emergency that has since been lifted.

Ethiopia's government has long been accused of arresting critical journalists and opposition leaders. Rights organizations and opposition groups have called for their release, saying they were arrested on trumped-up charges and punished for their points of view.

The academician-turned-politician has led Ethiopia since 2012 after the death of former strongman Meles Zenawi. He also served as deputy prime minister and foreign minister under the former leader before assuming power. He was also elected chairman of the African Union in 2013.

BARNABY JOYCE

DATE: 22nd February, 2018

Quit as Australia's deputy prime minister

Barnaby Joyce quit as Australia's deputy prime minister after having an extramarital affair with his former media adviser, leading to allegations that he breached ministerial guidelines. The revelations have damaged Joyce's credibility as a family man and he has also faced claims that he allowed Campion to work in his and another ministerial office during the affair — potentially breaching the ministerial code of conduct.

The issue dominated headlines in Australian media, taking the spotlight away from the prime minister's policy agenda, including his bid to legislate corporate and personal tax cuts. The affair has also spurred a debate about what parts of a parliamentarian's life are private and should be off-limits to media reporting. The Nationals will need to vote on a new party leader, with Michael McCormack, Darren Chester and David Littleproud expected to be among the frontrunners.

AMEENAH GURIB-FAKIM

DATE: 17nd March, 2018

Resigned as the president of Mauritius

Mauritian President Ameenah Gurib-Fakim has resigned after allegations of credit card fraud. Gurib-Fakim has been accused of buying jewellery and clothing using a credit card provided by an NGO, founded by an Angolan banker interested in doing business in Mauritius.

The allegations against the president, who is also a renowned biologist, stem from her joining the London-based Planet Earth Institute (PEI) in 2015 in an effort to further develop the scientific field in Africa.

In 2016, she received a credit card from PEI to pay for travel and other expenses related to her work for the organisation. Gurib-Fakim, 58, allegedly used the credit card to buy items worth $26,000 not related to her work for PEI.

PEI was founded by Alvaro Sobrinho, an Angolan businessman whose efforts to set up enterprises in Mauritius have come under scrutiny.

MARCH 18 ROUNDUP

EVENTS

NATIONAL

RS 2,900 CRORE APPROVED FOR NIRBHAYA FUND

DATE: 1st March 2018

OBJECTIVE: To make the eight major cities of the country safer for women

The Centre has approved projects worth ₹ 2900 crore under the Nirbhaya fund for eight major cities of the country in a bid to make them safer for women. The Nirbhaya Fund was set after the gruesome gang-rape and murder of a student in 2012 in Delhi.

The eight major cities are Delhi, Mumbai, Kolkata, Chennai, Bengaluru, Hyderabad, Ahmedabad and Lucknow.

The Empowered Committee headed by the secretary of Women and Child Development (WCD) sanctioned a total of ₹ 2,919.55 crore on this head. They have also given red signal to the trial of panic button feature on mobile phones in Uttar Pradesh which will be initiated later in March. They have also sanctioned setting up of a model forensic science laboratory in Chandigarh.

The national capital has been sanctioned ₹ 663.67 crore for using the latest technologies like facial recognition analytics, video monitoring, and tracking of people along with GPS equipped police patrol vans with the capability of sharing video feed.

Mumbai will get ₹ 252 crore for projects like strengthening of 'Police Didi' programme, mapping of criminal hotspots, video surveillance, etc.

Kolkata has been granted ₹ 181.32 crore and Bengaluru has got ₹ 667 crore for sanctioned projects.

1ST MEGA FOOD PARK INAUGURATED IN MAHARASHTRA

DATE: 1st March 2018

OBJECTIVE: To boost food processing industry such that agricultural sector grows exponentially

The first Mega Food Park, M/s Satara Mega Food Park Pvt. Ltd. has been inaugurated at Village Degaon, District Satarawas in Maharashtra by Smt. Harsimrat Kaur Badal, Minister of Food Processing Industries in the esteemed presence of Chief Minister of the state, Shri Devendra Fadnavis.

This is the 12th Mega Food Park to be operationalised in the country and the 10th to be operationalised during the tenure of the current government.

The main aim behind these is to double the farmer's income and to facilitate Make In India program of the government.

The Ministry of Food Processing Industries is implementing Mega Food Park Scheme in the country to give a boost to the food processing sector by adding value and reducing food wastage at every stage of the supply chain with main focus on perishables. Advanced and modern infrastructure facilities for food processing along the value chain from farm to market are being developed by Mega Food Parks.

Under this scheme, the Government of India provides financial assistance up to ₹ 50 Crore per Mega Food Park project. As informed by the Minister, the Mega Food Park will leverage an investment of estimated ₹ 250 crores in 25-30 food processing units in the park.

WINGS INDIA 2018

DATE: 8th March 2018

OBJECTIVE: To focus on fostering partnership to transform Indian aviation and the role of conducive regulatory framework to facilitate growth of civil aviation market

The four-day biennial event 'WINGS INDIA 2018' was inaugurated by Telangana IT and Industries Minister K T Rama Rao at the Begumpet Airport. The theme of the event this year is 'India-Global Aviation Hub'. The event saw presence of senior ministers of Telangana Government and senior officials of Ministry of Civil Aviation, DGCA, AAI and representatives from FICCI.

NATIONAL ELECTION QUIZ 2018

DATE: 11th March 2018

OBJECTIVE: To promote electoral literacy among youngsters in the age group of 14 to 17.

The National Election Quiz 2018 (NEQ 2018), organised by the Election Commission of India culminated with its grand finale in the capital city. The programme attracted a record participation of 13,63,982 students from 38,160 schools. The marathon quiz programme began in November 2017.

Winning teams from the six zones, Manipur, Puducherry, Goa, Delhi, Jharkhand and Jammu & Kashmir, contested for the prestigious trophy in the finale.

The NEQ 2018 trophy was lifted by Madhur Jain and Aditya Kumar of the DPS, Ranchi, Jharkhand. The first runner-up position was sealed by St. Patrick Matriculation Higher Secondary School, Puducherry, represented by V. Vishnu Priya and R.Mithun Krishna. The second runners-up were Shangker Singh

Laishram and Ashmaan Mainali of the Jawahar Navodaya Vidyalaya, Senapati, Manipur. The grand finale was anchored by the renowned quiz master Shri Vikram Joshi.

The winners got a cash reward of ₹ 1,00,000. The first runner-up team got ₹ 80,000 and the second runner up ₹ 60,000. The other three finalist teams took home the cash purse of ₹ 50,000.

SOLAR POWER PLANT INAUGURATED IN UP

DATE: 12th March 2018

OBJECTIVE: To generate electricity of around 75 MW and cater to the nearby areas

Uttar Pradesh's biggest solar plant was inaugurated in Mirzapur district's Chhanvey block by Prime Minister Narendra Modi and French President Emmanuel Macron.

The solar power plant has been built by French form ENGIE at a cost of roughly ₹ 500 crore. The 75 MW solar plant has come up at Dadar Kalan village on the hilly terrain of the Vindhyas range. The hilly slopes of the village were full of shrubs and thorny vegetation before the work began for setting up the solar power plant. Over an area of 380 acres, some 1,18,600 solar panels have been set up.

The power generated from the plant would be transmitted to Jigna sub-station of Mirzapur range of Uttar Pradesh Power Corporation Ltd. It will generate 15.6 crore units of electricity annually, about 1.30 crore units per month.

The plant has been built by a workforce of 800 people. Around 50 persons would be looking after the maintenance of the plant.

The solar panels were tested and immediately energized after Indian PM and the French President pressed the button and dedicated the facility to the nation.

105TH INDIAN SCIENCE CONGRESS INAUGURATED

DATE: 16th March 2018

OBJECTIVE: To focus on science disciplines which impact society and sustainable development

105th session of Indian Science Congress (ISC) was inaugurated by Prime Minister Narendra Modi at Manipur Central University in Imphal. The theme of this year's ISC is "Reaching the Unreached Through Science & Technology".

Under the given theme, the scientists from across world will look at bridging social gaps through innovations. The focal areas will be on science disciplines which impact society and sustainable development.

The five day event is organised by the Indian Science Congress Association (ISCA), a premier scientific organisation of India.

ISSUES

NATIONAL

RIGHT TO DIE WITH DIGNITY A FUNDAMENTAL RIGHT: SC

DATE: 9th March, 2018

SC has passed an order that allows passive euthanasia in the country. Court has held that right to die with dignity is a fundamental right. The Bench also held that a living will also legally valid. The Court has issued detailed guidelines in this regard.

"The right to life and liberty as envisaged under Article 21 of the Constitution is meaningless unless it encompasses within its sphere individual dignity. With the passage of time, this Court has expanded the spectrum of Article 21 to include within it the right to live with dignity as component of right to life and liberty."

The Bench also held that the right to live with dignity also includes the smoothening of the process of dying in case of a terminally ill patient or a person in Persistent vegetative state with no hope of recovery. It also laid down principles for execution of advance directives and spelt out guidelines and safeguards to give effect to passive euthanasia. The directive and guidelines shall remain in force till Parliament brings legislation in the field.

RAJASTHAN PASSES BILL FOR DEATH PENALTY FOR CHILD RAPE

DATE: 10th March, 2018

To protect girl child by laying down deterrent punishment, including death sentence Rajasthan passed a bill providing for the death penalty to the people convicted of raping girls under12 years of age or below. State Assembly has passed Criminal Laws (Rajasthan Amendment) Bill, 2018 by voice vote to amend Indian Penal Code (IPC), 1860. The Bill aims to protect girl child by laying down deterrent punishment, including death sentence, to offenders of child rape of girls below 12. The Bill inserts sections 376-AA and 376-DD in IPC, 1860. These sections provide, that whoever commits rape or gang-rape on a girl up to 12 years of age shall be punishable with death or rigorous imprisonment. The capital punishment under it will be not less than 14 years and 20 years respectively for sections and which may extend to imprisonment for life, which means imprisonment for remainder of offenders' whole life, and with fine.

National Crime Record Bureau (NCRB) 2016 report marks a steady rise in the cases of crimes against children in Rajasthan. The state recorded 3.8 % of the crimes against children (98,344) registered across the country. It stands fourth in the crime against women category. The Rajasthan government took the step in view of the rising crimes against women and children.

DEATH PENALTY SHOULD STAY: 12 OUT OF 14 STATES/UTS

DATE: 13th March, 2018

Death penalty should stay as it serves to act as deterrent in cases of heinous crimes 12 out of 14 States/UTs' reply to Home Ministry that capital punishment or death penalty should stay as it serves to act as deterrent in cases of heinous crimes such as murder and rape. In 2013, the Supreme Court had asked Law Commission to examine whether death penalty is deterrent punishment or is retributive justice. Justice A P shah had in its report proposed abolition of capital punishment for non-terrorism cases (i.e. it should be abolished for all crimes other than terrorism related offences and waging war). On the recommendation of Law commission of India, The Home Ministry had forwarded proposal to abolish death penalty to states/UTs. Gujarat, Chhattisgarh, Madhya Pradesh, Rajasthan, Jharkhand, Bihar, Tamil Nadu and Delhi vetoed abolition of capital punishment, while only two states, Karnataka and Tripura, want practice to be done away with.

India among a handful of countries such as China, Iran, Iraq and Saudi Arabia are still carrying out executions. At the end of 2014, 98 countries had abolished the death penalty, seven had abolished it for "ordinary crimes", and 35 were abolitionists in practice, making 140 countries abolitionists in law or practice. Among 140 countries, Suriname, Madagascar and Fiji formally abolished the death penalty in 2015.

TRIBUNAL TO SOLVE MAHANADI WATER DISPUTE BETWEEN ODISHA & CHHATTISGARH

DATE: 14th March, 2018

OBJECTIVE: To resolve the Mahanadi river water dispute with the neighboring Chhattisgarh

Union Cabinet approves to constitute of a Tribunal seeking to resolve the long-standing dispute between Odisha and Chhattisgarh on sharing Mahanadi river waters. Tribunal will be constituted under Section 4 of Inter-State River Water Disputes Act, 1956. The three members Tribunal required adjudicating the matter within a timeframe of maximum five years. Chief Justice of India has nominated Supreme Court Judge A M Khanwilkar as chairman of Tribunal, while Justice Ravi Ranjan of Patna High Court and Justice Indwermeet Kaur Kochar of Delhi High Court are two other members of this tribunal. The services of two assessors who are water resources experts having experience in handling sensitive water-related issues will also be provided to this tribunal. The Odisha government has long been demanding setting up the Tribunal to resolve the Mahanadi river water dispute with the neighbouring Chhattisgarh. The Tribunal will determine water sharing among basin states on the basis of the overall availability of water in the complete Mahanadi basin, the contribution of each state, the present utilization of water resources in each state and the potential for future development.

HARYANA PASSES BILL FOR DEATH PENALTY FOR CHILD RAPISTS

DATE: 16th March, 2018

To make the bill pertaining to sexual offences against women and children more stringent

In a move to make the law more stringent, Haryana assembly has passed a Bill pertaining to sexual offences against women and children in the state. Haryana will be third state after Rajasthan and Madhya Pradesh to have such a law. The new bill, Criminal Law (Haryana Amendment) Bill, 2018 will amend the Indian Penal Code 1860, the Code of Criminal Procedure 1973 and the Protection of Children from Sexual Offences Act 2012. The Bill passed would amend Section 376A, 376D, 354 and 354 D (2) of the IPC. The amendment (section 376AA) would mean death penalty or rigorous imprisonment of not less than 14 years extending to life imprisonment for those convicted of raping or gang raping a woman up to 12 years. Another new provision is section 376-DA for a woman up to 12 years who is raped by one or more persons constituting a group or acting in furtherance of a common intention. Now each perpetrator shall be deemed to have committed the offence of rape and will be punished with death or rigorous imprisonment for a term which will not be less than 20 years but which may extend to life imprisonment and with fine.

AMENDMENTS IN SURROGACY (REGULATION) BILL, 2016 APPROVED

DATE: 22nd March, 2018

The Union Cabinet approves for moving official amendments in the "Surrogacy (Regulation) Bill, 2016". The Surrogacy (Regulation) Bill, 2016 proposes to regulate surrogacy in India by establishing National Surrogacy Board at the central level and, State Surrogacy Boards and Appropriate Authorities in the States and Union Territories.

The proposed legislation ensures effective regulation of surrogacy, prohibit commercial surrogacy including sale and purchase of human embryo and gametes and allow altruistic surrogacy to the needy Indian infertile couples. The proposal is also to provide for rights of child born through surrogacy to that of a biological child and mandate for surrogacy clinics to be registered with the appropriate authorities in the states.

The amendments also seek 16 months of extended insurance coverage for the surrogate mother to cover all complications besides a strict clause to safeguard the surrogate mother from exploitation. Further, the rights of surrogate mother and children born out of surrogacy will be protected. The Bill shall apply to whole of India, except the State of Jammu and Kashmir.

SC SEEKS CENTRE'S VIEWS ON POLYGAMY, 'NIKAH HALALA'

DATE: 26th March, 2018

SC issues notices to the Centre and the Law Commission on petitions challenging the constitutional validity of the prevalent practices of polygamy and nikah halala among the Muslim community. Issuing notice, the court noted the grounds stating that though these practices, which come within the domain of Muslim personal law, were not immune from judicial review under the Constitution.

The court has been moved by Sameena Begum, Nafisa Khan, Moullium Mohsin and BJP leader and advocate Ashwini Kumar Upadhyay challenging the practice of polygamy, nikah halala (a requirement for a divorced couple to remarry), nikah mutah (temporary marriage in the Shias) and nikah misyar (short-term marriage among Sunnis) on the grounds of these being violative of Article 14, Article 15 and Article 21 of the Constitution.

One of the petitioners argued that the 2017 judgment of the Supreme Court, which had held instant triple talaq as unconstitutional, did not address these issues. The judge's bench comprising Chief Justice Dipak Misra and Justices A M Khanwilkar and D Y Chandrachud considered the submission and stated that a fresh five-judge constitution bench would be set up to deal with the constitutionality of 'nikah halala' and polygamy.

SC/ST (PREVENTION OF ATROCITIES) ACT: REVIEW PETITION TO BE FILED

DATE: 29th March, 2018

Union Law Ministry is "preparing" to file a review petition against the top court's ruling on the Scheduled Castes and the Scheduled Tribes (Prevention of Atrocities) Act, 1989 that puts a stop to immediate arrests in complaints filed under its provisions. The court further directed that public servants can only be arrested with the written permission of their appointing authority. SC also ruled that before arresting a public servant under the Act, a preliminary investigation by an officer not below the rank of deputy superintendent is a must.

The SCs & the STs (Prevention of Atrocities) Act, 1989 was amended recently to include new offences and to ensure speedy justice to victims. The amended law had come into effect from January 26, 2016. SC/ST (Prevention of Atrocities) Act was enacted in 1989. This Act defines not only atrocities against SCs &STs but also make several rules, regulations etc. for proper protection of these vulnerable classes.

One of the provisions of the law states that public servants (non SC/ST) neglecting his duties related to SCs/STs will be punished with imprisonment for a term of 6 months to 1 year. Ministry of Social Justice is the nodal ministry to enforce the SC & ST (Prevention of Atrocities) Act.

INTERNATIONAL

ONLY 13% OF TIGER CONSERVATION AREAS MEET GLOBAL STANDARDS

DATE: 1ˢᵗ March, 2018

In the survey of over a hundred tiger conservation areas by 11 leading conservation organizations and countries with tiger ranges that are part of the Conservation Assured Tiger Standards (CATS) Partnership, It is found that only 13% of tiger conservation areas meet global standards. The surveyed area is home to approximately 70% of the world's wild tigers. At least one-third of these areas are severely at risk of losing their tigers and most of these sites are in south-east Asia. According to survey, despite poaching being one of the greatest threats faced by the big cats, 85% of the areas surveyed do not have the staff capacity to patrol sites effectively and 61% of the areas in Southeast Asia have very limited anti-poaching enforcement. CATS is set of criteria that allow tiger conservation areas to check if their management will lead to successful tiger conservation. It is organized under seven pillars and 17 elements of critical management activity. Its purpose is to secure safe havens for wild tigers. It is important part of Tx2, WWF's global tiger programme that aims to double wild tiger numbers by the year 2022.

ETHNIC CLEANSING OF ROHINGYA CONTINUES: UN

DATE: 6ᵗʰ March, 2018

Myanmar's "ethnic cleansing" of Rohingya Muslims continues even after six months of insurgent attacks sparked a security response that has driven nearly 700,000 people into Bangladesh. UN Assistant Secretary-General for Human Rights Andrew Gilmour said after a four-day visit to refugee camps in Bangladesh's Cox's Bazar district, "The ethnic cleansing of Rohingya from Myanmar continues. I don't think we can draw any other conclusion from what I have seen and heard in Cox's Bazar." The nature of the violence has changed from the frenzied bloodletting and mass rape of last year to a lower intensity campaign of terror and forced starvation that seems to be designed to drive the remaining Rohingyas from their homes into Bangladesh.

According to Myanmar government, the Rohingyas are illegal immigrants from Bangladesh who were brought to Myanmar by the Britishers as builders and settlers. Government passed a law that limited the Rohingya Muslims' residence to two townships in the western state of Rakhine, which borders Bangladesh and also restricted them to have only two children.

India had also signed a MoU with Myanmar on December 20, 2017 to develop Rakhine state in order to restore normalcy to the region and enable the safe return of the displaced Rohingya community. Despite worldwide criticism, the Myanmar Government maintains that no abuse has been inflicted on the Rohingyas in Rakhine state.

FRANCE TO SET 15 YEARS AS LEGAL AGE OF SEXUAL CONSENT

DATE: 7th March, 2018

The French government has proposed making 15 the age of consent for sex after two high-profile cases in which men escaped rape convictions despite having intercourse with 11-year-old girls. In France, current laws criminalize sex with children under the age of 15 but prosecutors must prove that the sexual act was forced. The issue was brought to the fore after critics and lawmakers said French laws had allowed two men to escape rape charges when they were accused of sex with underage girls. Any sexual act by an adult with a child younger than 15 can be prosecuted as a sexual offence under current French law. But prosecutors hoping to charge an offender with rape must prove the sex was forced, a more complicated question when pre-teens are involved.

The law, once implemented, will set the age at which a person cannot agree to any sexual intercourse at 15 and will criminalize any sexual activity with any minor younger than that age.

PHILIPPINES WITHDRAWS FROM INTERNATIONAL CRIMINAL COURT

DATE: 16th March, 2018

The Philippines formally withdraws from the International Criminal Court(ICC). The Letter, dated March 15, 2018, submitted by Philippine Ambassador to the United Nations Teodoro Locsin Jr. to UN Cabinet Chief Maria Luiza Ribeiro Viotti, a Representative to Secretary General Antonio Guterres, has mentioned that the Philippines is withdrawing from the Rome Statute - which established the ICC in 1998 - as a "principled stand against those who politicise and weaponise human rights". Philippine President Rodrigo Duterte announced his country's withdrawal from the ICC, accusing the body of "baseless, unprecedented and outrageous attacks" against him and his administration, due to the ICC's attempts to investigate his anti-drugs campaign, which has led to over 12,000 deaths, according to Human Rights Watch. Under Article 127 of the Rome Statute, a state party's withdrawal from the treaty can only take effect a year after the written notification is received by the UN Secretary-General. The US and Russia withdrew from the Statute years after signing it, while China, India and the majority of Asian nations never ratified the treaty and are not part of the Hague-based court.

IDEAS

INDIA'S FIRST HELITAXI SERVICE TAKES OFF

DATE: 6th March, 2018

OBJECTIVE: To save the time of people who are in a rush to attend the business meetings at Electronic City

India's first and much awaited helitaxi service takes off in Bengaluru with people overjoyed with the utility. The helitaxi is ready to provide its services between Kempegowda International Airport and Electronic City. This innovative helicopter taxi service is started by Kochi based Thumby Aviation Private Limited, with a service intention of connecting prime locations from Bengaluru airport. The helitaxi service is operated during 6:30am to 9:30 am to 3:15 pm to 6:15 pm between KIA and Electronic City. Thumby Aviation has its own app "Heli Taxi" where the interested one can book their ride. This chopper can seat six passengers at a single trip and charged ₹ 4,130 per seat including GST. It includes pick up from airport terminal to the helipad and allows carrying 15 kg luggage, but would be charged extra for additional luggage. As Bengaluru is one of the busiest cities of India, It has at least 60000 fliers landing or taking off on working days.

BETI BACHAO BETI PADHAO PAN-INDIA EXPANSION

DATE: 9th March, 2018

OBJECTIVE: To save and educate the girl child

Modi government launched the Pan India Expansion of Beti Bachao-Beti Padhao (BBBP) scheme covering all 640 districts of the Country. BBBP, which was launched by PM Modi in 2015 at Panipat in Haryana, currently exists in 161 districts and will be taken to 640 more. Initial focus of BBBP had been on the districts which were either below national average or were the worse in their own states in terms of absolute values of Child Sex Ratio (CSR). As per data available in Health Management Information System, the sex ratio at birth (SRB) 918 in 2014 has improved to 926 in 2016-17.

The main objectives of scheme are to prevent gender biased sex selective elimination, ensuring survival and protection of the girl child. Its objectives also include ensuring education and the social status. It also focuses on awareness and advocacy campaign, and effective enforcement of Pre-Conception & Pre Natal Diagnostic Techniques (PC&PNDT) Act.

INDIA'S FIRST COASTAL POLICING ACADEMY

DATE: 11th March, 2018

OBJECTIVE: To train the police forces in safeguarding the shoreline

The Union home ministry recently sanctions the launch of the National Academy of Coastal Policing (NACP) from a campus of Gujarat's Fisheries Research Centre located in coastal Okha in Dwarka district. It is first-of-its-kind institution of the country that will be created and run by a multi-agency team of paramilitary and defence forces and sharpens the response and skills of the marine forces of multiple states which have sea lines.

As per the home ministry order, the navy and the Coast Guard will help in designing "the training curriculum, providing skilled trainers and ensuring access to jetties and boats" for the trainees of the academy.

HRD MINISTRY TO SET UP 'INNOVATION CELL'

DATE: 15th March, 2018

OBJECTIVE: To promote new ideas and innovation in the country

The HRD ministry has decided to create an innovation cell headed by a scientist and also includes a senior official and young professionals to brainstorm new ideas about promoting innovation in the country. The Union Minister has announced this after a high-level review meeting which deliberated upon the need for such a cell after India moved six ranks up the Global Innovation Index Ranking. The country stood at 66th position in 2016, whereas it ranked 60th in 2017, out of 127 countries.

Further, funds allocated through Higher Education Funding Agency (HEFA) for fast-tracking innovation and research infrastructure in the country's top central technical institutions and Prime Minister's Research Fellowship (PMRF) to 1000 top students from these institutions are also expected to grant the necessary push to India's Innovation and Research efforts.

OKLAHOMA TO BECOME FIRST US STATE TO USE NITROGEN GAS FOR EXECUTIONS

DATE: 15th March, 2018

OBJECTIVE: To provide painless execution

Oklahoma announces its plans to use Nitrogen Gas for executions. It will be the first US State to use Nitrogen Gas for executions once it resumes using the death penalty. State Attorney General Mike Hunter and corrections director Joe Allbaugh have announced the new form of capital punishment. They said nitrogen gas was easy to obtain and resulted in a painless death. Oklahoma has had one of the busiest death chambers in the U.S., but hasn't carried out an execution since 2015 after a series of mishaps, including a botched lethal injection in 2014 that left an inmate writhing on the gurney. In 2015, another inmate who was executed was injected with a drug that was not part of the state's approved procedures, the World reports.

INDIA'S FIRST SIGN LANGUAGE DICTIONARY LAUNCHED

DATE: 23rd March, 2018

OBJECTIVE: To bring uniformity in sign languages

Union Ministry for Social Justice and Empowerment launched the first Indian sign language dictionary. The dictionary has been developed by the Indian Sign Language Research and Training Centre (ISLRTC) and comprises 3,000 Hindi and English words with their corresponding graphic representation of the signs which are used in daily life. The dictionary is available both in print and video format. The basic aim of developing the Indian Sign Language (ISL) Dictionary is to remove communication barriers between the deaf and hearing-impaired communities.

The dictionary contains graphic representations of popular signs used by the hearing impaired and also includes regional variations. It will also enable government officials, teachers, professionals, community leaders and the public at large to learn and use sign language.

WORLD'S FIRST BRASS FUTURES CONTRACTS LAUNCHED

DATE: 23rd March, 2018

OBJECTIVE: To hedge the price risk of brass stakeholders

Multi Commodity Exchange of India (MCX) launches world's first futures trading in brass felicitating brass stakeholder to hedge their price risk. Brass futures will offer the stakeholder a more organized and robust price discovery platform and will help them to use benchmark price of national level. MCX Brass futures will be the first non-ferrous contract with compulsory delivery option. Its price will be quoted as per rate at ex-warehouse Jamnagar (delivery Centre) inclusive of taxes and duties.

This will enable them to reduce their price risk. Almost the entire scrap for making brass gets imported into India, but the importers are not sure on the price until the brass shipments lands in the country.

PEOPLE

NATIONAL

SHATRUGHAN SINHA

WHY IN NEWS? : Honoured with a lifetime achievement award in UK

Actor-politician Shatrughan Sinha has been honoured with a lifetime achievement award for his contribution to the fields of arts and politics at a ceremony in the UK's Parliament complex.

The annual 'Political and Public Life Awards' presented by Britain's Asian Voice weekly newspaper, now in its 12th year, recognises individuals who have made a significant impact on public life or made a difference in their local communities.

Sinha, who started his career as an actor in late 1960s, has to his credit over 225 Hindi feature films besides several in other Indian languages. A member of the ruling BJP, he represents Bihar state's Patna Sahib constituency in the Lok Sabha, the lower house of Parliament.

CONRAD SANGMA

WHY IN NEWS? : Sworn in as the 12th Chief Minister of Meghalaya

Conrad Sangma, son of former Lok Sabha Speaker P A Sangma and chief of National People's Party, sworn in as the 12th Chief Minister of Meghalaya. The 40-year-old was administered the oath by Governor Ganga Prasad at the lawns of the sprawling Raj Bhawan along with 11 ministers from alliance partners United Democratic Party, BJP, People's Democratic Front and Hill State People's Democratic Party.

The National People's Party-led five-party coalition has been named the Meghalaya Democratic Alliance (MDA). All the parties had come together to deny the Congress, which had emerged as the single largest party with 21 seats in the 60-member house, a shot at power. Home Minister Rajnath Singh, BJP president Amit Shah, BJP's North-east in-charge Himanta Biswa Sarma, Assam Chief Minister Sarbananda Sonowal, Arunachal Pradesh Chief Minister Pema Khandu, Manipur Chief Minister N Biren Singh, former Assam chief minister Prafulla Kumar Mahanta, former Meghalaya chief ministers Mukul Sangma and D D Lapang, and Nationalist Democratic Progressive Party chief Niephiu Rio attended the swearing-in.

Apart from Conrad, four MLAs of his party NPP, including his brother James Sangma, three of the UDP, two from the PDF and one each from the BJP and HSPDP took oath.

NEIPHIU RIO

WHY IN NEWS? : Sworn in as Nagaland chief minister

Nationalist Democratic Progressive Party (NDPP) leader Neiphiu Rio was sworn in as Nagaland chief minister by governor P.B. Acharya at a public function. This is Rio's fourth time as the chief minister of the northeastern state. Rio is heading the 'People's Democratic Alliance' government in partnership with the BJP in the state.

BJP's Y. Patton administered the oath as the deputy chief minister by the governor. Ten other ministers also administered the oath of office. These included five from the BJP, three from the Nationalist Democratic Progressive Party (NDPP), an independent and a JD(U) MLA.

Defence minister Nirmala Sitharaman, union minister Kiren Rijiju, BJP president Amit Shah and party general secretary Ram Madhav were present at the swearing-in ceremony. The outgoing chief minister T.R. Zeliang was also present at the function. The chief ministers of Assam, Arunachal Pradesh, Manipur and Meghalaya also attended Rio's swearing-in.

INTERNATIONAL

ARMEN SARKISSIAN

WHY IN NEWS? : Elected as the President of Armenia

Armen Sarkissian has been elected the fourth President of Armenia as a result of the vote in the National Assembly. Sarkissian was the only candidate for the presidency. His candidacy was presented by the ruling coalition - Republican Party of Armenia and ARF Dashnaktsutyun. One quarter of the deputies' votes was necessary to nominate a candidate for the presidency. The Tsarukyan bloc did not express a desire to nominate a candidate, while Yelq bloc lacked enough deputies to nominate a candidate.

In accordance with the amendments to the Constitution introduced in 2015, it is the first time when Armenia chooses the president not by way of nationwide elections, but by voting in the National Assembly. Since the Republic has adopted the parliamentary form of government, the prime minister becomes the first official of the state, and the powers of the president have significantly decreased. Armen Sarkissian will take over the office after the powers of the incumbent president expire on April 9.

KRISHNA KUMAR KOHLI

WHY IN NEWS? : Became the first-ever Hindu Dalit woman Senator in Pakistan

Krishna Kumari Kohli from Pakistan's Sindh province has become the first-ever Hindu Dalit woman Senator in the Muslim-majority country. Kolhi, 39, from Thar is a member of Bilawal Bhutto Zardari-led Pakistan People's Party (PPP). She was elected Senator on a minority seat from Sindh. The PPP awarded her the Senate ticket.

Her election represents a major milestone for women and minority rights in Pakistan.

She had joined the PPP as a social activist along with her brother, who was later elected as Chairman of Union Council Berano. Kolhi also actively participated and worked for the rights of downtrodden people of marginalised communities living in Thar and other areas.

EVENTS

NATIONAL

IISC TOPS THE LIST IN OVERALL NIRF RANKINGS 2018

DATE: 3rd April 2018

OBJECTIVE: To set the benchmarks of performance and improve quality of Higher Education

Indian Institute of Science, Bengaluru tops the list in overall rankings of National Institutional Ranking framework (NIRF)-2018 for higher educational Institutions. It also secured the top rank in University category. It is worth mentioning that this premier science institution in the country also secured the overall top ranking last year.

Indian Institute of Management, Ahmedabad bags the first rank in the Management category. AIIMS, New Delhi and NIPER, Mohali got the top ranking in the category of Medical and Pharmacy respectively.

IIT, Kharagpur secured 1st ranking in Architecture, while IIT, Madras in Engineering category. Miranda College, Delhi adjudged as Best College of the country. National Law School of India University, Bengaluru declared as the best Law Institution of India.

JNU, BHU and Anna University and IITs (Madras, Bombay, Delhi, Kharagpur, Kanpur and Roorkee) also made it to the top 10 in overall rankings.

The NIRF framework is an initiative of the Ministry of Human Resource Development to recognise excellence in higher educational institutions.

NATIONAL CONVENTION OF SWACHHAGRAHIS

DATE: 10th April 2018

OBJECTIVE: To spread the message of cleanliness

National Convention of Swachhagrahis was organised at Motihari, East Champaran. The city hosted the event to mark the centenary celebrations of the first Satyagraha led by Mahatma Gandhi inside India (1917). The theme of the convention was "Satyagraha se Swachhagraha".

Prime Minister Narendra Modi attended the event and addressed a gathering of about 20,000 Swachhagrahis. He also distributed awards to Champion Swachhagrahis.

Prime Minister launched the projects worth over Rs. 6600 crore, out of which 3000 crore have been already approved covering 11 projects dedicated to prevent waste water from polluting Ganga.

ISRO LAUNCHES IRNSS-1I

DATE: 12th April 2018

OBJECTIVE: To provide position information in the Indian region and adjoining area

Indian Navigation Satellite IRNSS-1I was launched from ISRO's Polar Satellite Launch Vehicle from Satish Dhawan Space Centre, Sriharikota.

1,425 kg IRNSS-1I was successfully lifted off by using PSLV-C41. This was 43rd flight of PSLV and till this flight it has successfully launched 52 Indian satellites and 237 customer satellites abroad.

After separation from the launch vehicle the solar panels of IRNSS-1I were deployed automatically. ISRO's Master Control Facility at Hassan in Karnataka then took over the control of the Indian navigation satellite.

NavIC or Indian Regional Navigation Satellite System is an independent regional navigation satellite system designed to provide position information in the Indian region and 1500 km around the Indian mainland.

CHENNAI HOSTS DEFEXPO 2018

DATE: 14th April 2018

OBJECTIVE: To find new meeting ground for developing military industrial enterprises

Defence Expo 2018 concluded at Thiruvidanthai in Kancheepuram district on the East Coast Road near Chennai. This was 10th edition of the biennial exhibition on Land, Naval and Internal Homeland Security Systems.

It was attended by Prime Minister Narendra Modi, Raksha Mantri Nirmala Sitharaman, Chief of the Army Staff, General Bipin Rawat, in addition to other dignitaries.

Chief of the Army Staff also interacted with myriad representatives from Governments, scientific community, academia, designers and developers during the exhibition.

The tagline of the DefExpo -'India: The Emerging Defence Manufacturing Hub' rightly reflected the India's Defence manufacturing capabilities to the world. It facilitated brand India as a defence exporter of defence systems and components.

47 official delegations from different countries have participated in DefExpo-18. Ministerial level delegations from USA, UK, Afghanistan, Czech Republic, Finland, Italy, Madagascar, Myanmar, Nepal, Portugal, Republic of Korea, Seychelles, Vietnam also discussed about issues related with defence procurement.

GRAM SWARAJ ABHIYAN LAUNCHED

DATE: 16th April

OBJECTIVE: To deliver welfare schemes to select villages which need particular attention

On the lines of rural development schemes like Antyodaya based on principle of convergence and saturation, Union Govt launched Gram Swaraj Abhiyan on the occasion of Dr. Babasaheb Ambedkar Jayanti (14th April). The initiative aspires for complete coverage of seven plans launched by Central Government for eligible beneficiaries in three-week home window from April 14 to May 5, 2018.

The seven schemes covered under this Abhiyan are Pradhan Mantri Ujjwala Yojana, Ujala scheme, Saubhagya, Pradhan Mantri Jan Dhan Yojana, Pradhan Mantri Jeevan Jyoti Bima Yojana, Pradhan Mantri Suraksha Bima Yojana and Mission Indradhanush. The objective of abhiyan is to market social harmony, get in touch with poor rural households, obtain feedback on ongoing programmes, enroll in new initiatives, concentrate on doubling farmers' income, enhance livelihood opportunities and re-emphasize nationwide priorities such as cleanliness and strengthen Panchayati Raj institutions.

This course of action will be implemented in 484 districts in 33 Union and States Territories, the maximum number of the villages is in Uttar Pradesh, Assam, Tamil Nadu, Meghalaya and Punjab.

RESEARCHERS DISCOVER A NEW SPECIES OF TERRESTRIAL FROG

DATE: 26th April

In the highland plateaus of the Western Ghats parts of Goa, a team of scientists led by KP Dinesh, from Zoological Survey of India, Pune identifies a new species of frog called Fejervarya goemchi. The new species was found in high elevation areas of laterite plateaus, temporary water bodies and paddy fields of Goa. This frog belongs to the genus Fejervarya and is named Fejervarya goemchi after the historical name of Goa. Fejervarya goemchi are large-sized terrestrial frogs. They sit next to water bodies making calls to attract females for mating and breeding. Although most of these frogs are terrestrial, they need water bodies to continue for survival.

Most Fejervarya species in South and South-East Asia are difficult to identify on the basis of morphology alone. The scientists have used a combination of morphology, geographic distribution range and molecular methods to describe the new species.

INTERNATIONAL

CABINET APPROVES INDO-AFGHAN COOPERATION AGREEMENT

DATE: 4th April 2018

OBJECTIVE: To co-operate in the field of Food Safety and allied fields

The Union Cabinet has approved the India-Afghanistan arrangement for co-operation in the field of food safety and allied fields. The agreement between the Food Safety & Standards Authority of India (FSSAI), Ministry of Health & Family Welfare (MoH&FW) and Ministry of Agriculture, Irrigation & Livestock (MAIL), Afghanistan for cooperation in the field of Food Safety and allied fields was approved by a cabinet committee chaired by PM Narendra Modi.

The cooperation arrangement will aid mutual information sharing, training, best practice, capacity building measure, etc. to improve overall food safety.

USA-SOUTH KOREA JOINT MILITARY EXERCISE

DATE: 2nd April 2018

OBJECTIVE: To make the forces of both countries combat ready

Foal Eagle- the annual joint military exercise between USA-South Korea began. It is one of the world's largest joint military exercises conducted annually. Armed forces of USA and Republic of Korea conduct the exercise under the combined Forces Command.

Foal Eagle will run for about two months. More than 11000 U.S. troops and nearly 300,000 South Korean forces will take part in these exercises.

In the changing scenario between USA and North Korea and between the Korean nations, the North Korea has not protested the annual joint exercise this time. As part of the agreement to meet with the US president, North Korea promised not to object.

The military exercise was delayed this year at the request of South Korea until after the Winter Olympics, which was organised in PyeongChang, the South Korean city.

NASA TESTS SUPERSONIC PARACHUTE

DATE: 2nd April 2018

OBJECTIVE: To test the capability of Supersonic Parachute in future Mars Missions

NASA tested its Advanced Supersonic Parachute Inflation Research Experiment (ASPIRE) to check its capability. The supersonic parachute is expected to be helpful in its future space explorations to Mars.

The Supersonic parachute was sent very high up in the sky through a rocket from NASA's Wallops Flight Facility in Virginia. The test was carried to mimic the conditions that a spacecraft would experience during its entry, descent and landing during Mars missions. The 18-meter-long Terrier-Black Brant-IX rocket carried the parachute to a maximum altitude of 51 km.

The payload splashed down in the Atlantic Ocean 40 miles from Wallops Island and will be recovered and returned to Wallops for further data retrieval and analysis.

ASPIRE is managed by NASA's Jet Propulsion Laboratory in Pasadena, California, with support from NASA's Langley Research Center in Hampton, Virginia, and Ames Research Center in Silicon Valley, California, for the agency's Science Mission Directorate in Washington.

UAE APPROVES EQUAL SALARIES FOR MEN AND WOMEN

DATE: 10th April 2018

OBJECTIVE: To ensure equal wages to female and male staff

The UAE Cabinet endorsed a draft law which will ensure equal wages to female colleagues on par with their male counterparts.

The Cabinet's approval of the Law on Equal Wages and Salaries comes in line with the government's objective to ensure the protection of women's rights and support their role in the national development process.

The UAE ranks second in the Middle East for 'wage equality for similar work' but studies have shown it to be otherwise. The country ranked 120 out of 144 countries overall in the 2017 World Economic Forum's Global Gender Gap Report.

Industry observers hailed the law as a major step in the right direction, though they cautioned that enforcement of the law may prove to be a challenge.

The UAE Government has made several moves towards narrowing the gender gap in past. In 2015, the UAE Council for Gender Balance was established and the UAE had launched the world's first Gender Balance Guide.

The guide was described in a statement from Dubai Media Office as a reference tool to "narrow the gender gap across the UAE's private and public institutions."

16TH INTERNATIONAL ENERGY FORUM MINISTERIAL MEETING

DATE: 11th April 2018

OBJECTIVE: To discuss the future of global energy supply and consumption

16th International Energy Forum (IEF-16) Ministerial Meeting was held in New Delhi. Energy Ministers from producing and consuming nations, Heads of International Organisations, CEOs of different firms, different dignitaries from the Government and Corporate sectors have participated in the forum

The biennial IEF Ministerial Meetings are the world's largest gathering of Energy Ministers who engage in a dialogue on global energy issues, IEF-16 witnessed ministers from 42 countries.

IEF-16 is hosted by India with China and South Korea as the co-hosts on the theme, "The Future of Global Energy Security - Transition, Technology, Trade and Investment". The main aim of this edition of the forum is to analyse and relate the issues of global shifts, transition policies, and introduction of new policies with market stability and future investment in the energy sector.

Delegates also engaged in energy technology neutral dialogue to strengthen energy market stability and achieve global goals through enhanced market transparency, trade, and investment.

IEF forum currently has 72 countries as members and they are signatories to the IEF Charter. In addition, 20 countries participated as special invitees in the IEF-16. IEF is unique forum as it also comprises Transit States and major players outside of IEA & OPEC members in addition to consuming and producing countries. IEF accounts for around 90% of global supply and demand for oil and gas.

UN LAUNCHES ROAD SAFETY TRUST FUND

DATE: 13th April 2018

OBJECTIVE: To save lives and prevent the loss of opportunity due to road accidents

United Nations launched a Road Safety Trust Fund to help save lives in road accidents. The main aim of the fund is to prevent the loss of opportunity due to road accidents in addition to primarily saving lives on the road.

The UN General Assembly also adopted a resolution on road safety, sponsored by Russia, in which it called for a host of measures to prevent road accidents and injuries. This Road Safety Trust Fund will serve as a catalyst for much-needed progress towards the road safety targets of the sustainable development goals.

Deputy Secretary General of UN during the launch of the fund and debate on road safety addressed road accidents as the foremost cause of death of young people and responsible for keeping millions of people in poverty each year.

The Fund will focus on strengthening the capacity of government agencies, local governments and city authorities to develop and implement road safety programmes, prioritizing projects in low and middle-income countries.

The Secretariat of the United Nations Road Safety Trust Fund will be hosted by UN Economic Commission for Europe (UNECE). Every $ 1500 contributed to the fund could save one life; prevent 10 serious injuries; and leverage $ 51,000 towards investments in road safety.

As per estimate, globally around 1.3 million people die each year and up to 50 million are seriously injured on the roads.

NHAI SIGNS AGREEMENT ON INDIA-MYANMAR-THAILAND HIGHWAY

DATE: 14th April 2018

OBJECTIVE: To upgrade India-Myanmar Friendship Road

National Highways Authority of India (NHAI) signed an agreement to upgrade India-Myanmar Friendship Road in Myanmar.

The agreement was signed between NHAI and joint-venture (JV) of Punj Lloyd Ltd-Varaha Infrastructure Limited. The upgradation of 120 km Yagyi-Kalewa section in Myanmar passes through mountainous terrain and will be upgraded to a two-lane road with paved shoulders. The project includes several new major and minor bridges, reconstruction of exiting bridges and culverts, 20 bus bays and one passenger rest area.

The 1000 km India-Myanmar-Thailand Trilateral Highway will run from Moreh in Manipur to Mae Sot in Thailand via Myanmar. The Rs 1177 crore-projects will be implemented on an engineering-procurement-construction (EPC) basis by the NHAI through the Ministry of External Affairs (MEA).

ISSUES

NATIONAL

BANKS TO STOP SERVICES TO BUSINESS DEALINGS IN VIRTUAL CURRENCIES

DATE: 6th April, 2018

RBI released a notification asking banks, NBFCs and payment service providers to disassociate themselves from entities dealing with virtual currencies (VCs), including bitcoins with immediate effect. It has repeatedly cautioned users, holders and traders of virtual currencies, including bitcoins. By its own admission, this move is an attempt to ring-fence regulated entities from the risks associated with crypto currencies. RBI has given three months to banks to end all existing relationships with bitcoin players.

However, the central bank also is keen on floating its own crypto currency or digital currency going ahead. Besides, in the last few weeks, several other countries, including Japan, the country where Bitcoin is rumoured to have originated, have also warned its people against the use of crypto currencies.

Going after the crypto currencies such as Bitcoin, Ripple, Ethereum and the exchanges dealing with these currencies, the apex bank in its monetary policy said that, "Technological innovations, including those underlying virtual currencies, have the potential to improve the efficiency and inclusiveness of the financial system. However, Virtual Currencies (VCs), also variously referred to as crypto currencies and crypto assets, raise concerns of consumer protection, market integrity and money laundering, among others."

GOVERNMENT DILUTES RULES ON CATTLE SALE IN ANIMAL MARKET

DATE: 14th April, 2018

The Centre wipes out its controversial notification on a ban on sale of animals for slaughter in livestock markets and come out with new draft rules doing away with the clause on "restrictions on sale of cattle". This means cattle, including cows, can be sold in animal markets, even for slaughter wherever it is legal.

The 2017 rules have been replaced with draft rules called Prevention of Cruelty to Animals in Animal Markets Rules, 2018. The ministry of environment, forest and climate change has also removed the word 'slaughter' from the draft rules. The new rules, condensed to half the original length, govern welfare of animals in the markets.

The previous rules on 'restriction on sale of cattle' clearly stated that no person would bring an animal to the market for slaughter. The only line that has been retained from this clause is "no unfit animal or young animal shall be sold in an animal market." Another clause which required a certification that the 'animal on sale was not for slaughter' too has been dropped.

MOTION TO REMOVE CJI REJECTED

DATE: 24th April, 2018

Rajya Sabha chairman Venkaiah Naidu rejected the Congress-led opposition's notice for removal of CJI Dipak Misra. Naidu held that there was no "substantial and verifiable" evidence of wrongdoing. Congress has announced that it would challenge the order in the apex court.

Article 124(4) of the Constitution lays down the procedure for removal of a judge of the Supreme Court, including the CJI, who can be removed on grounds of "misbehavior or incapacity". A removal motion signed by 100 members of Lok Sabha or 50 members of Rajya Sabha has to be submitted to the Speaker of the Lower House or Chairperson (i.e. Vice President) of the Upper House. This can be in either of the Houses of Parliament. The Speaker/Chairperson can then either accept or reject the motion.

On April 20, seven opposition parties led by the Congress had submitted a notice for the removal of the CJI on grounds of "misbehaviour" and "misuse of authority." The motion had been signed by 61 serving RS MPs and seven retired MPs.

Naidu held that the allegations emerging from the case had a serious tendency of "undermining" the independence of the judiciary. The notice lacks substantial merit, is neither tenable nor admissible. There is no credible or verifiable information on 'misbehavior' or incapacity.

SC SEEKS GOVT'S VIEWS ON PLEA AGAINST SECTION 377

DATE: 24th April, 2018

The Supreme Court seeks the response from the Centre on a plea filed by a batch of 20 current and former students of Indian Institutes of Technology for scrapping the law that makes homosexuality a crime. The plea challenges section 377 of the IPC which criminalizes homosexual activity and other unnatural sex. The court has already seized of the similar judgment of 2013, filed by Naz foundation. While agreeing to re-examine 2013 judgment, the court had on January 8, 2018, observed "a section of people or individuals who exercise their choice should never remain in a state of fear".

The 20 IITians, including scientists, teachers, entrepreneurs and researchers of different age groups, who all are Lesbian, Gay, Bi-sexual and Transgender (LGBT), have claimed that criminalization of sexual orientation has resulted in a "sense of shame, loss of self-esteem and stigma". The petitioners contend that the continued existence of section 377 severely curtails the protection of equality, dignity, liberty and expression that the Constitution guarantees to all Indian citizens".

Section 377 of the IPC refers to 'unnatural offences' and says whoever voluntarily has carnal intercourse "against the order of nature" with any man, woman or animal, shall be punished with imprisonment for life, or with imprisonment of either description for a term which may extend to ten years, and shall also be liable to pay a fine.

AFSPA LIFTED IN MEGHALAYA AND PARTS OF ARUNACHAL PRADESH

DATE: 25th April, 2018

The Union Home Ministry has removed Armed Forces (Special Powers) Act (AFSPA), 1958, from Meghalaya and reduced it to eight police stations in Arunachal Pradesh, with effect from April 1, 2018.

AFSPA gives powers to the Army and central forces deployed in "disturbed areas" to kill anyone acting in contravention of law, arrest and search any premises without a warrant and provide cover to forces from prosecution and legal suits without the Central government's sanction.

The Act has however been extended by another six months in three eastern districts of Arunachal Pradesh, Tirap, Longding and Changlang, which border Myanmar and specific areas under eight police stations of seven other districts bordering Assam. The three districts have been under the AFSPA since January 2016.

AFSPA is effective in the whole of Nagaland, Assam, Manipur (excluding seven assembly constituencies of Imphal). The state governments of Assam and Manipur now have the powers to keep or revoke the Act. In 2017, the Home Ministry gave up its power and asked the Assam government to take a decision on continuing AFSPA in the State.

REMOVE THE PROVISIONS DISCRIMINATING AGAINST LEPROSY PATIENTS: SC TO CENTRE

DATE: 25th April, 2018

Hearing a writ petition on behalf of the Vidhi Centre for Legal Policy on the gross violation of the fundamental rights of persons affected by leprosy under Articles 14, 19 and 21 of the Constitution of India by the continued existence of archaic, discriminatory provisions under 119 Central and State laws, the Supreme Court bench of Chief Justice Dipak Misra, Justice D. Y. Chandrachud and Justice A. M. Khanwilkar urged the Centre and the states "to rise to the occasion" in removing the 'disability and social stigma' attached to such persons. The bench also observed, "Be it noted that leprosy is absolutely curable. The Central Government shall monitor the states in adopting a sensitive approach. The court also takes objection to the Delhi Metro Railway Corporation (DMRC) requirement that passengers travelling in its trains must carry a certificate stating that the disease is not contagious.

Leprosy which also known as Hansen's disease (HD), is a chronic infection caused by the bacteria Mycobacterium leprae or Mycobacterium lepromatosis, which affects the skin and peripheral nerves. There are 119 laws which discriminate against leprosy patients. The laws bar them from occupying public posts or offices, impose disqualifications on them under personal laws and deny them access to public services.

INTERNATIONAL

INDIA AT RISK OF FOOD SHORTAGE: STUDY

DATE: 3rd April, 2018

A global study suggests that India is among the countries which are at the greatest risk of food insecurity due to weather extremes caused by climate change. A team of researchers led by the University of Exeter in the UK examined how climate change could affect the vulnerability of different countries to food insecurity-when people lack access to sufficient quantity of affordable, nutritious food.

The study, published in the journal Philosophical Transactions of the Royal Society A, looked at 122 developing and least-developed countries, mostly in Asia, Africa and South America.

According to Richard Betts, a professor at the University of Exeter, Climate changes are expected to lead to more extremes of both heavy rainfall and drought, with different effects in different parts of the world. Such weather extremes can increase vulnerability to food insecurity. Some change is already unavoidable, but if global warming is limited to 1.5 degrees Celsius, this vulnerability is projected to remain smaller than at 2 degrees Celsius in approximately 76% of developing countries.

INDIA THIRD MOST VULNERABLE COUNTRY TO CYBER THREATS

DATE: 5th April, 2018

According to **Internet Security Threat Report**, India is world's third most vulnerable country in terms of cyber threat risks including malware, spam, ransomware and one of the most recent and difficult-to-detect ones - crypto miners. About 5.09% global threats were detected in India in 2017.The Internet Security Threat Report' released by Symantec has illuminated that the US is most vulnerable to attacks at 26.61% followed by China at 10.95%.

India persists to be second most impacted by spam and bots, third most impacted by network attacks, and fourth most impacted by ransom ware. India has ranked ninth globally in terms of crypto mining activities. With the threat landscape becoming more diverse, attackers are working harder to discover new avenues of attack and cover their tracks. From the sudden spread of WannaCry and Petya/NotPetya, to the swift growth in coin miners, 2017 provided us with another reminder that digital security threats can come from new and unexpected sources.

Crypto jacking has captured the top slot at the attacker toolkit, which signals a massive threat to cyber and personal security. Crypto jacking is defined as the secret use of a computing device to mine crypto currency. There is also a 200% increase in attackers injecting malware implants into the software supply chain in 2017. Threats in the mobile space continue to grow year-over-year, including the number of new mobile malware variants rising 54%.

TURKEY HOSTS CRITICAL SUMMIT ON SYRIA

DATE: 6th April, 2018

OBJECTIVE: To speed up the peace process in Syria

The Iranian, Turkish and Russian presidents meet for their second tripartite summit of less than six months, aimed at speeding up the peace process in Syria and strengthening their influence in the country.

Turkish President Recep Tayyip Erdogan hosted his Russian and Iranian counterparts Vladimir Putin and Hassan Rouhani in Ankara at his presidential palace for a meeting that could have a critical bearing on developments in Syria. The meeting is the second such tripartite summit after the first hosted by Putin in November in Sochi and will be a new symbol of the increasingly deep cooperation.

The three powers have backed peace talks in Astana (Kazakh capital) which they argue are a parallel process to support UN-supported discussions in Geneva. Experts say that Ankara, Moscow and Tehran have quite different interests but have for now decided to team up to take advantage of the waning Western influence in Syria.

PAKISTAN'S TOP COURT DISQUALIFIES NAWAZ SHARIF FOR LIFE

DATE: 14th April, 2018

Pakistan's Supreme Court disqualifies former Prime Minister Nawaz Sharif and an influential opposition leader, Jehangir Tareen, who belongs to the Pakistan Tehrik-e-Insaf of cricketer-turned-politician Imran Khan, from holding public office or contesting elections for lifetime. A five-member bench delivered the verdict on the question of the period of the disqualification of an MP. The court had disqualified Sharif as Prime Minister over corruption charges in July last year but it had not mentioned the disqualification period in the verdict.

The ruling Pakistan Muslim League-Nawaz (PML-N) of Sharif rejected the verdict and said the former Prime Minister has been "punished for eliminating terrorism and carrying out development projects. A Minister told reporters in Islamabad that the verdict would not affect the PML-N's performance and the party would be victorious in the coming parliamentary elections, scheduled in July.

The ruling of the court has said the disqualification of any MP or a public servant under Article 62 (1)(f) of the Constitution would be permanent. Under this article, such a person cannot contest elections or become a Member of Majlis-e-Shoora (Parliament) unless he is sagacious, righteous, non-profligate and honest, there being no declaration to the contrary by a court of law.

WORLD PRESS FREEDOM INDEX: INDIA DOWN TWO RANKS TO 138

DATE: 27th April, 2018

India's rank falls by two places, from 136 to 138, in the 2018 World Press Freedom Index compiled by Reporters Without Borders (RWB), or Reporters Sans Frontières (RSF). RSF is a global non-profit body that works on the freedom of the press. The index is published annually by RSF since 2002; it measures the level of media freedom in 180 countries, including the level of pluralism, media independence, the environment and self-censorship, the legal framework, transparency, and the quality of the infrastructure that supports the production of news and information.

The 2018 report by the RWB mentions threat of sedition and hyper Hindu nationalism under the ruling disposition as reason behind the country's performance in press freedom index. The physical violence against journalists like Gauri Lankesh is largely responsible for India's low ranking. At least three journalists were murdered in connection with their work. More had been killed in circumstances that were unclear, as is often the case in rural areas.

IDEAS

NATIONAL

DIGITAL PLATFORMS FOR EASE OF FARM EXPORT LAUNCHED

DATE: 4th April, 2018

OBJECTIVE: To promote and protect farm brand of India

The government has developed three online portals for safe food export traceability, single laboratory for accreditation and approvals, and the third for monitoring export alerts from importing regulators. The purpose is to make easier to export farm products from India and reduce transaction costs. It will get a great boost due to these digital initiatives. The digital platforms, developed by the Export Inspection Council, have integrated the entire export food chain by linking primary production, chain catch, aquaculture pond, dairy farms and apiaries. The council is the official export certification body of the government and it has developed the portals for credible inspection and certification and to strengthen the confidence on Indian produce. As India has 7,600 km of coastline along 13 states, therefore the country has enormous potential in marine and fish exports. India has 35 agro-climatic zones in the country and can produce everything the world eats. There is the need in India to process according to world taste so that more agricultural products could be exported.

TAMIL NADU GOVERNMENT LAUNCHES 'UZHAVAN'

DATE: 8th April, 2018

OBJECTIVE: To provide proper information about agriculture

Tamil Nadu Government launches 'Uzhavan', a mobile app for farmers to provide complete real-time information about agricultural operations and offer nine services, including details on crop insurance. With the help of this App, the farmers could get weather updates for the next four days and price information about agricultural inputs. The app will also provide information on subsidies available for schemes under various categories — seeds, machinery, solar pump set, shade net, poly house, pack house, hi-tech nursery, small nursery, new tissue culture lab, anti-bird net, plastic mulching, beehives, pre-cooling chamber, reefer van, mobile vendor cart, low-cost onion storage and mushroom cultivation. The app can be downloaded from Google Play store and is available in two languages. The other highlights of the app, available in Tamil and English, include information on the available stocks of seeds and fertilizers in local government and private stores.

MOBILE APP OF NATIONAL COMMISSION FOR SAFAI KARAMCHARIS LAUNCHED

DATE: 10ᵗʰ April, 2018

OBJECTIVE: To help the Commission in addressing the grievances/complaints of petitioners in an efficient manner.

The Union Ministry of Social Justice & Empowerment launched new website and mobile app of the National Commission for Safai Karamcharis (NCSK). The new website is very user-friendly and as per Government of India Guidelines for official websites. It is a comprehensive website giving complete details about the Commission like its composition, mandate, manner of filing complaints, details of visits undertaken by its Chairman and Members, etc.

The petitioners can file their grievances/complaints, etc. on-line on the website and thereafter track their grievances/complaints. Simultaneously, the petitioner can also lodge their grievances/complaints through their android mobile phones by using the Commission's App which can be downloaded from the Google Play Store free of cost.

PEOPLE

NATIONAL

HIMANTA BISWA SARMA

WHY IN NEWS?: Elected as the president of the Badminton Association of India

Himanta Biswa Sarma has been elected as the president of the Badminton Association of India unopposed during the federation's annual general body meeting and election in Goa. Sarma, a cabinet ranked minister and convener of the North East Democratic Alliance (NEDA), took over as the interim president of BAI last year after the demise of former president Akhilesh Das Gupta. He will serve as the president for a term of four years.

MANU BHAKER

Why in news? : Chosen as brand ambassador for Measles and Rubella (MR) vaccination campaign

16-year-old Haryana shooter, Manu Bhaker, who won India's first gold in shooting at Commonwealth Games 2018, has been made brand ambassador for Measles and

Rubella (MR) vaccination campaign starting from April 25 in the State. Under this campaign, vaccination of about 85 lakh children from nine months to 15 years of age would be carried out in Haryana.

Haryana's Jhajjar girl, Manu Bhaker, won India's first gold in shooting with a new Commonwealth Games record score of 240.9 in the women's 10 M air pistol event at Belmont Shooting Ranges in Brisbane, Australia. Bhaker, who won gold in the same event in last month's ISSF World Cup in Mexico, edged out former world number one shooter Heena Sidhu in the final in Brisbane.

RISHAD PREMJI

WHY IN NEWS? : Appointed as the chairman of the NASSCOM

Rishad Premji, Board member of Wipro Ltd. has been appointed as the Chairman of the National Association of Software and Services Companies (NASSCOM) for 2018-19. Premji has been a member of NASSCOM's Executive Council and was the Vice Chairman for the previous year. He succeeds Raman Roy, Chairman and Managing Director, Quatrro Global Services, who served as Chairman of NASSCOM for the year 2017-18. Premji is the Chief Strategy Officer & Member of the Board, Wipro Ltd. As the Chief Strategy Officer, he leads Wipro's M&A Strategy and conceptualized Wipro Ventures – a $100M fund to invest in start-ups developing technologies and solutions that will complement Wipro's businesses with next generation services and products. In his role, he also leads the Investor Relations & Corporate Affairs functions for the company. NASSCOM also appointed Keshav Murugesh as the Vice Chairman for 2018-19. Keshav Murugesh serves as the Group Chief Executive Officer and Member of the Board of Directors of WNS Global Services.

TK RAJALAKSHMI

WHY IN NEWS?: Elected as the new president of the Indian Women's Press Corps

Senior journalist T K Rajalakshmi has been elected the new president of the Indian Women's Press Corps (IWPC), while Jyoti Malhotra and Shobhna Jain were declared vice-presidents of the media body. The IWPC, which was launched in 1994, is a reputed association of women journalists. It was set up to support women journalists in their professional work, in enhancing their knowledge and skills and to provide a forum for networking. The purpose of the organisation is to create a robust media network by making women's voices and bylines more visible.

INTERNATIONAL

JULIUS MAADA BIO

WHY IN NEWS? : Elected as Sierre Leone's new president

Sierra Leone election commission declared the main opposition candidate Julius Maada Bio as the nation's new President. The National Electoral Commission of Sierra Leone announced that Maada Bio of the Sierra Leone People's Party (SLPP) won the elections with 51.8 percent votes defeating ruling All People's Congress candidate Samura Kamara.

The elections were held on March 31 as the term of the outgoing President Ernest Bai Koroma was coming to an end and he could not seek a re-election due to term limits imposed upon him.

Julius Maada Bio along with former foreign affairs minister Kamara briefly ruled Sierra Leone as the military head in 1996. Both of them stood in the Presidential elections in opposition to each other in a bid to replace the outgoing President.

VIKTOR ORBAN

WHY IN NEWS? : Wins third term as Hungarian PM

Prime Minister Viktor Orban won a third straight term in power in elections after his anti-immigration campaign message secured a strong majority for his party in parliament, granting him two-thirds of seats based on preliminary results.

The rightwing nationalist prime minister projected himself as a saviour of Hungary's Christian culture against Muslim migration into Europe, an image which resonated with millions of voters, especially in rural areas.

According to preliminary results with 93 percent of votes counted, National Election Office data projected Fidesz to win 133 seats, a tight two-thirds majority in the 199-seat parliament. Nationalist Jobbik was projected to win 26 seats, while the Socialists were projected as third with 20 lawmakers.

That means Orban could have a two-thirds majority for a third time, and powers to change constitutional laws. The EU has struggled to respond as Orban's government has, in view of its criticisms, used its two landslide victories in 2010 and 2014 to erode democratic checks and balances.

MIGUEL DIAZ CANEL

WHY IN NEWS? : Elected as the new president of Cuba

Miguel Díaz-Canel was officially named as the new president of Cuba. It's the first time in nearly six decades that Cuba is being led by a man not named Castro. Díaz-Canel, 57, was selected by a vote of 603-1 as the unopposed candidate to replace Raul Castro, 86.

Díaz-Canel becomes president of the Cuban Council of States and Council of Ministers. Castro will still be a member of the National Assembly and, even if he is no longer president, remains the most powerful public figure on the island.

Castro's ringing endorsement of Díaz-Canel was a clear indication that members of the older generation that fought the revolution are banking on him to steer the government through an economic crisis and increasingly rocky relationship with the United States.

The transition marks a passing of a torch in Cuba from the revolutionaries who took power at the point of a gun to the younger generation of bureaucrats that have only ever known the Castros' socialist project.

PRINCE CHARLES

WHY IN NEWS? : Became the new head of Commonwealth

Britain's Prince Charles was approved as the successor to Queen Elizabeth as head of the Commonwealth at a meeting of the group's heads of government. The Commonwealth evolved out of the British empire in the mid-20th century and the queen has been its head since her reign began in 1952. Charles had long been expected to take on the role even though it is not strictly hereditary.

The position is largely symbolic, but the queen's commitment has been a major force behind the survival of the Commonwealth. She has visited almost every member country, often multiple times, over her 66-year reign. Charles is almost as well-travelled as his mother, and is a long-time champion of environmental causes, a priority for the Commonwealth. Its members include small island nations in the Caribbean and Pacific that are among the countries most vulnerable to rising seas, fiercer storms and other effects of global climate change.

British officials have been paying more attention to the Commonwealth since the U.K. voted in 2016 to leave the European Union. The Commonwealth could provide a platform for British diplomatic and cultural clout outside the EU.

EVENTS

NATIONAL

TATA STEEL ACQUIRES BHUSHAN STEEL LIMITED

DATE: 18th May 2018

Tata Steel's wholly-owned subsidiary Bamnipal Steel Limited (BNPL) has acquired 72.65 per cent stake in Bhushan Steel Limited (BSl). As per the approved resolution plan under the corporate insolvency resolution process (CIRP) the deal amounted to in the range of 36,000 crore.

Lauding the robust and transparent newly introduced Insolvency & Bankruptcy Code, Finance Minister Goyal said that lenders recovered almost entire principal loan of Bhushan Steel Limited through Rs 36,400 crore transparent bid by Tata Steel. They also got 12% stake in the company. He informed that creditors received almost four times the value of liquidation value of Bhushan Steel which was pegged at Rs 14,541 crore.

The Insolvency and Bankruptcy Code, 2016 (IBC) is the bankruptcy law of India which seeks to consolidate the existing framework by creating a single law for insolvency and bankruptcy. It was introduced in the Lok Sabha in December 2015 and was passed in May 2016.

The bankruptcy code provides a one-stop solution for resolving insolvencies which at present is a long process and does not offer an economically viable arrangement.

UGC APPROVES REGULATIONS FOR ONLINE COURSES

DATE: 25th May 2018

Country's top regulator in the education sector the University Grants Commission (UGC) has approved the UGC (Online Courses) Regulations.

Under the UGC (Online Courses) Regulations, 2018, any higher education institution will be able to apply for permission to offer such online programmes if they have been in existence for at least 5 years and are accredited by the National Assessment and Accreditation Council (NAAC) with a minimum score of 3.26 or A+ ranking on a 4 scale to maintain quality. Additionally, the institutions should also be in the top-100 in overall category in the National Institutional Ranking Framework (NIRF) for at least 2 years in the previous 3 years.

The regulations will be made applicable from the academic session 2018-19.

Institutions will be able to offer online degrees in all fields except engineering, medicine, dental, pharmacy, nursing, architecture and physiotherapy. In a nutshell, online programmes requiring practical/laboratory courses as a curricular requirement shall not be part of approval.

For authentication of Indian students, Aadhaar cards shall be used while passports will be required for foreign students.

ANDHRA PRADESH ANNOUNCES NEW STATE SYMBOLS

DATE: 31st May 2018

Andhra Pradesh has announced parakeet (Psittacula Krameri) as new state bird. It is locally known as the 'Ramachilaka'. The Indian Antelope (blackbuck) has been named the State Animal, locally known as Krishna Jinka. Neem (Azadirachta indica) or Vepa Chettu in local language got the status of state tree while Jasmine (Jasminum officinale) is new State flower. The state symbols were notified by the department of environment, forest, science and technology as per released order. It was informed that Government of Andhra Pradesh felt that it is necessary to have a separate set of symbols for the state of Andhra Pradesh after bifurcation of the combined state.

Telangana had dropped Krishna Jinka of undivided state and adopted Jinka or spotted deer as its state animal. The state bird of undivided Andhra Pradesh was Indian Roller (Coracias benghalensis) or Palapitta which is retained by Telangana.

The Telangana government had dropped neem (vepa chettu) and adopted Jammi Chettu (Prosopis cineraria) as state tree.

INTERNATIONAL

15TH MEETING OF CULTURAL MINISTERS OF SHANGHAI COOPERATION ORGANIZATION

DATE: 17th May 2018

OBJECTIVE: To create multilateral cultural cooperation among member states.

The 15th Meeting of Cultural Ministers of the Shanghai Cooperation Organization (SCO) member states was held in Sanya, China. The theme of the event revolved around achieving more in-depth and creative multilateral cultural cooperation among member states.

India, China, Kazakhstan, Kyrgyzstan, Russia, Tajikistan, Uzbekistan and Pakistan are the member states of SCO. India became full member of the SCO on 9th June, 2017 along with Pakistan during the SCO Heads of State Summit in Astana, Kazakhstan. SCO represents approximately 42% of the world's population, 20% of its GDP and 22% of the landmass.

WALMART BUYS 77 PERCENT STAKE IN FLIPKART

DATE: 9th May 2018

Global retail giant Walmart on May 9, 2018 formally signed a definitive agreement to acquire 77 percent stake in Flipkart with an investment of around USD 16 billion. The deal will value Flipkart at around USD 20.8 billion, up from its previous valuation of USD 12 billion.

Binny Bansal, Group Chairman at Flipkart, will continue to serve the company, after the completion of acquisition process. While, co-founder Sachin Bansal will encash his 5.96 per cent stake in the company which will amount to around USD 1.23 billion.

Some key takeaways of the deal are:

- Walmart will pay around USD 16 billion for an initial stake of approximately 77 percent in Flipkart. The remaining business will be held by Flipkart's existing shareholders, including Flipkart co-founder Binny Bansal, Tencent Holdings Limited, Tiger Global Management LLC and Microsoft Corp.
- Of the total deal amount of USD 16 billion, USD 2 billion will be new equity funding, while the rest will be utilised to buy stake from existing investors including Softbank, Naspers and co-founder Sachin Bansal.
- To finance the investment, Walmart will use a combination of newly issued debt and cash on hand.
- Upon the closing of the deal, Flipkart's financials will be reported as part of Walmart's International business segment.

TRUMP SIGNED 'FAITH INITIATIVE' TO PROMOTE RELIGIOUS FREEDOM IN USA

DATE: 3rd May 2018

US President Donald Trump signed an executive order to create a faith-based initiative at the White House, which would promote policies that recognize the vital role of faith in American life.

Objectives: The faith initiative aims to help design new policies that recognize the vital role of faith in American families and communities.

Significance: According to Trump, the order would among other things ensure that faith-based organizations have equal access to government funding and the equal right to exercise their deeply held beliefs.

INDIA LAUNCHES SECOND IT CORRIDOR IN CHINA

DATE: 27th May 2018

OBJECTIVE: To cash in on growing Chinese software market

India with the aim of tapping Chinese Market opened its second Information technology corridor in China. The National Association of Software and Services Companies (NASSCOM) has set up one more Digital Collaborative Opportunities Plaza (or SIDCOP platform) in China.

India's first IT corridor in China was launched in Dalian in December 2017 with a focus on Internet of Things (IOT). The focus of the second corridor will be on big data.

An agreement worth RMB 36 million (6 million USD) was signed with Indian IT companies and Chinese customers on the occasion of launch.

In China, Indian IT companies are present in 10 cities around the country, with a total workforce of around 25,000 employees. For India, getting access to China's IT market is important to address the massive trade deficit which has now reached to over 51 billion USD.

ISSUES

NATIONAL

THE GOVERNOR'S ROLE IN THE HUNG ASSEMBLY

DATE: 20th May 2018

The Assembly Elections in Karnataka produces an inconclusive verdict as no single party getting a simple majority to form the government. With the results of election throwing up a hung house, the role of the Governor has come into focus, in regard to whether the single largest party or the leader claiming majority with post-poll alliance should be invited to form the new government.

As a matter of convention, the Governor has to first invite the single largest party to form the government, but the decision has to be an "informed one" and "on sound basis," with a view to provide a stable government.

In a democratic system of Govt., the proper representation of public interest is of supreme importance. And the governments are chosen by the people. And, our constitution has clearly directed the ways how the government should be formed in case of Hung Assembly.

INTERNATIONAL

GravityRAT: MALWARE ALLEGEDLY DESIGNED BY PAKISTANI HACKERS

DATE: 5th May 2018

According to cyber crime cell report, Pakistani hackers recently updated a malware, GravityRAT. It has equipped with anti-malware evasion capabilities. The RAT was first detected by Indian Computer Emergency Response Team, CERT-In, on various computers in 2017. It is designed to infiltrate computers and steals the data of users, and relay the stolen data to Command and Control centres in other countries. The 'RAT' as its name stands for Remote Access Trojan, is a program capable of being controlled remotely and thus difficult to trace.

Unlike most malware, GravityRat lies hidden in the system that it takes over and keeps penetrating deeper. Its latest update enables this malware to function as Advanced Persistent Threat (APT), which, once it infiltrates a system, silently evolves and does long-term damage.

INDIA SLIPS TO 6TH SPOT IN BUSINESS OPTIMISM INDEX

DATE: 9th May 2018

As per the Grant Thornton's International Business Report (IBR), in the first quarter of 2018 India ranks 6th on Global Optimism Index. The report is prepared based on the results of a survey of 2,500 businesses in 37 economies. The top five nations in this index are Austria, Finland, Indonesia, the Netherlands and US. India ranks at the sixth place in the index with a score of 89. India had topped the chart for four years, but business optimism in India deteriorated while entering the last year of the current Government led by Prime Minister Narendra Modi. Underlying pessimism in India's Business Optimism reflects in other parameters as well including revenue, selling prices, profitability employment and exports expectations. Indian businesses have been citing regulations and red tape, availability of skilled workforce, lack of ICT infrastructure and shortage of finance as biggest growth constraints.

GENDER DISCRIMINATION IN INDIA: LANCET STUDY

DATE: 15th May 2018

As per the Lancet Global Health journals report that was released on May 14, 2018, around 239000 girls under the age of five die each year in India due to gender discrimination. The Lancet report is the first to examine the number of avoidable deaths among girls under the age of five in India at a district level, showing avoidable female mortality across India's 640 districts. The researchers utilized the UN population data from 46 countries to calculate the difference between the expected morality rate of girls under the age of five in countries without gender discrimination and the reality inside India. Avoidable mortality is defined as the difference between observed and expected mortality rates.

The numbers which are particularly higher in the northern states of Uttar Pradesh and Bihar are mostly due to unwanted child bearing and subsequent neglect.

In all, 29 out of 35 states in India had overall excess mortality in girls under five years old, and all states and territories bar two had at least one district with excess mortality.

IDEAS

NATIONAL

MAHARASHTRA FIRST TO ISSUE LAND DOCUMENT ONLINE

DATE: 2nd May

OBJECTIVE: To check irregularities and bring in transparency in land documents

Maharashtra has become the first state to issue a crucial land ownership document online and accept a digital signature on it as valid. The land ownership document is also known as 7/12 receipts. These receipts are extensively used by farmers for loan agreements, crop survey and for availing of government facilities. Till a few years ago, hand-written 7/12 receipts were prepared by talathis, who solely had the power to make changes in the documents. This resulted in several instances of misuse of authority. While talathis, who are local level revenue staff, would be supposed to issue the document as a matter of assistance, in reality many of them would demand bribes.

DIGITAL INDIA INTERNSHIP SCHEME PORTAL LAUNCHED

DATE: 10th May

OBJECTIVE: To ensure active participation of students in learning process

Ministry of Electronics and Information Technology (MeitY) launches Digital India Internship Scheme. The Scheme facilitates students to apply online for internship, provides opportunity for students to secure first hand and practical work experience under guidance of qualified and experienced Supervisor and Mentor. It ensures active participation of students in learning process through experimentation and putting into practice the knowledge acquired in the classrooms. Under this scheme, 25 interns will be inducted for period of three months. These interns will be paid a stipend of Rs. 10, 000 per month.

Any Indian students from recognized universities in India who have secured at least 60% marks in the last held degree or certificate examination , or students pursuing B.E/B.Tech or M.E/M.Tech or dual degrees and are in their course of study can apply for internships. The Internship will be offered two times in year i.e. summer Internship during May and June and winter Internship during December and January. The minimum duration of internship will be of two months and extendable up to three months, depending on the performance of the candidate.

CHENNAI ON TRACK FOR GLOBAL RAIL COACH EXPO

DATE: 16th May

OBJECTIVE: To create synergy for "Make in India"

Tamil Nadu hosts, the First-ever International Rail Coach Expo (IRCE) in Chennai, from 17th to 19th May, 2018. Many reputed rail car and equipment builders showcase their technology and products in this expo. The three day expo is hosted by Integral Coach Factory (ICF) Chennai, under the Ministry of Railways, in coordination with CII (Confederation of Indian Industries) and RITES Ltd. It would provide unique platform to bring different suppliers under one roof and create synergy for "Make in India". Train enthusiasts, railway suppliers, designers, developers, and general public will participate in this Expo.

SIDBI, CSC SPV TO PROVIDE FINANCIAL SUPPORT TO VILLAGE LEVEL ENTREPRENEURS

DATE: 25th May

Objective: To deliver electronic services in remote areas

Small Industries Development Bank of India (SIDBI) & Common Service Centres (CSC) sign a MoU for financial support to provide electronic services to village level entrepreneurs.

The existing VLEs (village level entrepreneurs) who have been operating CSCs for at least one year and looking to expand their operations are eligible for availing the financial support under the MoU, which is initially eyeing 50,000 VLEs. CSCs are working in 1.8 lakh gram panchayats and are set to reach 2.5 lakh gram panchayats by end of this year. Positioned as strategic cornerstones of Digital India programme, as many as 2.91 lakh CSCs operate in the country today. The MoU with SIDBI seeks to enhance financial viability of the CSCs by including additional offerings in their bouquet of products that currently includes services like banking, pensions, digital literacy and telemedicine.

INTERNATIONAL

10-YEAR RESIDENCY VISA PROGRAM FOR EXCEPTIONAL TALENTS BY UAE

DATE: 21st May

OBJECTIVE: To attract investors and economic competitiveness globally

UAE adopts a new system of entry visas, as per which it would be issuing long-term residency visas for up to 10 years to international investors and 'exceptional talents' including professionals and students. The programme will grant 10-year residency visas for specialists in medical, scientific, research and technical fields, as well as for all scientists and innovators. It will also provide five-year residency visas to the students studying in the UAE, the 10-year visas will be provided to exceptional students. UAE will also allow foreign companies to own 100 per cent of their business in the nation.

This programme will improve the country's position as a primary destination for international investors and global talents.

WORLD'S SECOND OLDEST ROCK FROM ODISHA

DATE: 10th May

Scientists discover world's second oldest grain of magmatic zircon (a mineral that contains traces of radioactive isotopes) from Champua from Singhbhum rock sample in Odisha's Kendujhar district. It is an estimated 4,240 million years old, making it world's second oldest rock ever to be discovered. It is oldest magmatic zircon on earth.

This rock sample was recovered nearly eight years ago and has put India at the forefront of geological research in the world. This discovery of great promise to study the earth's early years. It will also add valuable information about presence of water in the first few hundred million years of Earth's history. It will also give us clues to when plate tectonics began.

PEOPLE

NATIONAL

PAWAN CHAMLING

WHY IN NEWS? : Longest-serving Chief Minister in India

Sikkim's Pawan Chamling has created history by becoming longest-serving Chief Minister in India. He has completed 23 years, 4 months and 17 days of uninterrupted service in office. He surpassed earlier record held by Jyoti Basu, 5-term West Bengal CM who held office for 23 years. Jyoti Basu was in office from June 21, 1977 to November 6, 2000.

Pawan Chamling was born on September 22, 1950, at Yangang, South Sikkim. He had served as Minister for Industries, Information and Public Relations from 1989 to 1992 in Nar Bahadur Bhandari cabinet in the state. He formed Sikkim Democratic Front (SDF) in 1993, after a series of political upheavals in Sikkim. He was sworn in as chief minister of Sikkim for the first time on December 12, 1994 and now has been in office for fifth consecutive term.

JUNE 18 ROUNDUP

EVENTS

NATIONAL

CAUVERY WATER MANAGEMENT AUTHORITY FORMED

DATE: 2nd June

OBJECTIVE: To address the disputes over sharing of river water

Following directions from Supreme Court, the Central Government has constituted the Cauvery Water Management Authority (CMA) to address the dispute over sharing of river water among Tamil Nadu, Karnataka, Kerala and Puducherry. In February, 2018 judgement, the Supreme Court had directed centre to form the CMA within six weeks. In the same verdict, the court had also increased Karnataka's share in Cauvery Water marginally.

CAUVERY WATER MANAGEMENT AUTHORITY (CMA)

The newly constituted Cauvery Water Management Authority (CMA) has been created as per the Cauvery Management Scheme earlier framed by Centre and approved by Supreme Court.

Composition and Powers of CMA

The authority will comprise a chairman, a secretary and eight members. Out of the eight members, two will be full time, while two will be part time members from centre's side. Rest four will be part time members from states. The main mandate of the CMA will be to secure implementation and compliance of the Supreme Court's order in relation to "storage, apportionment, regulation and control of Cauvery waters". CMA will advise the states to take suitable measures to improve water use efficiency. It will do so by promoting use of micro-irrigation, changing in cropping pattern, improved farm practices and development of command areas.

INDIA, NEPAL FLAG-OFF JANAKPUR-AYODHYA BUS SERVICE

DATE: 11h June 2018

OBJECTIVE: To promote religious tourism in Nepal and India

Prime Minister Narendra Modi and his Nepalese counterpart KP Sharma jointly flagged-off a direct bus service between the two sacred cities Janakpur and Ayodhya, as part of the 'Ramayan Circuit'. The bus service was launched during PM Narendra Modi's visit to Nepal during May 11-12, 2018.

BACKGROUND:

- The bus service seeks to promote religious tourism in Nepal and India.
- As per mythological story 'Ramayana', Ayodhya is Lord Rama's birthplace, while, Janakpur is the birthplace of goddess Sita.
- Janakpur is known as the birth place of Sita, the wife of Lord Rama. The Janaki temple of Janakpur was built in memory of Sita in 1910.
- The bus service will provide Janakpur-Ayodhya-Janakpur transportation facility to pilgrims.

Ramayana Circuit

The Ramayana Circuit is among the thirteen thematic circuits identified for development under Swadesh Darshan Scheme of Union Ministry of Tourism.

Under the Ramayana Circuit, 15 destinations have been identified for development.

NITI AAYOG LAUNCHES COMPOSITE WATER MANAGEMENT INDEX

DATE: 24th June

OBJECTIVE: To assess and improve performance in efficient management of water resources

The NITI Aayog launched Composite Water Management Index as useful tool to assess and improve performance in efficient management of water resources. The index aims to inspire States/UTs towards efficient and optimal utilization of water and recycling thereof with a sense of urgency. The establishment of the Composite Water Management Index (CWMI) is a landmark achievement in the context of India's water management. The Index can help reinforce the principle of 'competitive and cooperative federalism' in the country and enable innovation in the water ecosystem. The CWMI is the country's first comprehensive and integrated national dataset for water.

Important Facts

The composite water management index comprises of nine parameters and 28 indicators. These include various aspects of ground water, irrigation, restoration of water bodies, farm practices, drinking water, policy and governance. For purpose of analysis, reporting states of index were divided into two special groups i.e. North Eastern and Himalayan States and Other States to take into account different hydrological conditions across these groups.

MAHARASHTRA GOVERNMENT IMPOSED BAN ON SINGLE USE PLASTICS

DATE: 23rd June 2018

OBJECTIVE: To prohibit the use, sale and manufacture of single use plastic and allied products

Maharashtra Government has imposed the statewide ban on single use plastics. The decision to ban the single use plastics was announced on 23rd March and the date of implementation was slated from 23rd June.

The plastic ban was issued under Maharashtra Plastic and Thermocol Products (Manufacture, Usage, Sale, Transport, Handling and Storage) Notification, 2018.

The notification cited the rising concerns of usage and disposal of plastic include accumulation of waste in landfills, water bodies and in natural habitats, physical problems for wild animals resulting from ingestion or entanglement in plastic, the leaching of chemicals from plastic products and the potential for plastics to transfer chemicals to wildlife and humans.

The ban covers plastic bags, disposable cups and plates, plastic cutlery, non-woven polypropylene bags, plastic pouches and packaging materials, thermocol items etc.

NATIONAL AWARDS IN THE FIELD OF PREVENTION OF ALCOHOLISM

DATE: 26th June 2018

OBJECTIVE: To award individuals and institutions working for prevention of Alcoholism and drug abuse

The President presented the Fourth National Awards for outstanding services in the field of Prevention of Alcoholism and Substance (Drug) Abuse. It was presented at a function in New Delhi to the institutions and individuals working in the field of Prevention of Alcoholism and Substance (Drug) Abuse.

Tapovan Nashamukti Evam Punarwas Sansthan (Rajasthan) was awarded for Best Integrated Rehabilitation Centre for Addicts (IRCA) for providing rehabilitation services to alcoholics and drug users, while *Lariapali Gram Panchayat* (Odisha) received the award for Best Panchayati Raj or Municipal Body working for prevention of alcoholism and substance (drug) abuse.

PRESIDENT INAUGURATES UDYAM SANGAM-2018

DATE: 27th June 2018

OBJECTIVE: To encourage partnerships among various MSME agencies for innovation and knowledge sharing

The President inaugurated the Udyam Sangam-2018 in New Delhi on the occasion of International Micro, Small & Medium Enterprises (MSME) Day. He also launched the Solar Charkha and MSME Sampark Portal.

The purpose of Udyam Sangam is to encourage dialogues and partnerships among various stakeholder of the MSME ecosystem for promoting innovation and knowledge sharing on MSME related issues.

Speaking on the occasion the Indian President said that the Udyam Sangam-2018 is an important effort in developing effective eco-systems for MSME sector.

NCST ORGANIZES SEMINAR ON CONSERVATION OF PARTICULARLY VULNERABLE TRIBES

DATE: 28th June 2018

OBJECTIVE: To Conserve the Particularly Vulnerable Tribes of Andaman and Nicobar Islands

National Commission for Scheduled Tribes (NCST) has organized a National Seminar on **Conservation of Particularly Vulnerable Tribes Groups (PVTGs) in New Delhi.** The theme of the seminar was "**Conservation of Particularly Vulnerable Tribes of Andaman and Nicobar Islands: The Way Forward.** This Seminar was organized in collaboration with Anthropological Survey of India (AnSI).

Various ministries and departments have attended the seminar and presented their strategies towards PVTGs in the Islands.

Exclusive Thematic Sessions held on tribes like the Sentinelese, Great Andamanies, Onge, Jarawa and Shompen.

DAHOD TOPS LIST OF DELTA RANKING ON ASPIRATIONAL DISTRICTS

DATE: 29th June 2018

OBJECTIVE: To identify sectors and indicator specific challenges in the districts

The first Delta ranking for the Aspirational Districts was released by NITI Aayog. Dahod (Gujarat), West Sikkim (Sikkim) and Ramanathapuram (Tamil Nadu) declared as top three ranked districts.

The rankings were released by CEO of NITI Aayog Amitabh Kant. It is based on self-reported incremental (Delta) data of districts between 31st March 2018 and 31st May 2018. The real time data points were collected on 49 key performance indicators in 5 main areas of Basic Infrastructure (Household Electricity Connections, Household Toilets and Rural Drinking Water), Health and Nutrition, Education, Agriculture and Water Resources, Skill Development and Financial Inclusion.

The ranking is a tool to identify sectors and indicator specific challenges and also take immediate corrective measures. The purpose of this ranking is to incite a sense of competition among the dynamic teams in the districts.

NATIONAL AWARDS IN THE FIELD OF PREVENTION OF ALCOHOLISM

DATE: 26th June 2018

OBJECTIVE: To award individuals and institutions working for prevention of Alcoholism and drug abuse

The President presented the Fourth National Awards for outstanding services in the field of Prevention of Alcoholism and Substance (Drug) Abuse. It was presented at a function in New Delhi to the institutions and individuals working in the field of Prevention of Alcoholism and Substance (Drug) Abuse.

Tapovan Nashamukti Evam Punarwas Sansthan (Rajasthan) was awarded for Best Integrated Rehabilitation Centre for Addicts (IRCA) for providing rehabilitation services to alcoholics and drug users, while *Lariapali Gram Panchayat* (Odisha) received the award for Best Panchayati Raj or Municipal Body working for prevention of alcoholism and substance (drug) abuse.

State Literacy Mission Authority (Bihar) and Punjab Institute of Medical Science (Punjab) were awarded for Best Awareness Campaign and Best Educational Institution doing outstanding work in awareness generation and prevention of alcoholism and substance (drug) abuse respectively.

Dr. R.C. Sahni (Rajasthan), Dr. Rajesh Tukaram Patil (Goa) and L.R. Madhujan (Kerala) received the award in individual category.

The Ministry of Social Justice and Empowerment celebrates 26th June every year as International Day against Drug Abuse and Illicit Trafficking. The Government of India has instituted a Scheme of the National Awards for outstanding services in the field of prevention of Alcoholism & Substance (Drug) since 2013.

AGARTALA AIRPORT BECOMES 'MAHARAJA BIR BIKRAM MANIKYA KISHORE AIRPORT'

DATE: 30th June 2018

OBJECTIVE: To pay tribute to erstwhile King of Tripura Bir Bikram Manikya Kishore

Agartala Airport, Tripura is renamed as 'Maharaja Bir Bikram Manikya Kishore Airport. The decision to rename the airport was taken by Union Cabinet under the chairmanship of Prime Minister.

The approval comes as a tribute to erstwhile king of Tripura Maharaja Bir Bikram Manikya Kishore Debbarman Bahadur who contributed a lot towards development of Tripura including the construction of Tripura Airport. It was a long pending demand from people of Tripura and the Tripura Governemnt to rename the airport in the name of previous ruler.

Maharaja Bir Bikram Manikya Kishore Debbarman Bahadur succeeded his father to the throne of the erstwhile Tripura Princely State at 13th August 1923. He is widely regarded as a caring and a sympathetic king who did philanthropic activites for welfare of people of Tripura and development of Tripura. He was instrumental in construction and design of aerodrome in Tripura and donated the land for the purpose.

The Agartala Airport is second busiest airport in entire north-eastern state of India after Guwahati Airport.

INTERNATIONAL

INDIAN UN PEACE KEEPING CONTINGENT AWARDED

DATE: 23rd June 2018

OBJECTIVE: To felicitate the contribution of Indian UN peace Keeping contingent

The 7 Garhwal Rifles Infantry Battalion of Indian Army which is part of United Nations peace Keeping Forces in South Sudan was awarded United Nations Peacekeeping Medal for selfless service. The Battalion is currently taking operational control of the Jonglei state.

The award ceremony witnessed drill parade by the Indian contingent in the presence of senior commanders and dignitaries.

Commander of the United Nations Mission in South Sudan (UNMISS), Brigadier General Mohammed Al Masoom congratulated the Indian Battalion for the Award.

Major General Bayarsaikhan Dashdondog, Deputy Force Commander, of the UNMISS congratulated the Indian contingent for carrying out numerous operational tasks with greatest professionalism and dedication to the UN mandate.

SAUDI LIFTS BAN ON WOMEN DRIVING

DATE: 24th June 2018

OBJECTIVE: To provide more power to female citizens

Adding more steps from a conservative society to a liberal nation towards Saudi Arabia has finally allowed its females to drive.

The lifting of the ban approved by a royal decree in September 2017 by King Salman is part of reforms in a bid to transform the economy of the world's top oil exporter and open up its restricted society.

The lifting of the ban has been welcomed by Western allies as proof of a new progressive trend in Saudi Arabia. The Islamic country has started issuing licenses to women at the start of the month and opening up of driving schools for women.

Saudi Arabia remains one of the most restrictive countries for women who need permission from legally mandated male guardians for important personal decisions like medical treatment, education, marriage, foreign travel etc.

PM INAUGURATES AIIB ANNUAL MEETING INAUGURATED

DATE: 26th June 2018

OBJECTIVE: To mobilize finance for infrastructure development

Prime Minister Narendra Modi inaugurated third annual meeting of the Asian Infrastructure Investment Bank (AIIB) in Mumbai.

Various Leaders from government and private sector shared their ideas and experiences on the theme of the meeting- "Mobilizing Finance for Infrastructure: Innovation and Collaboration. The Leaders expressed about the methods employed for sustainable future through sound infrastructure investment. Prime Minister also met these business leaders and discussed on issues ranging from economic growth, infrastructure development, policy initiatives, investment and innovation to job creation for the growing population.

Asian Infrastructure Investment Bank is a multilateral development bank with a mission to improve social and economic outcomes in Asia and globe. The bank commenced operations in January 2016 with 57 founding members. The current members of the bank are now 86. AIIB is viewed as Asia's response to the Asian Development Bank and the World Bank.

NEW ADDITIONS TO UNESCO'S WORLD HERITAGE SITES

DATE: 30th June 2018

OBJECTIVE: To preserve the world's cultural and natural heritage

UNESCO has added new sites to its list of world heritage sites. The announcement was made at ongoing meeting which is scheduled to add more world heritage site as part of its annual meeting in Bahrain.

The new world heritage sites include Aasivissuit-Nipisat (Denmark), Archaeological Border Complex of Hedeby and the Danevirke (Germany) and Victorian Gothic and Art Deco Ensembles of Mumbai (India) among others.

The decision was taken at the 42nd session of the World Heritage Committee of UNESCO, which has been meeting in Manama since June 24. The list also includes eight pre-Islamic sites in Iran, seven ancient Korean mountain Buddhist temples and old Christian sites in Japan.

INDIAN UN PEACE KEEPING CONTINGENT AWARDED

DATE: 23rd June 2018

OBJECTIVE: To felicitate the contribution of Indian UN peace Keeping contingent

The 7 Garhwal Rifles Infantry Battalion of Indian Army which is part of United Nations peace Keeping Forces in South Sudan was awarded United Nations Peacekeeping Medal for selfless service. The Battalion is currently taking operational control of the Jonglei state.

The award ceremony witnessed drill parade by the Indian contingent in the presence of senior commanders and dignitaries.

Commander of the United Nations Mission in South Sudan (UNMISS), Brigadier General Mohammed Al Masoom congratulated the Indian Battalion for the Award.

Major General Bayarsaikhan Dashdondog, Deputy Force Commander, of the UNMISS congratulated the Indian contingent for carrying out numerous operational tasks with greatest professionalism and dedication to the UN mandate.

More than 2000 personnel from Garhwal Rifles are participating in UN peace keeping operations since February 2018 in war torn South Sudan. The Indian peacekeepers in South Sudan have been deployed under Chapter VII which entails Peace Enforcement.

South Sudan became the 54th independent country in Africa on 9th July 2011 after a referendum of independence from Sudan was endorsed by more than 98% of the population.

ISSUES

NATIONAL

SUPREME COURT GIVES NOD FOR RESERVATION IN PROMOTION

DATE: 6th June 2018

OBJECTIVE: To enable the states to provide for reservation in matters of promotion to SC/ST

The Supreme Court has allowed Centre to go ahead with reservation in promotion for SC/ST employees as per the law. Reservations in promotions are mandated by Article 16 (4A) of the constitution. This article is an enabling provision and enables the state to provide for reservation in matters of promotion to SC/ST which in its opinion was not adequately represented in the services. The **Supreme Court** orally observed that promotions in government offices should go ahead in "accordance with law." The court was responding to the government's complaint that the entire promotion process was in limbo because of uncertainty over reservation in promotion for the Scheduled Caste/Scheduled Tribe employees.

A Bench of Justices A.K. Goel and Ashok Bhushan said nothing prevented the government from promoting employees in accordance with law. But the court was not clear about the law it was referring to. Promotions, according to the Centre, have come to a "standstill" due to the orders passed by various high courts. The apex court had also ordered for "status quo" in a similar matter in 2015.During the hearing, the ASG (Additional Solicitor General) cited the case laws on the issue of quota in promotion in government jobs and stated that the apex court's 2006 judgement in M Nagaraj case would be applicable.

UTTARAKHAND TO BAN USE OF POLYTHENE

DATE: 6th June 2018

The Uttarakhand Government has decided to completely prohibit the use of polythene or plastic from July 31, 2018. The move is aimed at curbing rampant use of plastic, which is increasingly becoming a huge environmental challenge. The announcement was made by the state on the occasion of World Environment Day on June 5, 2018.

Key Highlights

- All the polythene vendors in Uttarakhand have been asked to finish the polythene stock before July 31.

- The state would also be launching a comprehensive public awareness campaign on the environmental damage caused by polythene, one week before the complete ban on polythene.
- According to the state's Chief Minister Trivendra Singh Rawat, environmental conservation is a collective responsibility and so people's cooperation is necessary to make Uttarakhand polythene-free.

BACKGROUND: Sikkim became the first state in 1998 to ban disposable plastic bags. In 2016, it banned the use of packaged drinking water in government offices and government events and use of Styrofoam and thermocol disposable plates in the entire state. The Haryana government too has now decided to ban single-use plastic water bottles in all government offices in the state.

GENDER INEQUALITY EXTREMELY HIGH IN WORK & POLITICS IN INDIA: REPORT

DATE: 25th June

The McKinsey Global Institute (MGI) for the Asia-Pacific region releases a report in which it said gender inequality in India is extremely high at the workplace and in terms of legal protection and political voice. The report assessed inequality on the basis of a Gender Parity Score (GPS) that uses 15 indicators of gender equality in work and society. With 1.0 signifying parity, India's score was 0.30 in gender equality at work and 0.78 in legal protection and political voice. The report finds India behind the Asia-Pacific average in all four broad categories, but ahead of Bangladesh and Pakistan. However, as per the report, it pointed out that India has progressed faster than any other country in the Asia-Pacific region in the last 10 years, primarily due to advances in education and a reduction in maternal mortality. Advancing women's position in the countries of Asia Pacific, could add $4.5 trillion to their collective GDP annually in 2025, a 12% increase over a business-as-usual GDP trajectory.

This presumes a best-in-region scenario in which each country matches the rate of progress of the fastest-improving country in its region — China in the case of the Asia-Pacific. If this were achieved, India would add $770 billion in 2025 over and above its business-as-usual GDP.

INTERNATIONAL

WORLD'S HUNGRY POPULATION ON THE RISE AGAIN: UN REPORT

DATE: 22nd June

As per the report of United Nation releases on 20th of June, the number of hungry people in the world has risen for the first time in more than a decade. The report is an overview of progress towards achieving 2030 Agenda for Sustainable Development (SDG), which consists of 17 goals and 169 targets. It was adopted at the UN Sustainable Development Summit on September 25, 2015. The deadline to meet them is 2030. According to report there are now around 38 million more undernourished people in the world, rising from 777 million in 2015 to 815 million in 2016, the year for which the latest statistics are available. United Nation's Sustainable Development Goals (SDG) 2018 report, states that conflict is now one of the main drivers of food insecurity in 18 countries. Conflict, drought and disasters linked to climate change are among the key factors causing this reversal in progress. Violent conflicts also led to the forced displacement of a record high 68.5 million in 2017.

E SREEDHARAN COMMITTEE SET UP

DATE: 25th June

AGENDA/ISSUE: To lay down standards for metro rail systems in the country

TARGET APPLICATION: Prime Minister Narendra Modi approves a proposal to set up a committee, headed by E Sreedharan, a retired Indian Engineering Service (IES) officer. Sreedharan has served as the managing director of Delhi Metro from 1995 to 2012. He is also known as metro man in India. He is credited for changing face of public transport in India with his leadership in building Konkan Railway and

Delhi Metro. The committee will recommend standardization norms for various components of Metro rail systems that are currently imported. It will also look into all aspects rather that than evolving standards for each component separately. It will come up with uniform nationalize standards for various component of metro rail system, which aims at cutting costs in construction and operation of metro rail systems in the country. It will also focus and aid in manufacturing of various components of metro rail systems domestically, giving boost to government's Make in India policy. It will bring India to global standard, where every metro has same standards, same signaling system and track gauge, etc.

FINANCIAL ACTION TASK FORCE (FATF) PUTS PAKISTAN ON GREY LIST

DATE: 28th June

At its plenary meeting in Paris, France, The Financial Action Task Force (FATF) has officially placed Pakistan on its Grey List of countries involved in providing monetary assistance to terrorism and related causes for failing to curb terror financing on its soil. The announcement comes a day after Pakistan submitted a comprehensive 26-point action plan to the FATF to choke the funding of militants groups, including Mumbai attack mastermind Hafiz Saeed-led JuD and its affiliates, to avoid being blacklisted by it. FATF also has laid out 10-point action plan for Pakistan for compliance with its guidelines. If Pakistan fails in implementing the elaborate action plan, it may result in being included in FAFT's Black List in 2019. This is the second time Pakistan has been grey listed by FATF. For first time it was placed in the list for three years from 2012 to 2015. The placement of Pakistan on to grey list could hurt its economy as well as its international standing.

WORLD'S HUNGRY POPULATION ON RISE AGAIN DUE TO CONFLICT, CLIMATE CHANGE: UN REPORT

DATE: 22nd June

As per the report of United Nation releases on 20th of June, the number of hungry people in the world has risen for the first time in more than a decade. The report is an overview of progress towards achieving 2030 Agenda for Sustainable Development (SDG), which consists of 17 goals and 169 targets. It was adopted at the UN Sustainable Development Summit on September 25, 2015. The deadline to meet them is 2030. According to report there are now around 38 million more undernourished people in the world, rising from 777 million in 2015 to 815 million in 2016, the year for which the latest statistics are available. United Nation's Sustainable Development Goals (SDG) 2018 report, states that conflict is now one of the main drivers of food insecurity in 18 countries. Conflict, drought and disasters linked to climate change are among the key factors causing this reversal in progress. Violent conflicts also led to the forced displacement of a record high 68.5 million in 2017.

IDEAS

NATIONAL

24 DEGREES CELSIUS AS DEFAULT SETTING FOR AIR CONDITIONERS

DATE: 23rd June

OBJECTIVE: To promote energy efficiency

Government is considering making 24 degrees Celsius as mandatory default setting for air conditioners within a few months. At a meeting with the minister, AC makers were also advised to have labeling indicating the optimum temperature setting, which is between 24 and 26 degrees Celsius, for the benefits of consumers both from financial and their health points of view. Everyone degree increase in the air-conditioner temperature setting results in saving of 6 % of electricity consumed. Normal human body temperature is approximately 36-37 degrees Celsius, but large number of commercial establishments, hotels and offices maintain temperature around 18-21 degrees Celsius. This is not only uncomfortable but is actually unhealthy. Some countries like Japan have put in place regulation to keep the temperature at 28 degrees Celsius. The power ministry estimates indicate that if all the consumers adopt, this will result in savings of 20 billion units of electricity in one year alone.

'REUNITE', A MOBILE APP LAUNCHED

DATE: 30th June

'ReUnite' App launched to track missing kids

Objective: To track the missing and abandoned children

TARGET APPLICATION: Union Commerce Minister Suresh Prabhu and Nobel laureate Kailash Satyarthi, jointly launch mobile application for tracking missing and abandoned children in New Delhi. The app, christened as 'ReUnite,' will use Amazon Web Services based on face recognition technology to match the photographs of missing children with those in a Delhi Police database. The app, which was developed by the collaboration between Bachpan Bachao Andolan led by Satyarthi and IT major Capgemini, will be connected with the missing children's database of Delhi Police. It's a multi-user platform which can be used to upload photos of missing children. Parents of missing children will be able to report details of such children.

The app is multi user where parents and citizens can upload pictures of children, and provide detailed description like name, birth mark, address, report to the police station, search and identify missing kids. The app is available for both Android and iOS. It will use Amazon Web Services based on face recognition technology to match the photographs of missing children with a database to give result after face matching.

PEOPLE

A R RAHMAN

WHY IN NEWS? : Appointed as Brand Ambassador of Sikkim Government

Sikkim Government has appointed renowned music composer A R Rahman as Brand Ambassador of the state for a year. In his new role, he will promote and project Himalayan state's achievements nationally and globally. Earlier, he was made state's Brand Ambassador of tourism and business.

Sikkim, with its natural and pristine beauty, has over last two decades emerged as world famous eco-tourism destination. It also has attained distinct identity of being first fully organic farming state of India.

SHARAD KUMAR

WHY IN NEWS? : Appointed as Vigilance Commissioner in Central Vigilance Commission

Former National Investigation Agency chief Sharad Kumar has been appointed as Vigilance Commissioner in Central Vigilance Commission (CVC) by President Ram Nath Kovind. He will have a term of four years or till he attains the age of 65. Sharad Kumar was IPS officer of 1979 batch from Haryana cadre. He had retired in September 2017 after heading NIA for over four years. The Commission comprises of a Central Vigilance Commissioner and two vigilance commissioners. At present, K.V. Chowdhary is the CVC and T.M. Bhasin is the other vigilance commissioner.

Central Vigilance Commission (CVC)

Central Vigilance Commission (CVC) is an apex Indian governmental body created in 1964 to address governmental corruption. Recently, in 2003, the Parliament enacted a law conferring statutory status on the CVC. It has the status of an autonomous body, free of control from any executive authority, charged with monitoring all vigilance activity under the Central Government of India, advising various authorities in central Government organizations in planning, executing, reviewing and reforming their vigilance work.

S RAMESH

WHY IN NEWS? : Appointed as the chairman of Central Board of Indirect Taxes and Customs (CBIC)

The Appointments Committee of Cabinet (ACC) has appointed S Ramesh, member of Central Board of Indirect Taxes and Customs (CBIC) as its next Chairman. He will succeed present chairman Vanaja N Sarna.

Central Board of Indirect Taxes and Customs (CBIC)

The Central Board of Indirect taxes and Customs is the nodal national agency responsible for administering Customs, GST, Central Excise, Service Tax &

Narcotics in India. The Customs & Central Excise/CGST department was established in the year 1855 by the then British Governor General of India, to administer customs laws in India and collection of import duties / land revenue. It is one of the oldest government departments of India. Currently the Customs and Central Excise /CGST department comes under the Department of Revenue, Ministry of Finance, Government of India.

ANUKREETHY VAS

WHY IN NEWS? : Crowned as Femina Miss India 2018

Anukreethy Vas was crowned as Femina Miss India 2018 by the outgoing titleholder and Miss World 2017 Manushi Chhillar. During the competition, she was crowned Miss beautiful smile and won the Beauty with a Purpose award. Anukreethy will represent India at Miss World 2018 pageant to be held in Sanya, China on 8 December 2018.

Anukreethy Vas (born September 28, 1998) is an Indian model. She was born and brought up in Trichy, Tamil Nadu.

SHIKHAR DHAWAN

WHY IN NEWS? : Became the first Indian to score a hundred before lunch on the opening day of a Test Match

Shikhar Dhawan became the first Indian batsman to score a hundred before lunch on the opening day of a Test match. The Delhi left-hander achieved the feat in the opening session of the first day of the one-off Test match against Afghanistan in Bengaluru on Thursday. Dhawan joins five other cricketers who have reached the landmark before lunch and remained unbeaten 104 as India reached 158 for no loss at the break.

BACKGROUND: Shikhar Dhawan made his One Day International (ODI) debut against Australia in October 2010 at Visakhapatnam. His Test debut came against the same opposition in March 2013 at Mohali where he scored the fastest century by any batsman on Test debut.

MAHESH KUMAR JAIN

WHY IN NEWS? : Appointed as fourth deputy governor of RBI

The government on Monday named Mahesh Kumar Jain, managing director and chief executive officer of IDBI Bank, as the fourth deputy governor of the Reserve Bank of India (RBI), filling a post that has remained vacant since the retirement of S.S. Mundra in August 2017.

Jain's successful track record at Indian Bank as executive director first and CEO later, had prompted the government to name him as CEO of IDBI Bank in March 2017, in an abrupt swap with the then IDBI Bank boss Kishor Piraji Kharat. Jain has been appointed for a period of three years as RBI deputy governor.

ANANT BARUA

WHY IN NEWS? : Appointed as whole-time member of SEBI

The Union Government has appointed Anant Barua as whole-time member of the Securities and Exchange Board of India (SEBI). He has been appointed for three years.

BACKGROUND: Anant Barua is at present executive director in SEBI. He had taken charge as executive director of market regulator in May 2010. Prior to this assignment, he was legal adviser, Legal Affairs Department (LAD), SEBI. He had been working in LAD since 1992. Barua is a commerce graduate with LL.B from University of Delhi. He was on deputation to Central Bank of Bahrain as legal adviser and has also worked with National Fertilizers Ltd., Industrial Finance Corporation of India and DCM Ltd.

R PRAGGNANANDHAA

WHY IN NEWS? : Became the youngest Indian Grandmaster

R Praggnanandhaa of Chennai made history by becoming the youngest Indian Grandmaster and the second youngest overall by earning his GM norm during the Gredine Open in Italy at the age of 12 years and 10 months.

The title Grandmaster (GM) is awarded to chess players by the world chess organization FIDE. Apart from World Champion, Grandmaster is the highest title a chess player can attain. Once achieved, the title is held for life. This title can be awarded to the players with an Elo rating greater than 2500 who achieve the required three title norms.

BACKGROUND: Rameshbabu Praggnanandhaa (born 10 August 2005), is an Indian chess prodigy. He is the second-youngest person ever to achieve the title of grandmaster, behind Sergey Karjakin. Praggnanandhaa won the World Youth Chess Championship Under-8 boys title in 2013, and the Under-10 boys title in 2015. His elder sister, R. Vaishali, is a two-time youth chess champion. In 2016, Praggnanandhaa became the youngest International Master in history, at the age of 10 years, 10 months, and 19 days.

JANARDAN SINGH GEHLOT

WHY IN NEWS? : Elected as Chief of International Kabaddi Federation (IKF)

Janardan Singh Gehlot has been elected as the President of International Kabaddi Federation (IKF) for the next 4 years. This announcement was made after the Annual General Congress meeting of IKF.

The International Kabaddi Federation is the international governing body of Kabaddi. Its membership comprises 31 national associations. The federation was formed in 2004.

BACKGROUND: Janardhan Singh Gelhot is an Indian sports administrator. He was president of Amateur Kabaddi Federation of India (AKFI) for 28 years. In May 2013, he was made life president of AKFI. Gehlot is considered a father figure to Indian Kabaddi.

EVENTS

INTERNATIONAL

9TH MEETING OF THE EMINENT PERSONS GROUP (EPG) ON INDIA-NEPAL RELATIONS

DATE: 2nd July 2018

OBJECTIVE: To discuss various bilateral issues related to India-Nepal relations

Eminent Persons Group (EPG) on India-Nepal relations met in Kathmandu. It was 9th and final meeting of the EPG.

The Representatives from India and Nepal held discussions on various bilateral issues ranging from trade, transit, border policy to Peace and Friendship treaty of 1950.

Bhagat Singh Koshyari, Mahendra Lama, Jayant Prasad and Bhuvan Chandra Upreti represented the Indian side while Bhekh Bahadur Thapa, Nilamber Acharya, Dr. Rajan Bhattarai and Surya Nath Upadhyay represented the Himalyan nation.

The EPG is a joint mechanism consisting experts and intellectuals from India and Nepal. It was set up in February 2016 to make suggestions for updating all existing bilateral treaties and agreements between both the countries. The first meeting of EPG was held on July 5-6, 2016. The meeting seems to hold an important role to remove the confusions regarding 1950 treaty.

The EPG is expected to submit a report of the meeting to their respective governments.

EUROPEAN PARLIAMENT REJECTS CONTROVERSIAL COPYRIGHT LAW PROPOSAL

DATE: 5th July 2018

OBJECTIVE: To change the European Union's copyright laws

European Parliament rejected the controversial copyright law proposal. The proposed rules would have put more accountability on websites to check for copyright infringements, and forced platforms to pay for linking to news.

It was rejected by a margin of 318/278 with 31 abstentions. The parliament decided the changes needed more debate; and sent the proposals back to the Commission. The move was intended to bring the European Union's copyright laws in line with the digital age. A lot of oppositions arose against the bill from websites and internet users.

Supporters of the bill include celebrities Paul McCartney, Annie Lennox, David Guetta among others, who are of the opinion that websites are exploiting their contents without paying and aiding in copyright infringement.

On the other hand opponents of the proposal were of the view that the proposed legislation which seeks to overhaul EU copyrights rules would suppress internet freedom and creativity.

Article 11 of the proposed law was intended to protect newspapers and other agencies from internet giants like Google and facebook using their material without payment. Article 13 was also not less controversial as it was projected to put a greater responsibility on websites to enforce copyright laws. This was all set to enforce upon the websites to use filters that would stop users uploading various contents. Critics said that the new law would have suffocated the creativity and meme; remixes etc. would have been things of the past.

CHINA LAUNCHES TWO REMOTE SENSING SATELLITES FOR PAKISTAN

DATE: 9th July

China successfully launches two satellites; PRSS-1 and PakTES-1A, from the Jiuquan Satellite Launch Centre in northwest China. It has launched these remote sensing satellites for Pakistan, marking the first international commercial launch for the Long March-2C rocket in about 19 years. The PRSS-1 is China's first optical remote sensing satellite sold to Pakistan. It is the 17th satellite developed by the China Academy of Space Technology (CAST) for an overseas buyer. The PRSS-1 will be used for land and resources surveying, monitoring of natural disasters, agriculture research and urban construction and providing remote sensing information of road region.

The satellite, which has a designed life of seven years, is equipped with two panchromatic/multispectral cameras, with a resolution up to a meter and a coverage range of 60 km. The satellite can turn at wide angles to enable the cameras to cover a wider range. The PRSS-1 has an information security design, and the data can be encrypted. This launch is the 279th mission of the Long March rocket series. Long March-2C rockets are mainly used to send satellites into low Earth or Sun-synchronous orbits.

Chinese and Pakistani engineers have cooperated closely in the development of the satellite. French space experts were invited to supervise the manufacturing of key parts. Chinese space experts also helped train technologists from Pakistan on its operation.

ISSUES

NATIONAL

Discrimination against Gays will go if Criminality of Section 377 is removed: SC

DATE: 12th July

SC says the social stigma and discrimination attached to the lesbian, gay, bisexual, transgender and queer (LGBTQ) community would go if criminality of consensual gay sex is done away with, while maintaining that it would scrutinize the legal validity of section 377 of the IPC in all its aspects. The court stated this while maintaining that it would scrutinize the constitutional validity of section 377 of the IPC in detail. A five-judge bench comprising Chief Justice Dipak Misra and Justices R F Nariman, A M Khanwilkar, D Y Chandrachud and Indu Malhotra is currently hearing petitions challenging the constitutional validity of the 158-year-old penal law. The bench has rejected a proposal of the lawyers, seeking retention of section 377, that public opinion should be elicited on the matter, saying it did not want a referendum but would go by constitutional morality. The bench has said that it will try to see whether section 377 of the IPC can stand the test of fundamental rights enshrined under Articles 14 (right to equality), 19 (freedom of speech and association) and 21 (right to life and liberty) of the Constitution. The bench then said that the LGBTQ community faced discrimination and social stigma because of the criminality attached to the consensual same-sex relationship. It stated that once the criminality under section 377 goes, then the stigma and discrimination will also go.

IDEAS

NATIONAL

WINGS: BSNL LAUNCHES INDIA'S FIRST INTERNET TELEPHONY SERVICE

DATE: 11th July

OBJECTIVE: To stand in competitive environment of telecommunication

BSNL unveils the country's first internet telephony service that will allow users to dial any telephone number in India through its mobile app. Now BSNL customers will be able to make calls using the company's mobile app "Wings" to any phone number in the country. Before the launch of this app, phone calls on mobile apps were possible within users of a particular app and not on telephone numbers. To use this facility, customers will have to through the following methods:

- Customers will have to download the 'Wings App' and configure it with the Landline number
- Subsequently, User name and password will have to be generated
- Internet telephony service will require mobile data or wifi services
- The service will allow calls from mobile phone to any number, domestic or international
- Internet telephony service can also be used to send SMS
- 'Wings' will allow customers to make unlimited video or audio calls by paying annual fee of Rs 1,099

Telecom regulator TRAI had given its nod to the internet telephony service a month ago. 'Wings' service is set to give more impetus to Digital India and is being termed a game changer in the telecom sector. Registration for the service will start this week and the services will be activated July 25 onwards.

'JAL BACHAO, VIDEO BANAO, PURUSKAR PAO CONTEST' ON WATER CONSERVATION

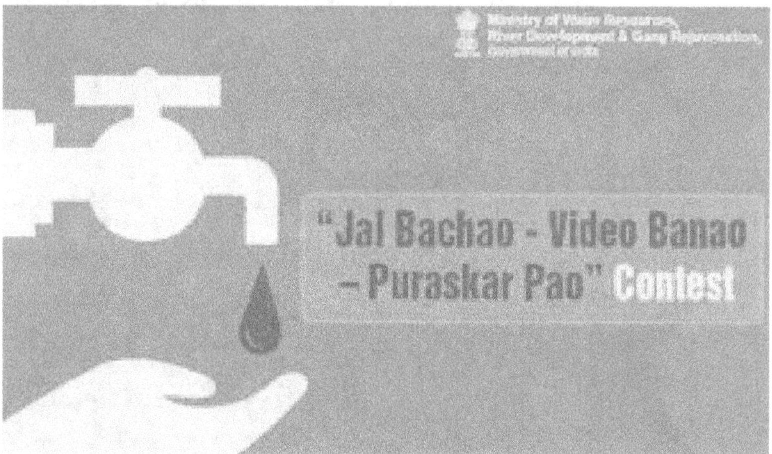

DATE: 14th July

OBJECTIVE: To aware the people about Water conservation

In an attempt to engage with the people of India on the important issues of water conservation and water management, the Ministry of Water Resources, River Development and Ganga Rejuvenation launches a video contest titled "Jal Bachao, Video Banao, Puruskar Pao". The Ministry has joined hands with My Gov portal of the GOI to run the contest. This contest will last till 4th November 2018 and three winners will be chosen every fortnight.

In the contest, any Indian citizen can upload their video entries on YouTube and enter the publicly accessible link on the Video link section of MyGov contest page www.mygov.in.

The participants will be judged on the basis of elements of creativity, originality, composition, technical excellence, artistic merit, quality of video, content and visual impact. The prize amount is Rs 25,000/-, Rs 15,000/- and Rs 10,000/- for first, second and third positions respectively.

The Ministry appeals to the people of India to make and upload videos capturing the efforts, significant contributions, best practices in the field of Water Conservation, Optimum Water Utilization and Water Resource Development and Management in different parts of the country. Any innovative advertisement/commercial on Water Conservation is also welcome. The duration of the videos should be minimum of 2 minutes and up to 10 minutes in any language and must not violate any provision of the Indian Copyright Act, 1957 or the Intellectual Property Rights of any third party.

INTERNATIONAL

UN SETS UP PANEL ON DIGITAL COOPERATION

DATE: 14th July

OBJECTIVE: To tackle cyber security threats

UN chief Antonio Guterres establishes a first-of-its-kind panel on digital cooperation that aims at addressing concerns of cyber security threats and rise in hate speech and named senior Indian diplomat Amandeep Singh Gill as the executive director of the panel's secretariat. The high-level panel on digital cooperation co-chaired by US philanthropist Melinda Gates and China-based Alibaba founder Jack Ma. It will coontain 20 members in total and include leaders from industry, civil society and academia. Senior Indian diplomat Amandeep Singh Gill along with former diplomat Jovan Kurbalija will be executive directors of panel's secretariat. It will map trends in digital technologies, identify gaps and opportunities and outline proposals for strengthening international cooperation. It will focus on cyber-bullying, abuse rise, fake news, cyber crime and security aspects. Digital technologies in modern era are expanding rapidly and are changing economies and societies at warp speed. At the same time, world is only beginning to address its dark side, such as cyber security threats, risks of cyber warfare magnification of hate speech and violations of privacy. Global community is also facing uncertainness about security, equity, ethics, and human rights in digital age. Fake news, poisoning of data, electoral manipulation are concern that have been highlighted by recent developments. So there is need to seize potential of technology while safeguarding against risks and unintended consequences.

NATIONAL

SBI, NABARD TIE UP TO PROMOTE JOINT LIABILITY GROUPS

DATE: 2ⁿᵈJanuary, 2018

OBJECTIVE: To repay loans jointly, taken by the group from a bank

State Bank of India and Nabard have signed an agreement with five NGOs in Bengal for the promotion of 2,500 joint liability groups (JLGs) in select districts of the State Bengal.

JLGs are informal groups of 4-10 members engaged in similar economic activities and willing to jointly undertake the responsibility to repay loans taken by the group from a bank. They are typically credit groups of small or marginal tenant farmers who do not have a proper title of their farmland. Through these JLGs, SBI plans to extend assistance to the financially excluded sections of the society, especially landless farmers in the districts of Purulia, Paschim Medinipur, Purba Medinipur, Burdwan and North 24 Parganas.

The bank hopes to be able to extend support to close to 12,500 tenant farmers under this arrangement. Plans are also afoot to scale up the project in a phased manner to cover the remaining districts.

Nabard has fixed a target of credit linking 80,000 JLGs in West Bengal in 2017-18. It has sanctioned assistance for the promotion of 60,000 JLGs by various NGOs in the State through 339 projects in different districts.

GOVT. FORECASTS GDP GROWTH AT 6.5% IN CURRENT FISCAL YEAR

DATE: 5ᵗʰ January, 2018

The Government has forecast 6.5 per cent growth in gross domestic product for the fiscal year ending in March, implying a quickening pace in the second half of that period as the economy bounces back from two major recent policy shocks. Economists say that growth in the current fiscal year has suffered from the aftershocks of the cancellation of high-value banknotes in November 2016, followed by the disruptive introduction of a new national goods and services tax in July last year.

Indian GDP growth was estimated by the Central Statistics Office at 5.7 per cent and 6.3 per cent, respectively, in the first and second quarters of the current fiscal year. This means that a significant acceleration would be needed to bring the full-year figure to 6.5 per cent – which would still be well below the 7.1 per cent growth estimate for the 2017 fiscal year. The government forecast growth of over 7 per cent in sectors such as financial services and transport. But manufacturing output was predicted to grow at 4.6 per cent, down from 7.9 per cent in the previous year.

CBDT RELAXES NORMS FOR MAT

DATE: 6th January, 2018

OBJECTIVE: To make Insolvency and Bankruptcy Code effective for insolvent companies

The income tax department decided rules around levy of minimum alternate tax (MAT) will be eased for insolvent companies as the government looks to make the Insolvency and Bankruptcy Code, 2016 more effective. Companies against whom Insolvency proceedings have been initiated will be allowed to reduce the entire amount of loss brought forward including absorbed depreciation from the book profit for calculation of MAT. This will be effective from assessment year 2018-19.

The decision follows representation made by various stakeholders about problems being faced due to restriction in allowance of brought forward loss for computation of book profit. As per the existing provisions of 115JB of the Income Tax Act dealing with levy of MAT, the amount of loss brought forward or unabsorbed depreciation, whichever is less as per books of account can be reduced from the book profit.

FDI POLICY LIBERALIZED IN KEY SECTORS

DATE: 10th January, 2018

OBJECTIVE: To make Economic Policy Investors-friendly

Under the Chairmanship of Prime Minister Shri Narendra Modi, Cabinet approves a number of amendments in the FDI Policy. These are intended to liberalize and simplify the FDI policy so as to provide ease of doing business in the country. In turn, it will lead to larger FDI inflows contributing to growth of investment, income and employment.

Major amendments approved are 100% FDI for Single Brand Retail Trading (SBRT) under automatic route, 100% FDI under automatic route in Construction Development, Foreign airlines allowed investing up to 49% in Air India under government approval route, FIIs/FPIs allowed investing in Power Exchanges through primary market and Definition of 'medical devices' amended in FDI Policy. Earlier the existing FDI policy on SBRT allows 49% FDI under automatic route and beyond 49% up to 100% is allowed through government approval route. The amendment now permits 100% FDI for SBRT under automatic route. It also permits SBRT entity to set off its incremental sourcing of goods from India for global operations during initial 5 years against mandatory sourcing requirement of 30% of purchases from India.

INDIA'S FIRST-EVER FDI IN FERTILIZER SECTOR

DATE: 14 January, 2018

A Norwegian fertiliser Giant Yara International acquires Tata Chemicals urea plant. The Rs. 2,682-crore acquisition deal includes transfer of all assets and liabilities (including working capital) relating to Babrala unit. It marks first foreign direct investment (FDI) in India's highly regulated urea sector.

The acquisition represents a major step of Yara as it deepens its footprint in India, world's second largest fertiliser market after China. Moreover, a Greenfield urea-ammonia plant of this size at Babrala will entail a setting up cost of $1 billion. It has acquired Agronomic Technology Corp. (ATC), an agricultural field modeling company for soil, water, crops, and fertilize. ATC is the maker of Adapt-N, a software tool for agronomists that combines data around soil types and weather with crop modeling and field management to provide farmers with detailed fertilizer prescriptions, to avoid overuse and wastage.

At present it does annual sales of $35-40 million in India. Much of it comprises premium micronutrients, complex and water-soluble fertilisers used in high-value crops such as banana, grapes, apples, sugarcane, chilli and vegetables grown mainly in Maharashtra, Karnataka, Andhra Pradesh and Himachal Pradesh.

GST COUNCIL REDUCES THE RATES

DATE: 19th January 2018

OBJECTIVE: To reduce GST rates on various goods and services

The Goods and Services Tax (GST) Council has reduced the rates on 29 goods and 53 categories of services. The announcement was made by Union Finance Minister Arun Jaitley following the Council's meeting in New Delhi.

In the services category the rates have been reduced in areas including , admission to theme parks (28% to 18%), common effluent treatment plans, petroleum and natural gas mining and exploration (18% to 12%), tailoring (18% to 5%).

Services relating to admission or conduct of examinations provided to all educational institutions, entrance fees for entrance examination and for transportation of students up to higher secondary schools have been exempted from taxation.

The goods on which the rates have been reduced include biodiesel buses used for public transport (28% to 18%), sugar boiled confectionery, biodiesel, fertiliser-grade phosphoric acid, drip irrigation system, drinking water packed in 20 litre containers (all from 18% to 12%), and LPG supplied to domestic consumers by private distributors (18% to 5%). New rates for all the revised services and goods would come into effect on January 25, 2018.

Although the inclusion of much awaited key sectors like petroleum and real estate in GST was not taken up in this meeting, it was expected to come up for discussion in council's next meeting.

ECONOMIC SURVEY 2017-18

DATE: 30th January 2018

OBJECTIVE: To review the progress of Indian Economy during the last financial year

Union Finance Minister Arun Jaitley tabled the Economic Survey for the year 2017-18 in the Parliament. Referring to the recently introduced Goods and Services

Tax (GST), the survey noted that with a policy change of such scale, scope and complexity, the transition unsurprisingly encountered challenges of policy, law and information technology systems, which especially affected the informal sector.

The survey mentioned about The Twin Balance Sheet (TBS) problem and how it was decisively addressed by sending the major stressed companies for resolution under the new Indian Bankruptcy Code and implementing a major recapitalisation package to strengthen the balance sheets of public sector banks. This led to the economy accelerated in the second half of 2017.

This is expected to boost real GDP growth to 6.75 per cent for the year as a whole and to 7-7.5 per cent in 2018-19, reinstating India as the world's fastest-growing major economy.

The survey noted that India should continue improving the climate for rapid economic growth on the strength of two truly sustainable engines, private investment and exports. India's performance in 14 out of the 17 indicators of women's agency, attitudes, and outcomes has also improved over the last 10-15 years. Other points it mentioned including, States' prosperity and its positive correlation with their international and inter-State trade, egalitarian structure of India's firm export, large increase in registered indirect and direct taxpayers, 50 % increase in unique taxpayers under the GST in comparison with the pre-GST system. Clothing incentive package boosted exports of readymade garments, Indian parents' preference for male progeny and raising farm productivity while strengthening agricultural resilience.

CABINET APPROVES AMENDMENT TO MSMED ACT, 2006

DATE: 8th February, 2018

The Union Cabinet has approved amendment to Micro, Small and Medium Enterprises Development (MSMED) Act, 2006 for classifying MSMEs from current investment in plant and machinery criteria to annual turnover criteria. At present Section 7 of MSMED Act classifies MSMEs on the basis of investment in plant and machinery for manufacturing units and investment in equipment for service enterprises. On the basis of new classification criteria, Micro enterprise will be unit with annual turnover does not exceed Rs. 5 crore, Small enterprise will be unit with annual turnover between Rs. 5 crore & Rs. 75 crore and Medium enterprise will be unit with annual turnover lies between 75 crore & Rs. 250 crore. The amendment empowers Central Government to vary turnover limits, provided not exceeding thrice the limits specified in Section 7 of MSMED Act by issuing notification.

The amendment will provide flexibility to the Government to fine-tune the classification of MSMEs in response to changing economic scenario without resorting to the amendment of MSMED Act. The change in the norms of classification will enhance the ease of doing business. The consequent growth and will pave the way for increased direct and indirect employment in the MSME sector of the country.

PNB'S $1.8 BILLION SCAM

DATE: 15th February, 2018

PNB, India's second-largest government bank, reports on that $1.8 billion or over Rs. 11,000 crore of taxpayers' money had been illegally transferred abroad to select customers from a single branch in Mumbai. The amount is nearly 1/3rd of the bank's total market capitalisation of Rs 36,000 crore. It is also 8 times of bank's fiscal year 2017 net profit of Rs 1,324 crore. With the sharp fall, investors have reportedly lost Rs 3,844 crore of wealth on a single day. Jeweller Nirav Modi allegedly acquired fraudulent letters of undertaking from a PNB branch in Mumbai to secure overseas credit from other Indian lenders, while PNB did not name the other lenders, Union Bank of India, Allahabad Bank and Axis Bank are reported to have offered credit based on letters of undertaking (LoUs) issued by PNB. Besides him, three other jewellers, Gitanjali, Ginni and Nakshatra are also under the interrogation with the CBI.

LoU is a letter of assurance or guarantee issued by one bank to branches of other banks to meet a liability on behalf of an importer, based on which foreign branches offer credit to buyers. An LoU involves four parties - an issuing bank, a receiving bank, an importer and a beneficiary entity overseas. It is used in international banking transactions. The bank that holds the LoU, then it goes back to the issuer bank and gets its due.

NATIONAL CONFERENCE ON DOUBLING FARMERS' INCOME BY 2022

DATE: 19th February 2018

OBJECTIVE: To double the income of Farmers by 2022

The conference ''Agriculture 2022 - Doubling Farmers' Income'' was inaugurated by Union Minister for Agriculture and Farmers Welfare Shri Radha Mohan Singh. Prime Minister Narendra Modi attended the last session of this two day conference organized at National Agriculture Science Complex (NASC), Pusa, New Delhi.

Addressing on the occasion PM proposed a four-pronged strategy to achieve his government's key agrarian agenda of doubling farmers' income by reducing cultivation costs, ensuring profitable prices, processing farm waste and creating non-farm sources of income.

The conference was organized in the backdrop of Ashok Dalwai Panel, which was set up for doubling of farmers' income. The panel pointed out that real income of farmers' need to register a compound annual growth rate of 10.4% for farmers' income to double by 2022.

The summit was attended by Farmers, senior officials from the Central and State Governments, scientists, economists, representatives from professional associations, academicians, Industry and NGOs.

BIHAR TOPS THE NATION WITH 10.3 % GROWTH RATE

DATE: 26th February 2018

Bihar topped the nation in growth rate during last fiscal year. The state witnessed a growth rate of 10.3 % in 2016-2017, as compared to national average of 7.0 %.

According to 12th Economic Survey tabled in the state Assembly, the growth rate of 10.3 % in 2016-2017 as against 7.5% in the corresponding fiscal a year ago is mainly due to the growth in services sector. The information was shared by Sushil Modi, Deputy Chief Minister of Bihar who is also holding the Finance portfolio.

As per the survey, the state has consistently been revenue surplus, which increased from Rs 5,101 crore in 2012-13 to Rs 10,819 crore in 2016-17. The surplus, projected to be Rs 14,556 crore during 2017-18, is considered to be the result of better financial management.

Additionally, the Gross Financial Deficit (GFD) of the state rose by Rs 4,418 crore in 2016-17 as compared to 2015-16. GFD is projected to grow to Rs 18,112 crore in current fiscal. Rice production stood at 82.39 LT in the fiscal, a hike of 21.1% over the previous year, whereas wheat output also recorded a rise from 47.36 LT (2015-16) to 59.86 LT (2016-17).

ZERO BUDGET NATURAL FARMING PROJECT LAUNCHED IN HP

DATE: 29th January, 2018

OBJECTIVE: To increase agriculture produce and the income of farmers

Himachal Pradesh Government launches Zero Budget Natural Farming (ZBNF) project to increase the income of farmers. ZBNF is set of natural farming methods where cost of growing and harvesting plants is zero. It is a farming practice that believes in natural growth of crops without adding any fertilizers and pesticides or any other foreign elements. The inputs used for seed treatments and other inoculations are locally available in form of cow dung and cow urine.

In Zero Budget system farmers need not purchase fertilizers and pesticides in order to ensure the healthy growth of crops. It requires almost no monetary investment and envisages use of 'Jeevamrutha' and 'Beejamrutha'. The main aim of ZBNF is to eliminate use of chemical pesticides and uses biological pesticides and promote of good agronomic practices. Farmers use low cost of inputs such as earthworms, cow dung, urine, plants, human excreta and such biological fertilizers for crop protection.

PRESIDENT INAUGURATES UDYAM SANGAM-2018

DATE: 27th June 2018

OBJECTIVE: To encourage partnerships among various MSME agencies for innovation and knowledge sharing

The President inaugurated the Udyam Sangam-2018 in New Delhi on the occasion of International Micro, Small & Medium Enterprises (MSME) Day. He also launched the Solar Charkha and MSME Sampark Portal.

The purpose of Udyam Sangam is to encourage dialogues and partnerships among various stakeholder of the MSME ecosystem for promoting innovation and knowledge sharing on MSME related issues.

Speaking on the occasion the Indian President said that the Udyam Sangam-2018 is an important effort in developing effective eco-systems for MSME sector.

It was organised by Ministry of Micro, Small & Medium Enterprises to celebrate the 2nd United Nations Micro, Small and Medium -Sized Enterprise Day. One of the main aims of the Sangam is to create public awareness about the MSME Sector along with the importance of the Sector in the national economy.

MSME sector acts as the backbone of Indian economy. This sector is the second largest employment provider after the agricultural sector. MSME sector generates more employment opportunities at a lower cost of capital and creates jobs in rural and backward areas.

DAHOD TOPS LIST OF DELTA RANKING ON ASPIRATIONAL DISTRICTS

DATE: 29th June 2018

OBJECTIVE: To identify sectors and indicator specific challenges in the districts

The first Delta ranking for the Aspirational Districts was released by NITI Aayog. Dahod (Gujarat), West Sikkim (Sikkim) and Ramanathapuram (Tamil Nadu) declared as top three ranked districts.

The rankings were released by CEO of NITI Aayog Amitabh Kant. It is based on self-reported incremental (Delta) data of districts between 31st March 2018 and 31st May 2018. The real time data points were collected on 49 key performance indicators in 5 main areas of Basic Infrastructure (Household Electricity Connections, Household Toilets and Rural Drinking Water), Health and Nutrition, Education, Agriculture and Water Resources, Skill Development and Financial Inclusion.

The ranking is a tool to identify sectors and indicator specific challenges and also take immediate corrective measures. The purpose of this ranking is to incite a sense of competition among the dynamic teams in the districts.

Total 108 districts participated in this ranking. The delta ranking is computed in a transparent manner for combined improvements made during April and May 2018.

It was launched by Prime Minister in January, 2018 with an aim to quickly and effectively transform some of the most underdeveloped districts of the country.

1ST GST DAY

DATE: 30th June 2018

Objective: To commemorate the first anniversary of GST implementation

The first Goods and Services Tax (GST) day was celebrated by Government of India.

The Act came into effect on 1st July 2017 as it was rolled out in the intervening night of June 30 and July 1, 2017 in a ceremony held in the Central Hall of Parliament.

As per the statement from Finance ministry GST subsumed over a dozen local levies and transformed India into "one nation, one Tax" and binds the country into an Economic Union. "The first year of GST has been an example to the world of the readiness of the Indian taxpayer to be a partner in this unprecedented reform of Indian taxation,"

To commemorate the event Union Minister Arun Jaitley addressed on the 1st year journey of GST over a live video link. Union Minister for Finance & Corporate Affairs and Railways, Coal, Piyush Goyal was the Chief Guest.

Mr. Jaitley recalled the pre-GST taxation system in India was one of the most complicated tax systems in the world.He said that this reform has created a unified market, the cascading of taxes has been eliminated, the weighted average of total taxation basket has come down. Mr. Goyal termed GST as a Game changer for small businesses and informed that enterprises having a turnover of Rs. 20 lakhs are exempted from GST and those with a turnover up to Rs. 1 crore have to pay 1% tax.

Speaking on the event Finance Secretary, Dr. Hasmukh Adhia called the '1st GST Day' as a day of celebration of the spirit of cooperative federalism that the functioning of the GST Council has upheld in the successful journey of GST.

Goods & Services Tax Law is a comprehensive, multi-stage, destination-based tax that is levied on every value addition. It is an indirect tax levied on the supply of goods and services. This law has replaced many indirect tax laws that previously existed in India and stated as one indirect tax for the entire country.

NASSCOM LAUNCHES THE CENTRE OF EXCELLENCE FOR DATA SCIENCE AND AI

DATE: 5th July 2018

OBJECTIVE: To support small and midsize business in various business domains

The National Association of Software and Services Companies (NASSCOM) opened the Centre of Excellence for Data Science and Artificial Intelligence (CoE -DSAI), in Bengaluru. The Centre of Excellence was launched in partnership with the Karnataka Government.

The CoE initiative is a nationwide programme on innovation, focusing on solutions in smart manufacturing, Internet of Things, healthcare, energy, banking and financial services, retail, telecommunication sector etc.

The aim of the CoE-DSAI initiative is to support small and midsize business, by fast-tracking their product development, provide market access to enterprises and assist them by co-creating programs along with other industry partners /start-ups to solve business problems.

The company also signed a Memorandum of Understanding with NITI Aayog to collaboratively foster applied research, accelerating adoption and ethics, privacy and security. The company is also supporting government's National Strategy for artificial Intelligence (AI) and facilitates collaboration between NITI Aayog and CoEs and will work with NITI Aayog as its knowledge partner. NASSCOM has partnered with Intel and IBM as its founding members and technology advisors for accelerating the data science and AI ecosystem in the country.

FIRST MEETING OF E-COMMERCE TASK FORCE HELD

DATE: 6th July 2018

OBJECTIVE: To prepare recommendations for India's national policy on e-commerce.

The first meeting of the Task Force on e-commerce was held in New Delhi. The meeting was chaired by was chaired by Commerce Secretary.

Senior officers from various ministries, government departments and institutes like Electronics and Information Technology, Corporate Affairs and Department of Telecommunications, Ministry of Micro Small and Medium Enterprises (MSME), Directorate General of Foreign Trade and Competition Commission of India attended the meeting.

The meeting discussed upon the suggestions raised during sub-group meetings held earlier. The meeting deliberated upon wide ranging issues like taxation, trade facilitation and logistics, Intellectual Property Rights, Future technologies, Foreign Direct Investment etc.

The task force was constituted as per the decision taken during the first meeting of the Think Tank, on the framework for national policy on e-commerce, under the chairmanship of, Minister of Commerce & Industry. The Task Force divided into nine sub-groups for preparing recommendations for India's national policy on e-commerce.

The suggestions and decisions taken during the Task Force meeting have been submitted to the Think Tank for consideration.

INTERNATIONAL

SAUDI ARABIA, UAE INTRODUCE VAT

Date: 1st January, 2018

OBJECTIVE: To increase revenue in Gulf countries

Value Added Tax (VAT) has been introduced in Saudi Arabia and the United Arab Emirates for the first time .The 5% levy is being applied to the majority of goods and services. Gulf states have long attracted foreign workers with the promise of tax-free living. But governments want to increase revenue in the face of lower oil prices. The tax kicked in on 1 January in both countries. The UAE estimates that in the first year, VAT income will be around 12 billion dirhams (£2.4bn; $3.3bn). Petrol and diesel, food, clothes, utility bills and hotel rooms all now have VAT applied. But some outgoings have been made exempt from the tax, or given a zero-tax rating, including medical treatment, financial services and public transport. In Saudi Arabia more than 90% of budget revenues come from the oil industry while in the UAE it is roughly 80%. Both countries have already taken steps to boost government coffers. In Saudi Arabia this included a tax on tobacco and soft drinks as well as a cut in some subsidies offered to locals. In the UAE road tolls have been hiked and a tourism tax introduced. But there are no plans to introduce income tax, where most residents pay 0% tax on their earnings.

AIIB PLANS TO ISSUE FIRST US DOLLAR BONDS

DATE: 7th January, 2018

OBJECTIVE: To issue dollar bonds in the market

The Asian Infrastructure Investment Bank (AIIB), the body set up and supported by China as part of its ambitious Belt and Road Initiative, may issue its first US dollar bonds by the end of June.

The earliest issuance could happen "toward the end of the first half of 2018." This would allow time for certain procedures, including the board of governors' approval of AIIB's 2017 financial statements as well as borrowing and swap documentation.

The bond would have a minimum size of $1 billion but after that the bank expects there might be strong demand after the first bond issue. The bond's maturity would be between three and five years depending on investor demand. The bank plans to cap its total borrowing at $3 billion in 2018.

INDIA AT 62ND PLACE ON INCLUSIVE DEVELOPMENT INDEX

DATE: 22nd January, 2018

World Economic Forum (WEF) ranks India at the 62nd place among emerging economies on an Inclusive Development Index, much below China's 26th position and Pakistan's 47th. India was ranked 60th among 79 developing economies last year, as against China's 15th and Pakistan's 52nd position.

The index takes into account the "living standards, environmental sustainability and protection of future generations from further indebtedness.

The 2018 index, which measures progress of 103 economies on three individual pillars i.e. growth and development; inclusion; and inter-generational equity.

The WEF index has also classified the countries into five sub-categories in terms of the five-year trend of their overall Inclusive Development Growth score — receding, slowly receding, stable, slowly advancing and advancing.

Among advanced economies, Norway is followed by Ireland, Luxembourg, Switzerland and Denmark in the top five. Lithuania, Hungary, Azerbaijan, Latvia and Poland are top-five most inclusive emerging economies

The neighboring countries rank above India includes Sri Lanka (40), Bangladesh (34) and Nepal (22). Mali, Uganda, Rwanda, Burundi, Ghana, Ukraine, Serbia, Philippines, Indonesia, Iran, Macedonia, Mexico, Thailand and Malaysia rank better than India.

According to the data of WEF released in Davos (Switzerland), Norway remains the world's most inclusive advanced economy, while Lithuania again tops the list of emerging economies.

IMF FORECASTS 7.4% GROWTH FOR INDIA IN FY19

DATE: 23rd January, 2018

According to IMF's January update of the World Economic Outlook (WEO), India's GDP growth rate is projected at 7.4 per cent for 2018-19 against 6.7 per cent this year. The IMF has projected a 7.8 per cent growth rate for India in 2019-20. Growth rate projections for both 2018 and 2019 remains unchanged since its October 2017 WEO projections. IMF further stated that this makes India the fastest growing economy among emerging economies following last year's slowdown due to demonetization and the implementation of GST.

The global economy is expected to grow 3.9% this year, faster than 3.7% forecast earlier in October. India's growth remains unchanged from the October forecast. Some 120 economies, accounting for three quarters of world GDP, have seen a pickup in growth in year-on-year terms in 2017, the broadest synchronized global growth upsurge since 2010. In the current year, China will grow 6.8%, just ahead of India but will slip to 6.6% next year. The US is forecast to grow 2.7% and 2.5% in 2018 and 2019, respectively, higher by 0.4 and 0.6 percentage points than earlier estimates. According to India's official estimates, the economy will grow 6.5% in the current fiscal with the second half clocking 7% growth.

WORLD ECONOMIC FORUM MEETING

DATE: 23rd January 2018

OBJECTIVE: To engage top political, business and other leaders of society to shape global, regional and industry agendas

The 48th annual meeting of the World Economic Forum (WEF) was held at Davos-klosters (Switzerland). In this 4 day event around 70 Heads of States and Governments and 45 Heads of International organizations including leaders from G7 and G20 countries participated. Additionally, more than 2000 CEOs of top global companies also participated in this global economic platform and discussed about various business projects and initiatives.

Prime Minister Narendra Modi delivered the keynote address at the forum. He listed out India's recent initiatives to transform the economy, such as, Jan Dhan Yojna, the International Solar Alliance among others. He listed terrorism, protectionism and climate change as three major world-challenges. Mr. Modi called for creating a shared future in a fractured world. He invited the corporate leaders to invest in India and reap the benefits out of the growing economy.

Professor Klaus Schwab is credited with founding of European Management Forum in 1971, which renamed as WEF later. The forum is a not-for-profit foundation and is headquartered in Geneva. It engages the foremost political, business and other leaders of society to shape global, regional and industry agendas. WEF strives in all its efforts to demonstrate entrepreneurship in the global public interest while upholding the highest standards of governance. The forum is one of the foremost International Organization for Public-Private Cooperation.

VENEZUELA BECOMES FIRST COUNTRY TO LAUNCH VIRTUAL CURRENCY PETRO

DATE: 22nd February, 2018

OBJECTIVE: To revive its failing economy and to counter the sanctions imposed by the US

Venezuela becomes first sovereign country to officially launch its own version of Bitcoin called Petro backed by oil, gas, gold and diamond reserves to circumvent US-led financial sanctions.

This crypto currency aims to help Venezuela to advance in issues of monetary sovereignty which will make financial transactions and overcome financial blockade. It is based on block chain technology. Its value will be pegged to price of barrel of Venezuelan oil from the previous day. Government of Venezuela will accept Petro as a form of payment of national taxes, fees, contributions and public services. The President has also authorised payments in crypto currency for Venezuela's consulate services and fuel on the border.

The government will issue 100 million coins of Petro of which 38.4 million are available for pre-sale and 44 million coins will be offered in Initial Coin Offerings (ICO) in March 2018. The rest 17.6 million coins will be retained by Venezuelan Superintendency of Currency and Related Activities (SUPCACVEN). Venezuelan officials have released few of details of how it will work ensuring investors that it is safe.

RE-DENOMINATION OF VENEZUELAN CURRENCY

DATE: 23rd March 2018

OBJECTIVE: To strengthen the economic crisis prevailing in Venezuela

The Venezuelan President announced the re-denomination of the ailing bolivar currency. President Nicolás Maduro outlined his monetary rescue plan by knocking three zeroes off bolivar currency amid hyperinflation and severe economic crisis.

The move illustrates the collapse of the bolivar, which has fallen 99.99% against the U.S. dollar since Maduro came to power five years back.

Amidst shortages of food and medicines during a fifth year of recession, millions of Venezuelans are suffering. The government is giving western hostility as the reason behind the crisis while critics put the onus on Maduro's incompetency.

The sinking of oil prices has played a major role in the current economical crisis as the Venezuelan government lost a large fraction of its revenue.

The Economists are of the view that the present move will not rescue the Bolivar from the economic crisis and is just a psychological ploy.

The Crisis is also important against a backdrop of scheduled May presidential elections in May for which Maduro is running and seeking his re-election.

FREE TRADE BLOC FOR AFRICA

DATE: 22nd March 2018

OBJECTIVE: To remove trade barriers between African countries

The African Continental Free Trade Area (AfCFTA) is all set to launch a long-held dream of the African Union: free trade across the continent. The 44 African countries signed the formal agreement to establish one of the largest trade blocs after WTO. The agreement was signed at Kigali the capital city of Rwanda.

The conceptualisation to establish a free trade bloc for African nations started since 2012. It was later shifted to negotiations stage which subsequently led to ratification by 44 countries and soon expected to be signed by all members of the African Union.

The free trade bloc is set to change the world trade scenario as it will bring together 1.2 billion people with a combine GDP of more than $2 trillion.

The AfCFTA aims to remove trade barriers like tariffs and import quotas, allowing the free flow of goods and services within trade bloc.

The draft agreement commits countries to removing tariffs on 90 percent of goods, with rest items expected to be phased out in subsequent stages.

INDIA AT 11TH SPOT IN AT KEARNEY FDI CONFIDENCE INDEX

DATE: 3rd May

India slips by three notches to 11th position in the FDI Confidence Index 2018 of global consultancy firm, A T Kearney. India was ranked 8th in 2017, while it was at 9th rank in the previous year. According to the report, some policies may have deterred investors, at least in the short term. The 2017 nationwide goods and services tax (GST), for example, has faced implementation challenges, and the 2016 demonetization initiative disrupted business activity and weighed on economic growth."

U.S. is at top position, followed by Canada, while Germany dropped to the third place. Overall, India remains among the top investment destinations due to its market size and rapid economic growth. The IMF projects India's economy will grow by 7.4% in 2018, the fastest growth rate of any major economy. Inward FDI flows already increased to an estimated $45 billion in 2017, a record high.

Global consultant AT Kearney releases the Foreign Direct Investment (FDI) Confidence Index. It is an annual survey which tracks the impact of political, economic and regulatory changes on the FDI preferences of Chief Executive Officers (CEOs) and Chief Financial Officers (CFOs) of the country. Investors are interested in developed markets across all regions including Europe, North America, Asia, and Australasia. Around 80 percent of investors believe FDI will become more important for corporate profitability and competitiveness in the next three years.

WORLD BANK SANCTIONS LOAN FOR USD 21.7 MILLION FOR RAJASTHAN PROJECT

DATE: 29th May 2018

OBJECTIVE: To strengthen the public financial management in Rajasthan

An Agreement was signed between India and World Bank for Credit of USD 21.7 million for the strengthening of public financial management in Rajasthan. The agreement was signed by Joint Secretary (FB and ADB), Department of Economic Affairs, Ministry of Finance on behalf of the Government of India and Acting Country Director, World Bank (India) on behalf of the World Bank.

The Project size is approximately USD 31 million, of which USD 21.7 million will be financed by the World Bank, and the remaining amount will be funded out of the State Budget.

The objective of the 5 year project is for contribution towards improved Budget execution, enhanced accountability and greater efficiency in Revenue Administration in Rajasthan. The Project involves Strengthening of the Public Financial Management Framework; Strengthening of Expenditure and Revenue Systems; and Project Management and Capacity Building among others.

'PUBLIC CREDIT REGISTRY' TO BE SET UP BY RBI

DATE: 7th June

OBJECTIVE: To curb bad loans

The Reserve Bank of India (RBI) has announced that it will set up a Public Credit Registry (PCR) as a repository of information regarding loan information of individuals and corporate borrowers. This decision has been taken as per recommendations of Y M Deosthalee committee set up by the central bank.

Y M Deosthalee Committee Recommendations

The Y.M. Deosthalee committee was set up by RBI and had submitted its report in April, 2018. The major recommendations of this committee report are as follows:

RBI should set up a Public Credit Registry in due course and this should be backed by a legal framework. The central bank may also consider moving such registry to a separate non-profit entity.

PCR should also capture data such as external commercial borrowings, market borrowings, and all contingent liabilities; and should provide a holistic picture about the borrower's indebtedness.

PCR will work as a repository of all loan contracts, duly verified by reporting institutions for all / any lending in India, regardless of the amount of the loan.

The registry should capture both positive and negative information about all loans. The borrowers should also be able to access their own history.

The PCR data should be available to all stakeholders such as banks on a need-to-know basis. There should be adequate safeguards on privacy protection.

Onus of data quality should be on reporting agencies and institutions and action should be taken against the institutions in case of any violations in rules.

The database should also be linked to defaulter databases such as those maintained by Export Credit Guarantee Corporation of India and GST network etc.

5TH RCEP INTERSESSIONAL MINISTERIAL MEETING

DATE: 1st July 2018

OBJECTIVE: To discuss on the issue of economic collaborations and agreements related to inclusive regional economic integration.

The 5th Regional Comprehensive Economic Partnership (RCEP) Intersessional Ministerial Meeting was held in Tokyo. It was attended by RCEP Participating countries.

During the meeting ministers from the participating countries discussed different developments, including the outcomes of the 22nd round of negotiations held in Singapore.

The Ministers welcomed the progress made by the negotiators across all areas, and agreed to work in a collaborative manner with a greater focus on finding breakthroughs for conclusion of the RCEP negotiations, in line with the RCEP Leaders' mandate, 2017.

As a prelude to this meeting the intersessional meetings of selected working groups and sub-working groups; as well as the 4th RCEP Intersessional TNC and Related Meetings held on 25-29 June 2018 in the same city. It witnessed participation from Working Group on eCommerce, Working Group on Intellectual Property, and the Sub-Working Group on Customs Procedures and Trade Facilitation and intensification of market access bilateral negotiations.

The Ministers recognised the importance of swiftly and successfully concluding the RCEP negotiations and reaffirmed their resolve to work together and see through the RCEP negotiations towards conclusion, and to achieve an agreement that would allow economies of different levels of development to actively participate in and benefit from an open and inclusive regional economic integration.

Representatives from India, China, Singapore, Philippines, Australia, Brunei, Cambodia, Indonesia, Japan, Korea, Laos, Malaysia, Myanmar, New Zealand and Thailand participated in the event

RCEP is a free trade agreement (FTA) between ASEAN and the Asia-Pacific states with which ASEAN has existing FTAs (Australia, China, India, Japan, South Korea and New Zealand). It is one of the largest economic blocs in the world

PHILIPPINES PRESIDENT INAUGURATES JV OF GMR-MEGAWIDE CONSORTIUM NEW TERMINAL

DATE: 1ST July 2018

OBJECTIVE: To look over the operations of Mactan Cebu International Airport

Philippines President inaugurated the new terminal Terminal T2 at Mactan Cebu International Airport (MCIA, Philippines). It is operated by joint Venture of New Delhi based GMR infrastructure and Megawide construction Corporation (Philippines)-GMR-Megawide Cebu Airport Corporation (GMCAC).

The President Rodrigo appreciated the GMCAC for constructing the world-class transportation facility. Speaking on the occasion he cited MCIA as the most beautiful airport in the Philippines.

In the joint venture, Mega wide Construction Corporation and GMR Infrastructure Ltd. having 60% and 40% shareholding respectively. GMCAC has been given responsibility to look over the construction, development, renovation, expansion on build, operate and transfer (BOT) basis for a period of 25 years since 2014 when it took over the operations of MICA.

The new terminal has been constructed with a view to lessen congestion in MCIA. It is all set to transform MCIA into a world-class facility and resort gateway. As

MCIA is the second largest airport in the Philippines and it connects Cebu to the rest of the Philippines and to the world.

BUDGET 2018

S. No.	Years/Segments	2016-2017 Actuals	2017-2018 Budget Estimates	2017-2018 Revised Estimates	2018-2019 Budget Estimates
1	**Revenue Receipts**	**1374203**	**1515771**	**1505428**	**1725738**
2	Tax Revenue (Net to Centre)	1101372	1227014	1269454	1480649
3	Non-Tax Revenue	272831	288757	235974	245089
4	**Capital Receipts[1]**	**600991**	**630964**	**712322**	**716475**
5	Recovery of Loans	17630	11933	17473	12199
6	Other Receipts	47743	72500	100000	80000
7	Borrowings and Other Liabilities	535618	546531	594849	624276
8	**Total Receipts (1+4)**	**1975194**	**2146735**	**2217750**	**2442213**
9	**Total Expenditure (10+13)**	**1975194**	**2146735**	**2217750**	**2442213**
10	On Revenue Account of which	1690584	1836934	1944305	2141772
11	Interest Payments	480714	523078	530843	575795
12	Grants in Aid for creation of capital assets	165733	195350	189245	195345
13	On Capital Account	284610	309801	273445	300441
14	**Revenue Deficit (10-1)**	**316381** (2.1)	**321163** (1.9)	**438877** (2.6)	**416034** (2.2)
15	**Effective Revenue Deficit (14-12)**	**150648** (1.0)	**125813** (0.7)	**249632** (1.5)	**220689** (1.2)
16	**Fiscal Deficit [9-(1+5+6)]**	**535618** (3.5)	**546531** (3.2)	**594849** (3.5)	**624276** (3.3)
17	**Primary Deficit (16-11)**	**54904** (0.4)	**23453** (0.1)	**64006** (0.4)	**48481** (0.3)

[1] Excluding receipts under Market Stabilisation Scheme

[2] Includes drawdown of Cash Balance

Notes: (i) GDP for BE 2018-2019 has been projected at ₹ 18722302 crore assuming 11.5% growth over the estimated GDP of ₹ 16784679 crore for 2017-18 (RE).

(ii) Individual items in this document may not sum up to the totals due to rounding off.

(iii) Figures in parenthesis are as a percentage of GDP.

Rupee Comes From (Budget 2018-2019)

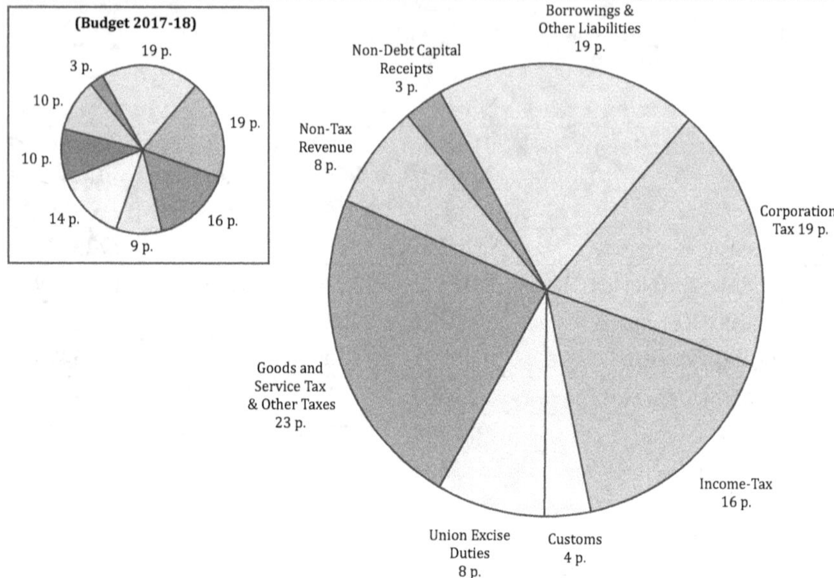

Notes: 1.   Total receipts are inclusive of States' share of taxes and duties which have been netted in the table on page 1.

      2.   Represents Service tax and other taxes in BE 2017-18.

Rupee Goes To (Budget 2018-2019)

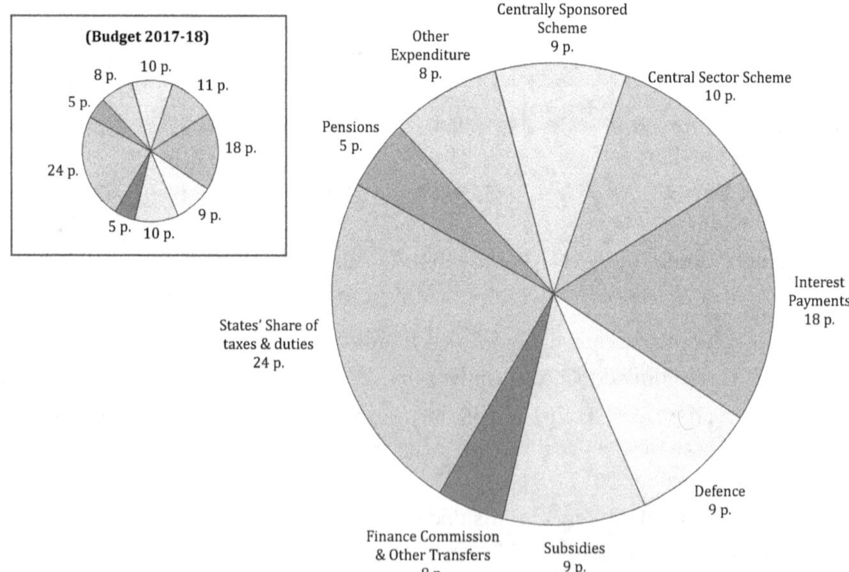

Note: Total expenditure is inclusive of the states' share of taxes and duties which have been netted against receipts in the table.

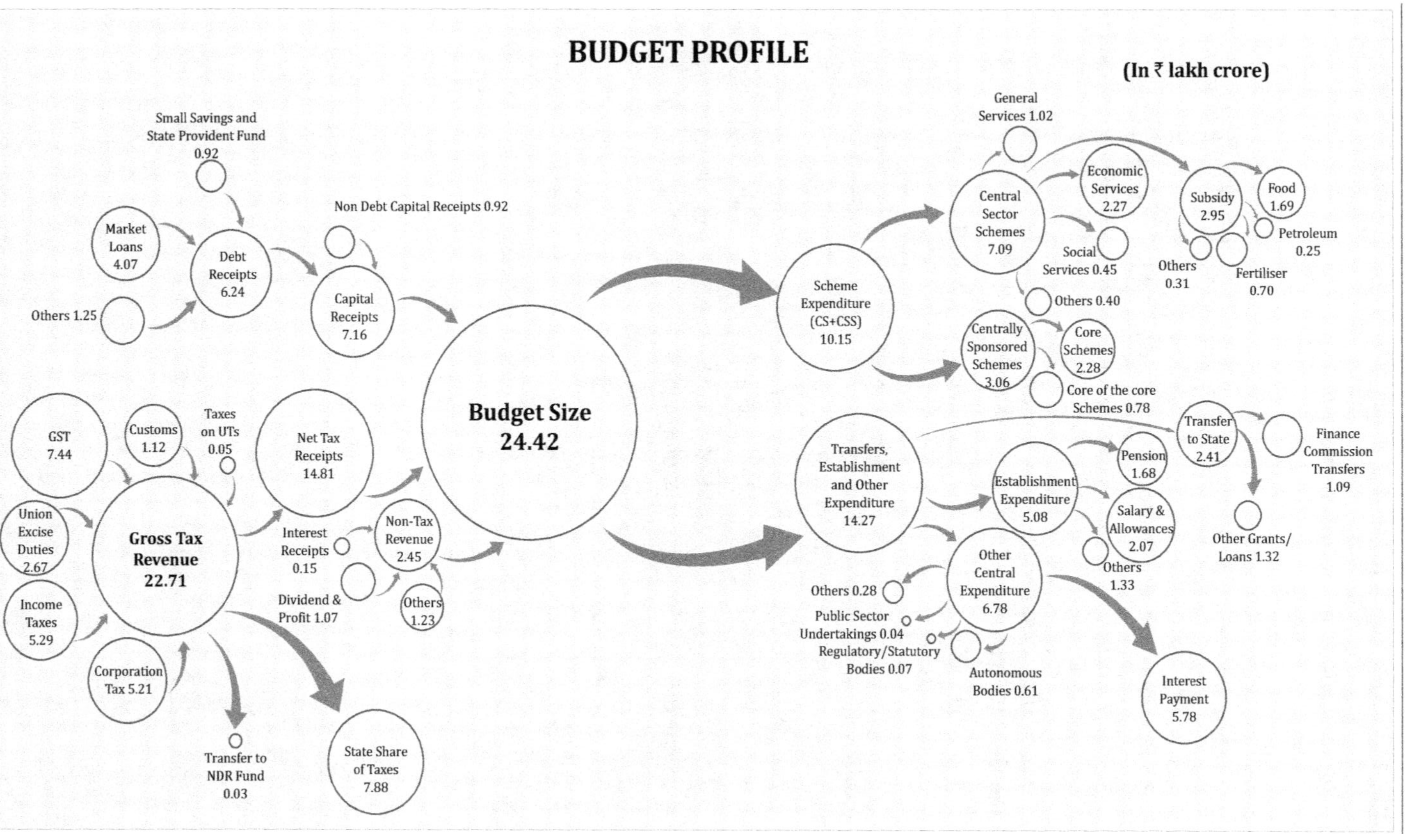

BUDGET PROFILE
(In ₹ lakh crore)
Budget Size 24.42
Small Savings and State Provident Fund 0.92
Market Loans 4.07
Others 1.25
Debt Receipts 6.24
Non Debt Capital Receipts 0.92
Capital Receipts 7.16
GST 7.44
Customs 1.12
Taxes on UTs 0.05
Union Excise Duties 2.67
Income Taxes 5.29
Corporation Tax 5.21
Gross Tax Revenue 22.71
Transfer to NDR Fund 0.03
State Share of Taxes 7.88
Net Tax Receipts 14.81
Interest Receipts 0.15
Dividend & Profit 1.07
Non-Tax Revenue 2.45
Others 1.23
Scheme Expenditure (CS+CSS) 10.15
General Services 1.02
Central Sector Schemes 7.09
Economic Services 2.27
Social Services 0.45
Others 0.40
Subsidy 2.95
Food 1.69
Petroleum 0.25
Fertiliser 0.70
Others 0.31
Centrally Sponsored Schemes 3.06
Core Schemes 2.28
Core of the core Schemes 0.78
Transfers, Establishment and Other Expenditure 14.27
Transfer to State 2.41
Finance Commission Transfers 1.09
Other Grants/ Loans 1.32
Establishment Expenditure 5.08
Pension 1.68
Salary & Allowances 2.07
Others 1.33
Other Central Expenditure 6.78
Others 0.28
Public Sector Undertakings 0.04
Regulatory/Statutory Bodies 0.07
Autonomous Bodies 0.61
Interest Payment 5.78

Union Budget 2018

1. *Commodities that are now cheaper*
IMPORTED ITEMS

- Raw cashew nuts
- Solar tempered glass or solar tempered glass used for manufacture solar panels/modules
- Raw materials, parts or accessories used in making cochlear implants
- Select capital goods and electronics such as ball screws and linear motion guides.

2. *Commodities that will cost you more*
IMPORTED ITEMS

- Cars and motorcycles
- Mobile phones
- Silver
- Gold
- Vegetable, fruit juices
- Sunglasses
- LCD/LED TV panels
- Furniture
- Mattresses
- Lamps
- Watches and clocks
- All toys
- Miscellaneous food except Soya
- Perfumes/Deodorants
- Sunscreen
- Dental hygiene
- Shaving preparations
- Video game consoles
- Outdoor games, including pools
- Cigarette and other lighters, candles
- Kites
- Truck and Bus radial tyres
- Silk Fabrics
- Footwear
- Jewellery
- Smart watches
- Edible/vegetable oils such as olive oils, groundnut oil

Note: No change in Income Tax Slabs except in Cess

ECONOMIC SURVEY 2018

Union finance Minister Arun Jaitley tabled the Economic Survey 2017-18 in Parliament during 2018 budget session. The survey was authored by chief economic adviser Arvind Subramanian. The survey projects economy to grow in the range of 7% to 7.50% in the next fiscal year 2018-19 in the post-demonetization year. Survey 2017-18 was in pink colour to highlight gender issues.

KEY HIGHLIGHTS OF SURVEY GROWTH FORECAST:

1. Goods and Services Tax (GST) has given a new perceptive of the Indian economy and new data has emerged. There has been a fifty percent increase in the number of indirect taxpayers. There has also been a large increase in voluntary registrations.
2. India's formal sector, especially formal non-farm payroll, is substantially greater than what it currently is believed to be. It became evident that when formality was defined in terms of social security provisions like EPFO/ESIC the formal sector payroll was found to be about 31 percent of the non-agricultural work force. When formality was defined in terms of being part of the GST net, such formal sector payroll share was found to be 53 percent.
3. For the first time in India's history, data on the international exports of states has been dwelt in the Economic Survey. Such data indicates a strong correlation between export performance and states' standard of living.
4. India's exports are unusual in that the largest firms account for a much smaller share of exports than in other comparable countries. Top one percent of Indian firms account only for 38% of exports unlike in other countries where they account for substantially greater share – (72, 68, 67 and 55 percent in Brazil, Germany, Mexico and USA respectively). Such tendencies were also found to be true for the top five or ten per cent of the Indian companies.
5. It was pointed out that the Rebate of State Levies (ROSL) has increased exports of readymade garments (man-made fibers) by about 16 per cent but not of others.
6. The data highlighted another seemingly known fact that Indian society exhibits a strong desire for a male child. It pointed out that most parents continued to have children until they get number of sons.
7. The survey pointed out that tax departments in India have gone in for contesting against in several tax disputes but also with a low success rate which is below 30 per cent. About 66 per cent of pending cases accounted for only 1.8 per cent of value at stake.
8. Extrapolating the data the survey indicated that growth in savings did not bring economic growth but the growth in investment did.
9. The survey mentions that collection of direct taxes by Indian states and other local governments, where they have powers to collect them is significantly lower than their counterparts in other federal countries.
10. The survey captures the footprints of climate change on the Indian territory and consequent adverse impact on agricultural yields.

NABARD (AMENDMENT) BILL, 2017

DATE: 2nd January, 2018

The Parliament on 2nd Jan 2018 passed the NABARD (Amendment) Bill, 2017 after Rajya Sabha's approval. It seeks to amend the National Bank Agriculture and Rural Development Act, 1981 that established NABARD for providing and regulating facilities like credit for industrial and agricultural development in rural areas.

- The bill allows Union government to increase authorised capital of NABARD from Rs. 5000 crore to Rs. 30,000 crore which is subject to increase further with consultation with the RBI, if needed.

- The Bill replaces MSME Development Act, 2006. It extends the provision of investment of up to Rs. 20 lakh in machinery and plant to up to Rs. 10 crore in manufacturing sector and Rs. five crore in services sector.

- It allows central government only to hold at least 51% of share capital of NABARD, while the 1981 Act provided for holding at least 51% of share capital of NABARD by central government and the RBI.

- References to provisions of the Companies Act, 1956 have been substituted with references to the Companies Act, 2013 under the NABARD Act, 1981. The provisions it includes are definition of a government company and qualifications of auditors.

AMENDMENTS TO COMPANIES ACT

DATE: 7th January, 2018

OBJECTIVE: To make insolvency process more effective

The government notified amendments to the Companies Act 2013, aimed at making the insolvency process more effective. The Companies (Amendments) Act 2017, which received Parliament's nod in the just-concluded winter session, have put restrictions on managerial remuneration when a company has defaulted in its dues.

Companies, which have defaulted on their dues to financial institutions, will now require the prior approval of these creditors, besides approval in a general meeting in case the payment of managerial remuneration exceeds 11% of the net profits. Earlier, only the company's prior approval in a general meeting was required.

The amendments have also allowed issuance of shares at a discount to the creditors in cases where debt is converted into shares in pursuance of a resolution plan under the Insolvency or Bankruptcy Code or a debt restructuring scheme.

The changes to the Act also bar a registered valuer from undertaking valuation of any asset in which he has direct or indirect interest for a period of three years before or after his appointment. These changes are a part of the government's efforts to remove or change laws that are impeding the effective resolution of bankrupt companies.

ANCIENT MONUMENTS AND ARCHAEOLOGICAL SITES AND REMAINS (AMENDMENT) BILL, 2017

DATE: 2ⁿᵈ January, 2017

OBJECTIVE: To enable government to take up infrastructure projects near monuments

Lok Sabha has passed The Ancient Monuments and Archaeological Sites and Remains (Amendment) Bill, 2017 to allow government to take up infrastructure projects within prohibited areas around protected monuments. The Bill amends the Ancient Monuments and Archaeological Sites and Remains (AMASR) Act, 1958. AMASR Act, 1958 - The AMASR Act provides for preservation of ancient and historical monuments and archaeological sites and remains of national importance. It provides for the regulation of archaeological excavations and for protection of sculptures, carvings and other like objects. It was passed in 1958. The Archaeological Survey of India functions under the provisions of this act. The Act prohibits construction in 'prohibited area', an area of 100 meters around protected monument. It does not permit construction in such prohibited areas even if it is for public purposes, except under certain conditions. The central government can extend the prohibited area beyond 100 meters.

The Bill empowers central government to allow public works based on recommendation of National Monuments Authority (NMA) on application forwarded by relevant central government department, that seeks to carry out construction for public purposes in a prohibited area.

BILL TO HIKE SALARIES OF JUDGES

DATE: 4ᵗʰ January, 2018

A bill to hike the salaries of judges of the Supreme Court and the 24 high courts by over two folds was passed by the Lok Sabha. Once the bill is cleared by Parliament and becomes a law, the Chief Justice of India will get a monthly salary of Rs 2.80 lakh from the present Rs one lakh. Similarly, judges of the Supreme Court and Chief Justices of the high courts will draw a monthly salary of Rs 2.50 lakh from the current Rs 90,000.

The judges of the high courts, who get Rs 80,000 per month now, will get Rs 2.25 lakh per month, the bill states. The salary hike, which is in line with the recommendations of the 7th Pay Commission for officers of all-India services, will come into force retrospectively from January 1, 2016.The High Court and Supreme Court Judges (Salaries and Conditions of Service) Amendment Bill, 2017 also seeks to revise the rates of house rent allowance with effect from July 1,

2017 and the rates of sumptuary allowance with effect from September 22, 2017.

In 2016, then Chief Justice of India T S Thakur had written to the government seeking a hike in the salaries of Supreme Court and high court judges. As against the approved strength of 31, the Supreme Court today has 25 judges. The high courts have an approved strength of 1,079, but 682 judges are today handling work in the 24 high courts. The move will also benefit 2,500 retired judges. Once the hike is effected, the salary of judges will be on a par with those of the bureaucrats following the implementation of the recommendations of the 7th pay panel.

FUGITIVE ECONOMIC OFFENDERS BILL, 2018

DATE: 1st March, 2018

The Union Cabinet chaired by Prime Minister Narendra Modi, has approved the proposal of the Ministry of Finance to introduce the Fugitive Economic Offenders Bill, 2018 in Parliament.

The Bill would help in laying down measures to deter economic offenders from evading the process of Indian law by remaining outside the jurisdiction of Indian courts.

The cases where the total value involved in such offences is Rs.100 crore or more will come under the purview of this Bill.

Impact

- The Bill is expected to re-establish the rule of law with respect to the fugitive economic offenders as they would be forced to return to India to face trial for scheduled offences.
- It is expected that the special forum to be created for expeditious confiscation of the proceeds of crime, in India or abroad, would coerce the fugitive to return to India to submit to the jurisdiction of Courts in India to face the law in respect of scheduled offences.

Salient features of the Bill

- Application before the Special Court for a declaration that an individual is a fugitive economic offender;
- Attachment of the property of a fugitive economic offender;
- Issue of a notice by the Special Court to the individual alleged to be a fugitive economic offender;
- Confiscation of the property of an individual declared as a fugitive economic offender resulting from the proceeds of crime;
- Confiscation of other property belonging to such offender in India and abroad, including benami property;
- Disentitlement of the fugitive economic offender from defending any civil claim; and
- An Administrator will be appointed to manage and dispose of the confiscated property under the Act.

Background: There have been several instances of economic offenders such as Vijay Mallya and Nirav Modi, fleeing country to evade clutches Indian law to remain outside jurisdiction of Indian courts. The absence of such offenders from Indian courts has several deleterious consequences. It hampers investigation in criminal cases, wastes precious time of courts of law, undermines rule of law in India.

DEATH PENALTY ORDINANCE FOR CHILD RAPISTS

DATE: 22nd April, 2018

President Ram Nath Kovind approved an ordinance to provide death penalty for those convicted of raping girls below age 12 years. The President promulgated The Criminal Law (Amendment) Ordinance, 2018, which was approved by the cabinet and which seeks to provide effective deterrence against rape and instil a sense of security among women, particularly young girls.

The ordinance follows outrage over rape and murder of an eight-year-old girl in Kathua in Jammu and Kashmir and similar crimes in other parts of the country. However, a large number of people do not find capital punishment to be a solution rather they are of the view that India should instead work towards abolishing the death penalty which is inherently cruel and irreversible, with little evidence that it serves as a deterrent. Following the President's approval, POCSO, IPC and The Evidence Act stand amended. The development puts in place a number of measures for speedy investigation and trial of rape cases including a two-month time limit for investigation, two months for completion of trial and six months for disposal of appeals.

THE INSOLVENCY AND BANKRUPTCY CODE (AMENDMENT) ACT, 2018

DATE: 6th June, 2018

The insolvency and Bankruptcy Code (Amendment) Bill, 2017 was introduced to replace the ordinance. The bill was passed by both houses of the parliament and received President's assent on 18th January, 2018 to become the Insolvency and Bankruptcy (Amendment) Act, 2018.

The Provisions of this Code apply to-

(a) Any company incorporated under the Companies Act, 2013 (18 of 2013) or under any Previous Company Law;

(b) Any other company governed by any special Act for the time being in force, except in so far as the said provisions are inconsistent with the provisions of such special Act;

(c) Any Limited Liability Partnership incorporated under the Limited Liability Partnership Act, 2008;

(d) Such other body incorporated under any law for the time being in force, as the Central Government may, by notification, specify in this behalf; and

(e) Personal guarantors to corporate debtors;

(f) Partnership firms and proprietorship firms; and

(e)   Personal guarantors to corporate debtors;

(f)   Partnership firms and proprietorship firms; and

(g)   Individuals, other than persons referred to in clause (e), in relation to their insolvency, liquidation, voluntary liquidation or bankruptcy, as the case may be.

DAM SAFETY BILL 2018

DATE: 14th June, 2018

OBJECTIVE: To adopt uniform safety procedures to ensure safety of reservoirs

The Union Cabinet has approved the proposal for introduction of Dam Safety Bill, 2018 in the Parliament. The bill aims to help all States and Union Territories to adopt uniform dam safety procedures which will ensure safety of dam and safeguard benefits from such dams. This will also help in safeguarding human life, livestock and property.

Important features of the Bill

The bill addresses all issues concerning dam safety including regular inspection of dams, comprehensive dam safety review, emergency action plan, adequate repair and maintenance funds for dam safety, instrumentation and safety manuals. It lays onus of dam safety on dam owner and provides for penal provisions for commission and omission of certain acts.

The Bill provides for proper surveillance, inspection, operation and maintenance of all specified dams in the country to ensure their safe functioning. It mandates constitution of National Committee on Dam Safety (NCDS) which will evolve dam safety policies and recommend necessary regulations as may be required for the purpose.

The Bill also provides for establishment of National Dam Safety Authority (NDSA) as regulatory body which shall discharge functions to implement policy, standards and guidelines for dam safety in the country. It also provides for constitution of State Committee on Dam Safety (SCDS) by State Government.

ELECTORAL BOND SCHEME

DATE: 2nd January, 2018

OBJECTIVE: To bring transparency in electoral funding

The government notified electoral bonds, as a new instrument for donations to political parties, in a bid to clean up election funding in India. The bonds will bring substantial transparency in political donations against the present system of anonymous contributions. Though called 'bonds', it is an interest-free instrument in the nature of a promissory note, which can be purchased for any value, in multiples of Rs 1,000, Rs 10,000, Rs 1 lakh, Rs 10 lakh and Rs 1 crore from specified branches of the State Bank of India (SBI).

The bonds can be bought only once KYC norms of SBI are fulfilled and the payment for it has to be from a bank account. The bonds will not carry the name of the donor. And this is where political analysts said that electoral bond will fail in its objective to inject transparency into political funding. Electoral bonds would have a life of only 15 days during which it can be used for making donation only to the political parties registered under section 29A of the Representation of the Peoples Act, 1951, and can be redeemed only through registered bank accounts of parties.

The bonds will be available for purchase for a period of 10 days in January, April, July and October and an additional period of 30 days that will be notified by the government during general elections. These bonds will be part of the returns filed by political parties with the Election Commission.

CYBER SURAKSHIT BHARAT YOJNA

DATE: 19th January, 2018

Minister of State for Electronics & Information Technology, KJ Alphons launched Cyber Surakshit Bharat initiative on 19th January, 2018. It aims to strengthen the cyber security ecosystem in India. The Ministry of Electronics and Information Technology (MeitY), launched this yojna in association with National e-Governance Division (NeGD) and industry partners.

Microsoft, Intel, Redhat, Wipro and Dimension Data are the founding partners while

Organizations such as Cert-In, NIC, CISCO, NASSCOM and the FIDO Alliance, and consultancy firms Deloitte and EY are knowledge partners for this initiative.

Objectives: The objective of the programme is to educate & enable the Chief Information Security Officers (CISO) & broader IT community to address the challenges of cyber security.

- Create awareness on the emerging landscape of cyber threats
- Provide in-depth understanding on key activities, new initiatives, challenges and related solutions
- Applicable frame works, guidelines & policies related to the subject Share best practices to learn from success & failures
- Provide key input stotake informed decision on Cyber Security relate dissues in their respective function alarea

CHEAP SANITARY PAD SCHEME, "ASMITA YOJANA" FOR RURAL WOMEN

DATE: 18th February, 2018

Maharashtra State Government launched cheap sanitary pad scheme "Asmita Yojana" which aims at providing subsidized sanitary pads to girl student and women in rural areas. It was launched on the eve of international women day on 8th March.

Key Features

- Under this yojana, girls in Zilla Parishad schools will get a sanitary napkin packet at Rs 5 while rural women can avail it at a subsidised rate of Rs 24 and Rs 29.
- "Umed'- the Maharashtra State Rural Livelihood Mission will be the nodal agency for implementation of this scheme.
- Task of procurement and sale of sanitary pads and counseling the girls and women has been entrusted to Women Self Help Groups (SHGs) while beneficiary girls will be given "Asmita Cards",for availing subsidized sanitary pads.

Significance

The scheme will promote menstrual hygiene and increase awareness among young girls on usage of sanitary pads in rural areas. It will also help to reduce school absenteeism i.e. boost school attendance among school girls. Similarly, it will help to create employment opportunities for women in rural areas and create awareness about health and education.

AMMA 2-WHEELER SCHEME

DATE: 24th February, 2018

Prime Minister Narendra Modi launched the subsidized scooter scheme for working women on the occasion of the 70th birth anniversary celebrations of late leader Jayalalithaa. He handed over the keys and registration certificate copies to five women beneficiaries. The beneficiaries included women who worked in the private sector, an accountant, a salesperson and an assistant in a private store.

Key Features

- Under the new scheme the state government will offer the beneficiary with a subsidy for the purchase of the scooter. The subsidy offered will be equivalent to around 50 percent of the overall cost of the two wheel vehicle.

- The state government has also made it clear that the subsidy under the scheme will be offered to the beneficiary by the state government, rest amount for purchase will be funded by the beneficiaries. A subsidy amount of 25000 will be offered by the government at the time of sanction.

- The government has also ensured that to offer with efficient benefit under the scheme the subsidy amount will be directly credited in the beneficiaries bank account. The disbursement of the amount will be done once all legal documents have been submitted.

- The beneficiary will also be offered with financial assistant for purchasing the vehicle directly by the non banking and banking financial institutions. The disbursement will be made after considering the RBI norms.

- The state government also expects to offer benefit of the new scheme to over 1 lakh women of the state under the scheme once they fulfill the eligibility criteria.

VAN DHAN SCHEME

DATE: 27th April, 2018

The Prime Minister Narendra Modi launched the Van Dhan Scheme of Ministry of Tribal Affairs and TRIFED on April 14, 2018. It was launched during the celebrations of Ambedkar Jayanti at Bijapur, Chattisgarh. It seeks to improve tribal incomes through value addition of tribal products.

Key Highlights

- Under Van Dhan, 10 Self Help Groups of 30 Tribal gatherers would be constituted.

- The groups will then be trained and provided with working capital to add value to the products that they collect from the jungle.

- These groups would then be able to market their products, by working under the leadership of collector, not only within the states but also outside the states.

- The Tribal Cooperative Marketing Development Federation of India (TRIFED) would be providing all the required training and technical support.

- The SHGs will be appropriately trained on sustainable harvesting/collection, primary processing & value addition and be formed into clusters so as to aggregate their stock in tradable quantity and link them with the facility of primary processing in a Van Dhan Vikas Kendra.

- The stock after primary processing shall be supplied by these SHGs to the State Implementing Agencies or direct tie up for supply to the corporate secondary processor.

- Big corporates shall be involved under PPP model for the creation of secondary level value addition facility at district level and tertiary level value addition facility at the state level. The PPP model will be based on utilising Private entrepreneur skills in undertaking processing as well as marketing of the produce.
- The central and state government would provide support by creating infrastructure and providing enabling environment for undertaking value addition of systematic scientific lines.

GANGA HARITEEMA YOJANA

DATE: 8th April, 2018

The Uttar Pradesh Chief Minister launched the Ganga Hariteema Yojana at Allahabad in a function organized on the bank of Sangam, the confluence of rivers of Ganga, Yamuna and mythical Saraswati. This Scheme is also known as Ganga Greenery scheme. It was launched on April 7, 2018 in the 27 districts of Uttar Pradesh that are located on the bank of river Ganga.

Highlights

- To enhance green cover in the catchment areas of the river Ganga and to control the land erosion, it envisages carrying out plantation drives in one-kilometre areas from the banks of river.
- Common people will also be encouraged for plantation on their private lands under 'One Person One Tree' slogan.
- Uttar Pradesh's Department of Forest has been nominated as nodal department for this scheme.
- The scheme will be carried out till September 16, 2018 (Ozone Day)

SAMAGRA SHIKSHA SCHEME

DATE: 24th May, 2018

The Union H R D Minister launches Samagra Shiksha scheme for school education from pre-school to senior secondary levels.

Objectives

- To improve quality of education,
- To enhance the learning outcomes, and
- To use digital technology to empower children and teachers

Major Features

- Single Scheme for the School Education Sector from Classes I to XII-extension of interventions to senior secondary stage.
- Treat school education holistically as a continuum from Pre-school to Class 12
- Supporting States to initiate pre-primary education.
- Inclusion of senior secondary levels and pre-school levels in support for School education for the first time.

- Single and unified administrative structure leading to harmonized implementation.
- Flexibility to States to priorities their interventions under the Scheme.
- Key focus on quality education emphasizing capacity building of teachers in online and offline mode as well as strengthening of Teacher Education Institutions SCERT/DIET/BRC/CRC/CTEs/IASEs.
- Annual Grant per school for strengthening of Libraries
- Support 'Operation Digital Board' in all secondary schools over a period of 5 years, which will revolutionize education- easy to understand, technology based learning classrooms will become flipped classrooms.
- Enhanced use of digital technology in education through smart classrooms, digital boards and DTH channels.
- Digital initiatives like Shala Kosh, Shagun, Shaala Saarthi to be strengthened.
- "DIKSHA", digital portal for teachers to be used extensively for upgrading skills of teachers
- Enhanced Transport facility to children across all classes from I to VIII for universal access to school
- Composite school grant increased and to be allocated on the basis of school enrolment.
- Specific provision for Swachhta activities – support 'Swachh Vidyalaya'
- Empowerment of girls with education and physical training
- Allocation for uniforms and text book under RTE Act enhanced per child per annum.
- Allocation for Children with Special Needs (CwSN) increased from Rs. 3000 to Rs. 3500 per child per annum. Stipend of Rs. 200 per month for Girls with Special Needs from Classes 1 to 12.
- Commitment to 'Sabko Shiksha Achhi Shiksha'
- Exposure to Vocational Skills at Upper Primary Level would be extended.
- Strengthening of vocational education at secondary level as an integral part of curriculum
- Vocational education which was limited to Class 9-12, to be started from class 6 as integrated with the curriculum and to be made more practical and industry oriented.
- Reinforce emphasis on 'Kaushal Vikas'
- Sports Education to be an integral part of curriculum and Sport equipment will be provided to all school under this component.
- Support 'Khelo India'.
- Preference to Educationally Backward Blocks (EBBs), LWEs, Special Focus Districts (SFDs), Border areas and the 115 inspirational districts identified by Niti Aayog.

GOBAR DHAN YOJNA

DATE: 7th April, 2018

During Budget Session for 2018-19, Gobar Dhan Yojna was officially announced by the Finance Minister Arun Jaitely. The new scheme is expected to help in enhancing and improving the condition of rural areas within the country.

Objectives:

- To promote the use of cattle dung as bio-fuel.
- Improve the lifestyle of the people with homes in the rural areas.
- Make India a clean country with removal and reuse of cattle dung.
- The scheme aims to promote health and awareness in the villages.

Key Features

- The scheme is for the proper management of cattle dung.
- It is also a helping hand to the 'Swach Bharat Mission' in India.
- Farmers will be able to use the cow dung as composts and fertilizers.
- People will make use of cow dung as bio-fuel and biogas.

GOVT. LAUNCHES SAMAGRA SHIKSHA SCHEME

DATE: 25th May

OBJECTIVE: To improve the quality of school education

The Union H R D Minister launches Samagra Shiksha scheme for school education from pre-school to senior secondary levels. The objectives of the scheme are improving quality of education, enhancing the learning outcomes and using technology to empower children and teachers. It will be focused on digital education and will enhance use of digital technology in education through smart classroom and digital boards.

The scheme will provide holistic education for holistic development. It will focus on teachers and technology which will improve the quality of education. Ministry will provide an annual grant of Rs 5000- 20,000 for strengthening of libraries in the schools.

Samagra Shiksha scheme is an integrated scheme for school education from pre-school to senior secondary levels. The scheme is an integration of three already existing schemes; Sarva Shiksha Abhiyan (SSA), Rashtriya Madhyamik Shiksha Abhiyan (RMSA) and Teacher Education (TE). States would have the flexibility to prioritise their interventions under the scheme, learning outcomes and steps taken for quality improvement would be the basis for allocation of grants under the scheme.

BPO PROMOTION SCHEME FOR RURAL YOUTH

DATE: 19th June

OBJECTIVE: To expand BPO promotion scheme to generate employment

Ministry of Electronics & Information Technology is planning to expand its India BPO Promotion Scheme to 1 lakh seats from current 48,000 seats. It will also set up 5th and India's largest National Data Centre (NDC) in Bhopal, Madhya Pradesh with capacity of 5 lakh virtual servers. NDCs host government websites, services and apps, are currently operational at four locations viz. Pune, Hyderabad, Delhi and Bhubaneswar. These initiatives will help to create new job opportunities and also ensure that people in smaller towns find employment closer home.

India BPO Promotion Scheme (IBPS)

This scheme was approved under Digital India Programme to incentivize BPO/ IT – ITES operations sector in the country. It was launched in 2014. The scheme aims to incentivize establishment of BPO firms and their extension to Tier II and Tier III cities (as per census 2011) to provide employment, distributed across various states in proportion to population of state with financial support in form of Viability Gap Funding (VGF).

The Software Technology Parks of India (STPI), an autonomous society of Ministry of Electronics & Information Technology is nodal implementing agency of the scheme. It will be implemented to incentivize setting up of BPO/ITES operations across the country (excluding certain cities and north eastern states which are covered separately under North-East BPO Promotion Scheme).

FIRST APEX CONFERENCE FOR (CEOs) OF SMART CITIES

DATE: 8th May

Objective: To share learning among the CEOs of Smart Cities

Union Urban Affairs Ministry organized the First Apex Conference for CEOs of Smart Cities in Bhopal, Madhya Pradesh. The conference aims to provide single platform for convergence of all best practices in Smart city missions across country to help city leaders to use collective learning to accelerate progress of work. It also aims to provide momentum to cities and platform for cross-learning, sharing and disseminating experience gained over past two and a half years. It enables the CEOs to learn from the experiences of all city leaders to understand in greater details both successes and failures, which aims to promote sustainability, innovation and participatory approaches in the Smart Cities.

This is the first such conference after the launch of Smart Cities Mission on June 25, 2015. The conference also includes exhibition and presentations by the Smart Cities CEOs. The representatives from municipal, State and Central Government and various other stakeholders also participate in Smart City Mission.

Raisina Dialogue: 'Discussing ways to fight terror'

DATE: 16th January 2018

The third edition of the Raisina Dialogue hosted by Observer Research Foundation, an independent think tank with the Ministry of External Affairs of India took place on 16th January 2018 with this year's theme as "Managing Disruptive Transitions: Ideas, Institutions and Idioms". Israel's Prime Minister Benjamin Netanyahu was the main guest with PM of India and External Affairs Minister Sushma Swaraj. It is a multilateral conference held annually in New Delhi since 2016 and has emerged as India's flagship conference on geopolitics and geo-economics. The highlights are as follows:

- The Israeli PM discussed ways to strengthen security cooperation against menace of Islamist extremism.

- He also discussed ways to strengthen the two nations in civilian areas, in security areas and in every area.

- Netanyahu emphasised on his focus on 'hard power' such as submarines, cyber capabilities, science and technology, interceptors to ensure security for countries in the present day world.

- He said that our way of life is being challenged by radical Islam and its terrorist offshoots from a variety of corners and so joining hands with democracies would help in overcoming "radical Islam" and would help in fighting terrorism.

ASEAN-INDIA COMMEMORATIVE SUMMIT

DATE: 25th January 2018

OBJECTIVE: To deepen partnership for combating terrorism and radicalisation through information sharing

ASEAN-India Commemorative Summit was inaugurated in New Delhi. It was held to celebrate the 25th anniversary of establishment of sectoral dialogue between two sides. Delhi declaration was adopted at the summit. India and the ASEAN decided to deepen partnership for combating terrorism and radicalisation through information sharing, law enforcement cooperation and capacity-building projects. The Delhi Declaration reaffirmed "the importance of maintaining and promoting peace, stability, maritime safety and security, freedom of navigation and overflight in the region, and other lawful uses of the seas and unimpeded lawful maritime commerce and to promote peaceful resolutions of disputes, in accordance with the United Nations Convention on the Law of the Sea (UNCLOS). The top agenda for the plenary session was countering terrorism and maritime security cooperation. The session was addressed by all 10 southeast Asian leaders - PMs of Vietnam, Cambodia, Singapore, Thailand, Malaysia and Laos, the President of the Philippines and Indonesia, Myanmar State Councillor Aung San Suu Kyi, Sultan of Brunei Darussalam and Indian PM Narendra Modi.

The leaders further stressed that there can be no justification for acts of terror on any grounds whatsoever. They also decided to strengthen cooperation between ASEAN and India on cybersecurity and policy coordination.

ASEAN was established on 8 August 1967 in Bangkok, with the signing of the Bangkok Declaration. Indonesia, Malaysia, Philippines, Singapore and Thailand were the founding nations. The motto of ASEAN is "One Vision, One Identity, One Community".

INTERNATIONAL SOLAR ALLIANCE SUMMIT

DATE: 22nd February 2018

OBJECTIVE: To make available solar energy at an affordable price and establish a solar credit mechanism

India will host the founding conference of the International Solar Alliance (ISA) summit. The Conference will be held on 11th March at Rashtrapati Bhawan cultural centre in New Delhi. The daylong summit, which is expected to culminate in a 'New Delhi Declaration', will focus on prioritising solar energy and ensuring 'power for all'. With hosting this important global event, India is all set to assume leadership in the battle against climate change. The summit will also enable India in power projection in a fashion that empowers common citizens. International Solar Alliance is jointly led by India and France as part of an outreach programme. It aims to create solar projects in the Pacific nations.

Various Heads of state/government representatives from Asia, Africa, Pacific and South America of nations that are signatories to the ISA alliance are expected to attend this global summit. Additionally representatives of global banks, firms specialising in solar energy and NGOs will be present at the summit.

French President Emanuel Macron, who will be the co-host for the summit and Sri Lankan President M Sirisena and president of Venezuela Nicolas Maduro are expected to hold bilateral discussions with PM Narendra Modi.

The summit will underline India's commitment to fulfilling global commitments in a time-bound manner, thereby increasing global confidence in India's capacities.

INTERNATIONAL CONFERENCE ON SUSTAINABLE BIO-FUELS

DATE: 26th February 2018

OBJECTIVE: To share information, experiences and challenges related to development and scaling of sustainable bio-fuels

The International conference on Sustainable Bio-fuels was organized in New Delhi. The two day international conference was jointly organized by Department of Biotechnology (DBT), Govt. of India and Bio-future platform at Stein Auditorium, India Habitat Centre, New Delhi.

The conference was organized keeping in mind the sustainable Bio-fuels sector to take stock of current knowledge, share information and best practices, and build consensus on the actions most needed to move forward.

The event witnessed presence of around 400 experts and delegates from 19 countries. Country representatives from mission innovation member countries, International Energy Agency, Biofuture Platform member countries, International Renewable Energy Agency and Below50 have attended the conference. Representatives from all co-leads of sustainable bio-fuel challenge India, Brazil, Canada and China, presented the status of bio-fuel development in their countries.

The event provided a common platform to research community, Government policy makers, industry and investors to exchange experiences and challenges related to development and scaling of advance bio-fuels. Besides it also focused on concerns of the private sectors to speed up large scale production of sustainable bio-fuels.

The roles played by sustainable bio-fuels are highly significant considering its ability to reduce the emission of Green House Gases (GHGs).

WORLD OCEAN SUMMIT 2018

DATE: 9th March 2018

OBJECTIVE: To address issues facing the world's seas and to come up with solutions to protect the planet's vast ocean resources.

The fifth World Ocean Summit which was held on Riveria Maya, Mexico concluded on 9th March 2018. The event focussed on five main pillars viz. sustainable fisheries, pollution, climate change, finance and technology. During the event, conservationists, business and government leaders tussled with some of the ocean's most intractable problems—and explored new possibilities.

The event saw participation from the world's leaders who discussed ways to evaluate strategies and devise new solutions to urgent threats facing the oceans. More than 70 world leaders spoke at The Economist event including Enrique Peña-Nieto, the President of Mexico; Guðni Th. Jóhannesson, the President of Iceland as well as members of businesses and organizations. The sixth World Ocean Summit event will be held in Abu Dhabi in March 2019.

First Indo-French Knowledge Summit

DATE: 11th March 2018

OBJECTIVE: To mutually recognise educational qualifications between India and France

First Indo-French Knowledge Summit concluded successfully on 11th March, 2018 with a landmark agreement on mutual recognition of educational qualifications between India and France. 15 other MoUs were also taken up between universities and research institutions on partnerships and joint initiatives.

The two day summit was held in New Delhi and organised by the French Embassy in India and co-hosted by the Union Ministry of Human Resource Development, Government of India. It was attended by more than 350 people from around 80 Indian Institutions and 70 French Institutions along with some key enterprises. The Summit was supported by Ministry of Science and Technology, Campus France and Confederation of Indian Industry.

At the closing session, a Franco-Indian Education Trust was also unveiled which will offer educational scholarships and merit based financial support to the Indian students. It will be funded by the Indian industry and French companies in the country.

The broader objective of the summit is to design a roadmap of cooperation between the two countries in collaboration with companies. The common goal of both the nations was to increase the student mobility, enlarge Research & Development collaborations and link campuses to companies by focusing on employability.

BAKU HOSTS THE NAM MINISTERIAL CONFERENCE

DATE: 6th April 2018

OBJECTIVE: To promote cooperation and coordination among NAM Members

Baku, the capital of Azerbaijan hosted the mid-term ministerial conference of the Non-Aligned Movement. The two-day conference was organised for the purpose of promoting cooperation and coordination among NAM Member and observer states and organizations.

Presently the Non- Aligned Movement is a strong organization of 120 member countries, while NAM observer countries are 17. Ten organizations are part of NAM observers.

The 18th mid-term ministerial conference was preceded by a two day senior officials meeting at the same venue under the theme, "Promoting international peace and security for sustainable development."

External Affairs Minister Sushma Swaraj attended the conference. Speaking on the occasion she gave emphasis about the relevance of Non-Alignment Movement in the changing world scenario.

As head of the host country, President of Azerbaijan addressed the NAM representatives gathered at the venue. It was followed by Jorge Arreaza, Venezuelan Foreign Minister and current chair of the NAM ministerial conference.

The Non-Aligned Movement was formed during the Cold War as an organization of States that did not seek to formally align themselves with or against any major power blocs. These states sought to remain independent or neutral and thus NAM was formed.

Jawaharlal Nehru (India), Josip Broz Tito (Yugoslavia), Sukarno (Indonesia), Gamal Abdel Nasser (Egypt) and Kwame Nkrumah (Ghana) are regarded as the founding fathers of NAM. The First NAM Summit Conference took place in Belgrade (1961).

INDIA HOSTS 15TH ASIA MEDIA SUMMIT

DATE: 10th May 2018

OBJECTIVE: To encourage dialogue and cooperation in Media Sector in the region

The Union Ministry of Information and Broadcasting in collaboration with the Indian Institute of Mass Communication (IIMC), New Delhi and Broadcast Engineering Consultants India Limited (BECIL), is hosting the 15th Asia Media Summit (AMS-2018) in New Delhi from May 10-12, 2018.

The Union Minister for Information & Broadcasting and Textiles, Smriti Zubin Irani presided over the inaugural ceremony of the summit as the chief guest.

The summit is a prestigious annual event in the Asia Pacific Region, which is organised by the Asia-Pacific Institute for Broadcasting Development (AIBD) in collaboration with its partners and international organizations. India is hosting the event for the first time.

Goals:

The theme aims to encourage dialogue and cooperation in Media Sector in the region. The summit mainly aims to provide a unique opportunity to the broadcasters in Asia to share their thoughts on broadcasting and information.

It aims to encourage regional and bilateral dialogue and cooperation to respond to challenges to the broadcasting sector in the region. Over 200 foreign delegates representing 39 countries of SAARC, ASEAN, East Asia, Africa, Oceania, Europe, Syria, Uzbekistan, USA and China are expected to attend the summit. There would be over 100 Indian delegates as well.

RASHTRAPATI BHAVAN HOSTS NOBEL LAUREATES SEMINAR

DATE: 5th February 2018

OBJECTIVE: To engage Indian scientific and policy community for advancement of Scientific Research

One-day Nobel Laureates Seminar was organised by the Department of Biotechnology, Government of India in association with the Nobel Foundation. The event was hosted by Rashtrapati Bhavan. This was part of the Nobel Prize Series, a regular and landmark engagement between the Indian scientific and policy community and the Nobel Foundation.

Addressing to the Seminar, the President gave emphasis on a creative schooling system as root of Research and Innovation Culture in the country.

He said that in the 70 years since India became independent, belief in science has shaped our society and developmental process. From agriculture to harnessing the energy of the atom, from vaccine innovation to advances in space technology, science has helped us build our nation. He also added that Science is nothing without a global enterprise and stressed upon the idea of building world class institutions and universities and how these connect to the society.

Nobel Laureates Christiane Nusslein-Volhard, Sir Richard John Roberts, Serge Haroche and Dr Tomas Robert Lindahl also addressed the Seminar.

INTERNATIONAL SOLAR ALLIANCE SUMMIT

DATE: 22nd February 2018

OBJECTIVE: To make available solar energy at an affordable price and establish a solar credit mechanism India will host the founding conference of the International Solar Alliance (ISA) summit. The Conference will be held on 11th March at Rashtrapati Bhawan cultural centre in New Delhi. The daylong summit, which is expected to culminate in a 'New Delhi Declaration', will focus on prioritising solar energy and ensuring 'power for all'. With hosting this important global event, India is all set to assume leadership in the battle against climate change. The summit will also enable India in power projection in a fashion that empowers common citizens. International Solar Alliance is jointly led by India and France as part of an outreach programme. It aims to create solar projects in the Pacific nations.

Various Heads of state/government representatives from Asia, Africa, Pacific and South America of nations that are signatories to the ISA alliance are expected to attend this global summit. Additionally representatives of global banks, firms specialising in solar energy and NGOs will be present at the summit.

French President Emanuel Macron, who will be the co-host for the summit and Sri Lankan President M Sirisena and president of Venezuela Nicolas Maduro are expected to hold bilateral discussions with PM Narendra Modi.

The summit will underline India's commitment to fulfilling global commitments in a time-bound manner, thereby increasing global confidence in India's capacities.

INTERNATIONAL CONFERENCE ON SUSTAINABLE BIOFUELS

DATE: 26th February 2018

OBJECTIVE: To share information, experiences and challenges related to development and scaling of sustainable biofuels

The International conference on Sustainable Biofuels was organized in New Delhi. The two day international conference was jointly organized by Department of Biotechnology (DBT), Govt. of India and Biofuture platform at Stein Auditorium, India Habitat Centre, New Delhi.

The conference was organized keeping in mind the sustainable Biofuels sector to take stock of current knowledge, share information and best practices, and build consensus on the actions most needed to move forward.

The event witnessed presence of around 400 experts and delegates from 19 countries. Country representatives from mission innovation member countries, International Energy Agency, Biofuture Platform member countries, International Renewable Energy Agency and Below50 have attended the conference. Representatives from all co-leads of sustainable biofuel challenge India, Brazil, Canada and China, presented the status of biofuel development in their countries.

The event provided a common platform to research community, Government policy makers, industry and investors to exchange experiences and challenges related to development and scaling of advance biofuels. Besides it also focused on concerns of the private sectors to speed up large scale production of sustainable biofuels.

The roles played by sustainable biofuels are highly significant considering its ability to reduce the emission of Green House Gases (GHGs).

ANDAMAN AND NICOBAR COMMAND HOSTS MILAN 2018

DATE: 6th March 2018

OBJECTIVE: To foster cooperation through naval exercises and professional interactions with the underlying theme of 'Friendship across the Seas'

The Indian Navy will host Milan 2018, a multinational mega event conducted biennially by Indian Navy at the Andaman and Nicobar Islands, under the aegis of the Andaman and Nicobar Command. The get-together of foreign navies will be held at Port Blair from 6 March to 13 March 2018. The command has been organising the get-together since 1995.

With the underlying theme of 'Friendship Across the Seas', MILAN 2018 will have participation from 16 countries with 38 delegates coming for the event. It will have diverse mix of professional exercises and seminars, social events and sporting fixtures.

The theme of this year's MILAN International Maritime Seminar is **'In Pursuit of Maritime Good Order - Need for Comprehensive Information Sharing Apparatus'**. The interactions during the MILAN are directed towards sharing of views and ideas on maritime good - order and enhancing regional cooperation for combating unlawful activities at sea.

The social interactions planned include display by bands of the Indian Navy and Indian Army, ship visits and colourful cultural evenings.

The inaugural address will be delivered by Admiral Sunil Lamba, PVSM, AVSM, ADC, Chairman Chiefs of Staff Committee (COSC) and Chief of the Naval Staff (CNS).

Some events will also be open to the general public including displays by sky diving team, beating the retreat and Naval continuity drill.

Milan 2018 aims at showcasing the rich heritage and natural beauty of Andaman and Nicobar Islands to the foreign visitors. The event will culminate with all the participating naval ships doing the Passage Exercise at sea.

WORLD ATM CONGRESS 2018 CONCLUDED

DATE: 8th March 2018

OBJECTIVE: To bring together the world's leading product developers, experts, stakeholders, and air navigation service providers (ANSPs)

The 6th annual World ATM Congress held in IFEMA - Feria de Madrid in Madrid, Spain concluded on 8th March 2018 with an overwhelming response from the exhibitors. The three day exhibition saw a record breaking registration with 8,542 registrants and 237 exhibitors from 136 countries and territories.

The event was organised in collaboration between the Civil Air Navigation Service Organisation (CANSO) and Air Traffic Control Association (ATCA).

The world's largest air traffic management (ATM) exhibition brings industry and academia together. The event highlights on commercial and defence air, airlines, air traffic, airports, air safety, airplanes, air transport and air security issues.

The Airports Authority of India (AAI) also participated and showcased its initiatives and achievements.

WORLD OCEAN SUMMIT 2018

DATE: 9th March 2018

OBJECTIVE: To address issues facing the world's seas and to come up with solutions to protect the planet's vast ocean resources.

The fifth World Ocean Summit which was held on Riveria Maya, Mexico concluded on 9th March 2018. The event focussed on five main pillars viz. sustainable fisheries, pollution, climate change, finance and technology. During the event, conservationists, business and government leaders tussled with some of the ocean's most intractable problems—and explored new possibilities.

The event saw participation from the world's leaders who discussed ways to evaluate strategies and devise new solutions to urgent threats facing the oceans. More than 70 world leaders spoke at The Economist event including Enrique Peña-Nieto, the President of Mexico; Guðni Th. Jóhannesson, the President of Iceland as well as members of businesses and organizations. The sixth World Ocean Summit event will be held in Abu Dhabi in March 2019.

FIRST INDO-FRENCH KNOWLEDGE SUMMIT

DATE: 11th March 2018

OBJECTIVE: To mutually recognise educational qualifications between India and France

First Indo-French Knowledge Summit concluded successfully on 11th March, 2018 with a landmark agreement on mutual recognition of educational qualifications between India and France. 15 other MoUs were also taken up between universities and research institutions on partnerships and joint initiatives.

The two day summit was held in New Delhi and organised by the French Embassy in India and co-hosted by the Union Ministry of Human Resource Development, Government of India. It was attended by more than 350 people from around 80 Indian Institutions and 70 French Institutions along with some key enterprises. The Summit was supported by Ministry of Science and Technology, Campus France and Confederation of Indian Industry.

At the closing session, a Franco-Indian Education Trust was also unveiled which will offer educational scholarships and merit based financial support to the Indian students. It will be funded by the Indian industry and French companies in the country.

The broader objective of the summit is to design a roadmap of cooperation between the two countries in collaboration with companies. The common goal of both the nations was to increase the student mobility, enlarge Research & Development collaborations and link campuses to companies by focusing on employability.

MINISTERIAL MEETING OF WORLD TRADE ORGANISATION

DATE: 19th March 2018

OBJECTIVE: To provide an opportunity to engage in free and frank discussions with the hope that it will lead to political guidance on some major issues

The two-day informal World Trade Organisation (WTO) ministerial meeting is scheduled to begin on 19th March in New Delhi. Representatives of the 50 members will be in attendance for the event. Ministers and Vice Ministers from 27 countries are part of the delegations. WTO Director General Roberto Azevedo will also be participating.

With India hosting the meeting, Commerce and Industry Minister Suresh Prabhu welcomed the participants. In his address, he said that he hoped that it will provide an opportunity to the participating countries to engage in free discussions.

As per the officials, the ministerial meeting will provide an opportunity for ministers to explore in greater detail options on different issues for re-invigorating the WTO.

One of the major agendas of the meeting is to find a permanent solution to the food stock-holding by WTO members.

The meeting is significantly important as the global trade appears fragile with some developed countries threatening to retaliate the duty hike on steel and aluminum products by the Trump administration.

INDIA TO HOST INTERNATIONAL COMPETITION NETWORK ANNUAL CONFERENCE

DATE: 21st March 2018

OBJECTIVE: To provide an international platform in the field of competition law and policy.

17th Annual Conference of International Competition Network 2018 (ICN2018) will commence from 21st March 2018 in New Delhi. This is the first time that India is hosting the conference ever since it joined International Competition Network (ICN) in 2009.

The conference will be inaugurated on the first day by Union Minister for Finance and Corporate Affairs Shri Arun Jaitley while Union Minister for Railways and Coal Shri Piyush Goyal will attend the valedictory on the final day of the conference.

The Annual Conference offers key international platform in the field of competition law and policy. ICN2018 will bring together over 500 heads and senior officials of competition authorities, non-governmental advisors, distinguished legal experts and economists from over 100 countries.

Competition Commission of India's Chairperson Shri Devender Singh Sikri, along with CCI members Shri Sudhir Mital, Shri Augustine Peter, Shri U.C. Nahta and Justice G.P. Mittal addressed queries by media persons.

The Annual Conference will comprise seven plenary sessions and twenty four breakout sessions encompassing the themes viz. Special Project on Cartel Enforcement and Competition, Advocacy for the Good Times, the Bad Times or Any Time, Perspectives from the Bench: Litigating competition cases, Vertical Mergers, Online Markets and Vertical Restraints: the Same Old Story, Incentives, Deterrence and Compensation, Implementation in ICN.

SEMINAR ON CONSERVATION OF PARTICULARLY VULNERABLE TRIBES

DATE: 28th June 2018

OBJECTIVE: To Conserve the Particularly Vulnerable Tribes of Andaman and Nicobar Islands

National Commission for Scheduled Tribes (NCST) has organized a National Seminar on Conservation of Particularly Vulnerable Tribes Groups (PVTGs) in New Delhi. The theme of the seminar was "Conservation of Particularly Vulnerable Tribes of Andaman and Nicobar Islands: The Way Forward. This Seminar was organized in collaboration with Anthropological Survey of India (AnSI).

Various ministries and departments have attended the seminar and presented their strategies towards PVTGs in the Islands.

Exclusive Thematic Sessions held on tribes like the Sentinelese, Great Andamanies, Onge, Jarawa and Shompen.

Directors of Tribal Research Institutes, Vice Chancellors of six Universities in different States, Domain experts, NGOs working for welfare of Tribals along with civil Society representatives presented/discussed their mode of strategy on the theme of the seminar.

75 tribal groups have been categorized by Ministry of Home Affairs as Particularly Vulnerable Tribal Groups. PVTGs reside in 18 States and Union Territory of Andaman and Nicobar Islands.

National Commission for Scheduled Tribes is a Constitutional body set up under Article 338(A) of the Constitution to protect the interests of Scheduled.

MOU BETWEEN INDIA & UK TO IMPROVE PUBLIC TRANSPORT

DATE: 3rd January, 2018

OBJECTIVE: To improve public transport in India

The Union Cabinet chaired by the Prime Minister Narendra Modi has approved the signing and implementation of the Memorandum of Understanding (MoU) between Ministry of Road Transport & Highways and 'Transport for London', a statutory body established under the Greater London Authority Act, 1999 (UK) to improve Public Transport in India.

The MoU will help to improve the overall public transport system in the country, improve passenger services and promote the use of high capacity buses in India. It will go a long way in strengthening ties and promoting bilateral relations between India and United Kingdom. The MoU will help in strengthening the integrated public transport for all. This will help people from poorer strata of the society to have access to a quality public transport system.

AGREEMENT BETWEEN INDIA & MYANMAR ON LAND BORDER CROSSING

DATE: 3rd January, 2018

OBJECTIVE: To facilitate the movement on border areas of India and Myanmar

The Union Cabinet chaired by the Prime Minister Narendra Modi has approved the Agreement between India and Myanmar on Land Border Crossing. The Agreement will facilitate regulation and harmonization of already existing free movement rights for people ordinarily residing in the border areas of both countries. It will also facilitate movement of people on the basis of valid passports and visas which will enhance economic and social interaction between the two countries.

The Agreement is an enabling arrangement for movement of people across India-Myanmar border. It is expected to provide connectivity and enhance interaction of the people of North Eastern States of India with the people of Myanmar. The Agreement would give a boost to the economy of the North East and allow us to leverage our geographical connections with Myanmar to boost trade and people to people ties. The Agreement will safeguard the traditional rights of the largely tribal communities residing along the border which are accustomed to free movement across the land border.

MOU BETWEEN INDIA & SRI LANKA ON MEDICINE

DATE 3rd January, 2018

OBJECTIVE: To regulate teaching, practice, drugs and drugless therapies, Traditional Medicine and Homeopathy

The Government is planning to sign a memorandum of understanding (MoU) with Sri Lanka for cooperation in areas of traditional systems of medicine & Homoeopathy. The Memorandum of Understanding envisages the following salient areas for cooperation between the two countries in the field of traditional medicine and homeopathy:

- Promotion including the regulation of teaching, practice, drugs and drugless therapies, Traditional Medicine and Homeopathy
- Exchanging experts for training of practitioners, paramedics, scientists, teaching professionals and students in Traditional Systems of Medicine and Homeopathy
- Accommodating interested scientists, practitioners, paramedics and students in institutions for research, educational and training programmes on Traditional Medicine
- Mutual recognition of officially recognised systems of medicine, educational qualifications in Traditional Systems of Medicine and Homeopathy, pharmacopoeias and formularies
- Setting up of Academic Chairs on Traditional Systems of Medicine and Homeopathy

The financial resources necessary to conduct activities under the MoU will be met from the existing allocated budget under this ministry's Central Sector Scheme for promotion of International Cooperation in AYUSH.

HDFC BANK AND RAJASTHAN GOVT. PARTNER TO PROMOTE STARTUP

DATE: 4th January, 2018

OBJECTIVE: To encourage the businesses to grow in initial stages

HDFC Bank and state government of Rajasthan have partnered with each other for the promotion and nurturing startups in the state. Under this partnership, HDFC Bank will team up with the state government to provide end-to-end solutions like current accounts, credit cards and other solutions to startups under its SmartUp programme. HDFC bank also plans to assist startups in showcasing their offerings to the general public through its various platforms.

As per the HDFC, currently the bank has been working with more than 150 startups across the country and is growing. In future, bank has plans to extend its support to startups by launching Smartup Zones in 65 more of its branches across 30 cities which will also include tier II and tier III cities.

This partnership between HDFC bank and Rajasthan Govt. will be very helpful for Start-ups in the state and will encourage the businesses to grow in initial stages.

MoUs BETWEEN INDIA AND ISRAEL

DATE: 15th January 2018

OBJECTIVE: To co-operate in several fields including Cyber Security and Space

Technology

India signed several Memorandums of Understanding (MoUs) with Israel on 15th January 2018. Altogether nine MoUs in the field of Cyber Security, Oil and Gas Sector, Space technology, Air transport, Concentrated solar thermal technologies, Research in Homeopathic Medicine, Film co-production, Investment and Metal-air batteries were signed.

The agreements were signed following delegation-level talks headed by Indian and visiting Israeli Prime Ministers Narendra Modi and **Benjamin Netanyahu** respectively.

The Israeli business delegation which consists of 100 companies, 20 startups and 30 government officials were enthusiastic about collaboration with Indian companies' stalwarts. Along with these collaborations, Indian and Israel Government are also launching together a R&D fund of $40million which will support businesses from both the countries. Each company will bear 25% of the R&D cost while the governments together will sponsor 50% of the cost.

Israel is also keen to team up with Indian business bodies like ASSOCHAM, CII and FICCI to nurture business. NASSCOM Product Council is also signing MoU with Israel-based startup accelerator MassChallenge.

INDIA-CAMBODIA AGREEMENTS

DATE: 27th January 2018

OBJECTIVE: To prevent human trafficking, mutual legal assistance in Criminal Matters to Culture

India and Cambodia signed agreements ranging from prevention of human trafficking, mutual legal assistance in Criminal Matters to Culture. The agreements were signed after the talks between Indian PM Narendra Modi and his Cambodian counterpart Samdech Hun Sen.

Both the countries have also agreed on a $ 20 million concessional Line of Credit (LoC) by India for construction of transmission line in Cambodia. India has offered additional LoC for infrastructure projects in Cambodia, including in health sector for setting up of super specialty hospitals and for road, rail & digital connectivity. India has also agreed to provide soft loans through LoC to finance the 'Stung Sva Hab Water Resource Development Project' worth $ 36.92 million.

Indian Prime Minister also mentioned the Archaeological Survey of India's efforts in the restoration on Angkor Wat and Ta Prohm Temples in Cambodia. He also reaffirmed India's commitment to undertake restoration and conservation work at the ancient temple of Lord Shiva at Preah Vihear.

Both sides also agreed to explore the possibility of extending the India-Myanmar-Thailand Trilateral Highway further to Cambodia and beyond. Expansion of air connectivity to facilitate people-to-people contacts and promote tourism between the two countries was also discussed.

BOTANICAL SURVEY OF INDIA SIGNS MOU WITH NATURAL HISTORY MUSEUM, UK

DATE: 16th February 2018

OBJECTIVE: To collaborate on scientific issues dealing with plant species and habitat

The Memorandum of Understanding was signed between Botanical Survey of India (BSI) and Natural History Museum (NHM), UK. The MoU was signed for the purpose of cooperation in the field of genetic studies, research and training, species and habitat conservation in India, including species and habitat conservation assessments and on other related issues.

The MoU will facilitate the BSI staff to work in Natural History Museum, London and vice-versa. Both the premier scientific institutes will also share the benefits that may arise from the collection, study and conservation of the samples and associated data & images.

The agreement was signed by Director, BSI Dr Paramjit Singh and Head of the Algae, Fungi and Plants Division, NHM, Dr Sandra Knapp. Union Minister for Environment, Forest & Climate Change Dr Harsh Vardhan was also present on the occasion.

This scientific collaboration is set to benefit both India and the UK in matters related to plant sciences and research. Both countries have also expressed their commitment to the use of scientific evidence for supporting the goals of the Convention on Biological Diversity, CITES and the Nagoya Protocol on Access and Benefit Sharing (ABS).

INDIA JOINS ASHGABAT AGREEMENT

DATE: 6th February 2018

OBJECTIVE: To facilitate transportation of goods between Central Asia and Persian Gulf.

India has been admitted formally to Agreement on the Establishment of an International Transport and Transit Corridor between Iran, Oman, Turkmenistan and Uzbekistan known as Ashgabat Agreement.

Ashgabat Agreement envisages facilitation of transit and transportation of goods between Central Asia and the Persian Gulf. Accession to the Agreement would diversify India's connectivity options with Central Asia and have a positive influence on India's trade and commercial ties with the region. This agreement will also complement India's presence in Chabahar Port, INSTC (International North–South Transport Corridor) as well as future accession to Eurasian Economic Union. India's accession to the agreement is a hint at diversification of connectivity options that India has with central Asia. In that manner, a trade route will have a positive influence on India's trade and commerce.

MoUs BETWEEN INDIA AND OMAN

DATE: 11th February 2018

OBJECTIVE: To strengthen cooperation between India and Oman in different sectors

India and Oman signed Memorandums of Understanding in different areas like trade and investment, energy, defence, security, food security and regional issues.

The agreements were signed during Indian Prime Minister Narendra Modi's visit to Oman. During his maiden visit to Gulf nation, the Indian PM held delegation-level talks with the Sultan of Oman, Qaboos bin Said al Said about measures to strengthen cooperation between both nations including healthcare, tourism, trade , energy, defence, food security and about other major issues.

Prime Minister had embarked on a three-nation tour with Oman being his last destination. He had arrived in Muscat, capital of Oman and on his arrival, he was given a ceremonial reception at the Royal Airport by Sayyid Fahd Bin Mahmoud Al Said, the Deputy Prime Minister for Council of Ministers of Oman.

INDIA GERMANY AGREEMENT ON SUSTAINABLE URBAN DEVELOPMENT

DATE: 23rd February 2018

OBJECTIVE: To provide technical cooperation and support approaches in integrated planning, affordable housing & basic services.

India and Germany have signed the Memorandum of Understanding for an "Implementation Agreement in Sustainable Urban Development and Smart Cities in India". The main objective of the program is to develop and subsequently apply concepts related to sustainable urban development for the provision of urban basic services and housing in selected Indian cities.

The 'Sustainable Urban Development Programme - Smart Cities in India' project is supported by the German Federal Ministry for Economic Cooperation and Development (BMZ) and jointly implemented by the Ministry of Housing and Urban Affairs, Government of India and Deutsche Gesellschaft für Internationale Zusammenarbeit (GIZ). Both the countries will work for the implementation of technical cooperation and support approaches in integrated planning, affordable housing & basic services. The Germany is contributing approx. 8 million EUR in the project.

Drinking water, waste water treatment and solid waste management and mobility will be prime focus under the implementation stages of provision of affordable housing and basic services. The project will continue till December 2020 that is for duration of three years.

International Trade

INDIA AND IRAN SIGN AGREEMENT ON AVOIDANCE OF DOUBLE TAXATION

DATE: 17th February 2018

OBJECTIVE: To Avoid Double Taxation and prevent fiscal evasion of taxes on income

India and Iran signed an agreement for the Avoidance of Double Taxation (DTAA) and the prevention of fiscal evasion with respect to taxes on income. The agreement was signed in the presence of Indian Prime Minister Narendra Modi and visiting Iranian President Hassan Rouhani. As per information by CBDT the agreement is expected to stimulate flow of investment, technology and personnel from India to Iran and vice-versa, and will check double taxation. The pact will facilitate exchange and sharing of information between India and Iran in line with the latest international standards. This is significant and expected to improve transparency in tax matters and curbing of tax evasion and tax avoidance as well. The accord also meets treaty related minimum standards under G-20 OECD Base Erosion and Profit Shifting (BEPS) Project, in which India participated on an equal footing.

INDIA, WORLD BANK SIGN USD 200 MILLION LOAN AGREEMENT FOR NATIONAL NUTRITION MISSION

DATE: 8th May

OBJECTIVE: To support Indian Government's National Nutrition Mission

India signed a loan agreement with the World Bank worth USD 200 million for the National Nutrition Mission (POSHAN Abhiyaan).

The loan will support Indian Government's National Nutrition Mission that aims to reduce stunting in 0-6 years old children from 38.4 percent to 25 percent by the year 2022.

Goals:

The mission aims to reduce stunting, under-nutrition, anaemia among young children, women and adolescent girls and reduce low birth weight by at least 2 percent per annum.

- Though the target to reduce stunting is at least 2 percent per annum, the mission will strive to achieve reduction in stunting from 38.4 percent to 25 percent by 2022.
- More than 10 crore people are expected to be benefitted by the program.
- It will cover all the states and districts in a phased manner. While 315 districts will be covered in 2017-18 and 235 districts will be covered in 2018-19, the remaining districts will be covered in 2019-20.

INDO-CANADA ECONOMIC CO-OPERATION

DATE: 23rd February 2018

OBJECTIVE: To expand economic co-operation between India and Canada

India and Canada signed MoUs in various fields. The agreements were signed in the presence of Indian Prime Minister Narendra Modi and visiting Canadian Prime Minister Justin Trudeau.

Memorandums of Understanding were signed in various fields including civil nuclear science and technology, intellectual property, education, sports, audio-visual co-production and information technology.

Both the leaders welcomed the signing of agreements which is expected to create new economic opportunities and jobs in both countries. In addition, it was felt to encourage the private sectors to further explore investment opportunities in both countries, through India's flagship programmes like Make in India, Start-Up India, Digital India as well as Canadian programs such as the Innovation and Skills Plan, the Canadian Technology Accelerators, the Start-Up VISA Program and the Global Skills Strategy.

The Prime Ministers also reaffirmed the extent and scope of Indo-Canadian relations, based on the fundamental principle of respect for sovereignty, unity and territorial integrity of both countries.

ENVIRONMENT UPDATES

NATIONAL

ENVIRONMENT MINISTRY REFUSES CAPTIVE BREEDING OF CHIRU

DATE: 13th January, 2018

The Ministry of Environment and Forests and Climate Change (MoEFCC) has refused to allow captive breeding of Chiru (Tibetan antelope), whose underfur is used for making famous shahtoosh shawls. Chiru for long time have been hunted for their underfur, which is renowned for its quality which is traditionally woven into an extremely fine fabric to make Shahtoosh shawls. It takes three to five hides to make a single shawl. At present, Shahtoosh shawls' sale and possession is banned in India and in many countries.

Chiru is assessed as 'near threatened' by the International Union for Conservation of Nature (IUCN) 2017. Their current low population can only be maintained with continued high levels of protection in its natural. Any relaxation in protection regime of animal will lead to rapid population decline due to commercial poaching.

The suggestion for captive breeding was made by Parliamentary Standing Committee on Science & Technology, Environment & Forests asking to consider captive breeding as it will add to livelihood of people of Kashmir.

DELHI BECOMES THE FIRST INDIAN CITY TO INTRODUCE BS-VI

DATE: 1st April 2018

OBJECTIVE: To combat alarming levels of air pollution in Indian cities

Delhi becomes the first Indian city to introduce BS-VI (equivalent to fuel meeting Euro-VI emission norms) grade petrol and diesel from BS-IV (equivalent to fuel meeting Euro-IV emission norms) grade.

In a bid to combat alarming levels of air pollution in Indian cities in general and Delhi in particular the Indian Government has advanced the introduction of BS VI by 2 years and directly shifted from BS-IV to BS-VI.

BS-VI grade fuel contains maximum 10 ppm of sulphur as against max. 50 ppm in BS-IV fuels. State-owned oil firms have begun supplying the BS-VI petrol and diesel (equivalent to fuel meeting Euro-VI emission norm) at all their 391 petrol pumps in the national capital territory. To meet the new fuel requirement the Mathura refinery in Uttar Pradesh, Panipat refinery in Haryana, Bina in Madhya Pradesh and Bhatinda in Punjab have started producing Euro-VI grade fuel.

FIMBRISTYLIS AGASTHYAMALAENSIS: NEW PLANT SPECIES DISCOVERED IN WESTERN GHATS

DATE: 3rd April, 2018

A team of researchers recently discovered a grass like plant species called **'Fimbristylis agasthyamalaensis'**. This plant has been discovered in Ponmudi hills within the **Agasthyamala Bio reserve of Western Ghats.** It has been classified as sedge, the grass-like plant has been named, after the locality from which it was found. Researchers have recommended the protection of the plant because this plant is in serious danger. In this area, this plant can become a food for livestock in the wild. The habitat of this plant is counted in the Tourism hub of Kerala, which puts extra pressure on this plant and increases the risk of its endangered species. The plant of Fimbristylis agasthyamalaensis is related to the family of cypress. In India, 122 plants related to cypress are found in which 87 are found on Western Ghats. Most of these plants are used in medicines or used as fodder.

DIU SMART CITY BECOMES FIRST TO RUN ON 100% RENEWABLE ENERGY

DATE: 23rd April

OBJECTIVE: To make city clean, green and environment-friendly

Diu Smart City becomes the first city in India that runs on 100% renewable energy during daytime setting a new benchmark for other cities to become clean and green. Diu had been importing 73% of its power from Gujarat until last year. It now adopts a two-pronged approach whereby a 9 MW solar park spread over 50 hectares rocky barren land has been developed besides installing solar panels on the rooftops on 79 government buildings thereby generating 1.3 MW annually. To further enhance its solar capacity, Diu offers its residents a subsidy of Rs 10, 000-50,000 for installing 1-5KW rooftop solar panels. Diu is saving about 13,000 tons of carbon emissions every year. Due to low-cost solar energy, power tariffs have been cut in residential category by 10% last year and 15% this year.

Like Diu other smart cities such as Bengaluru Smart City is working on implementation of solution to improve traffic management, while Jaipur Smart City Ltd (JSCL) has planned to develop night bazaar at Chaura Rasta, in the heart of Pink city.

BACTERIA HELP PRODUCE LOW-SULPHUR FOSSIL FUELS

DATE: 23rd April

OBJECTIVE: To make low-sulphur fossil fuels

Scientists from CSIR-Institute of Minerals and Materials Technology (CSIR-IMMT) in Bhubaneswar used four bacterial strains (Rhodococcus rhodochrous, Arthrobacter sulfureou, Gordonia rubropertinita and Rhodococcus erythropolis) that use dibenzothiophene as an energy source thereby getting rid of the sulphur.

Fossil fuels contain sulphur, which contributes to environmental pollution by emitting sulphur oxides and creating acid rain. Existing methods that utilize micro-organisms cannot efficiently remove organic sulphur from fossil fuels.

Previously bacterial strains removed between 70% and 90% of the sulphur, while the novel bacterial strains remove 99% of the sulphur, suggesting their potential to make low-sulphur fossil fuels. It can potentially be used to remove sulphur from petrochemicals and coal with an energy-saving process.

The process of bio-desulfurization using these four bacterial strains is also eco-friendly and economical. These bacterial strains can be potentially used on commercial scale for removal of sulphur from fossil fuels.

ENVIRONMENT MINISTRY LAUNCHES GAJ YATRA

DATE: 28th May 2018

OBJECTIVE: To raise awareness about securing elephant corridors and conservation of elephants

Gaj Yatra was launched by Ministry of Environment, Forest and Climate Change (MoEFCC) from Tura in Garo Hills of Meghalaya. It is a campaign to raise awareness about shrinking space for India's national heritage animal and the importance of securing elephant corridors.

It is being led by Wildlife Trust of India (WTI) and motivates people from all walks of life in conservation of elephants.

First time the Gaj yatra was launched on the occasion of National Elephant Day (12th August) in 2017.

The main aim of Gaj Yatra is to secure around 100 elephant corridors across India. The campaign has been launched from the Garo Hills to acknowledge local community who have created community forests for human-elephant harmony and conservation of animals such as hoolock gibbon. In 2014, villagers in Meghalaya's Garo Hills set aside a part of their community-owned land to create village reserve forests giving right of passage to elephants. Four of the elephant corridors are in Meghalaya, including the Siju-Rewak corridor that some 1,000 elephants use to travel between the Balpakram and Nokrek National Parks in the State.

Elephant corridors are vital natural habitat linkages that enable elephants and other wildlife to move through the degraded habitats lying between larger protected forests freely, without being disturbed by humans. India has about 30,000 wild Asian elephants (Elephas maximus); over 50% of the species' estimated global population. The growing resource needs of India's human population have led to the destruction and fragmentation of wild habitats across the country which is the main cause of man-wild animal conflict.

UTTARAKHAND TO BAN USE OF POLYTHENE

DATE: 6th June

OBJECTIVE: To curb rampant use of plastic which is increasingly becoming a big environmental issue

The Uttarakhand Government has decided to completely prohibit the use of polythene or plastic from July 31, 2018. The move is aimed at curbing rampant use of plastic, which is increasingly becoming a huge environmental challenge. The announcement was made by the state on the occasion of World Environment Day on June 5, 2018.

Key Highlights

- All the polythene vendors in Uttarakhand have been asked to finish the polythene stock before July 31.
- The state would also be launching a comprehensive public awareness campaign on the environmental damage caused by polythene, one week before the complete ban on polythene.
- According to the state's Chief Minister Trivendra Singh Rawat, environmental conservation is a collective responsibility and so people's cooperation is necessary to make Uttarakhand polythene-free.

Background: Sikkim became the first state in 1998 to ban disposable plastic bags. In 2016, it banned the use of packaged drinking water in government offices and government events and use of Styrofoam and thermocol disposable plates in the entire state. The Haryana government too has now decided to ban single-use plastic water bottles in all government offices in the state.

TAJ DECLARATION TO BEAT PLASTIC POLLUTION

DATE: 3rd June

OBJECTIVE: To make Taj Mahal premises litter-free

With an aim to make 500-meter area around Taj Mahal litter free and phase out single use plastic, Union Minister Mahesh Sharma administered a pledge to the residents of Agra. The pledge called "Taj Declaration to Beat Plastic Pollution" was made in the presence of United Nations Environment Program (UNEP) Executive Director Erik Solheim and UNEP Goodwill Ambassador Diya Mirza.

The declaration came ahead to the World Environment Day, June 5. Well before the declaration was undertaken, workshops were conducted to deal with problem. The major focus of the workshop is to curb littering around 17th century monument. Short term and long term plans are worked up on.

It was also highlighted that India and the whole world is facing a huge problem of pollution caused by the use of plastic. According to an official statement, a pledge was taken to make the 500-metre area around the Taj Mahal litter-free and take steps to phase out single-use plastic from the area.

MAHARASHTRA GOVERNMENT IMPOSED BAN ON SINGLE USE PLASTICS

DATE: 23rd June 2018

Objective: To prohibit the use, sale and manufacture of single use plastic and allied products

Maharashtra Government has imposed the statewide ban on single use plastics. The decision to ban the single use plastics was announced on 23rd March and the date of implementation was slated from 23rd June.

The plastic ban was issued under Maharashtra Plastic and Thermocol Products (Manufacture, Usage, Sale, Transport, Handling and Storage) Notification, 2018.

 The notification cited the rising concerns of usage and disposal of plastic include accumulation of waste in landfills, water bodies and in natural habitats, physical problems for wild animals resulting from ingestion or entanglement in plastic, the leaching of chemicals from plastic products and the potential for plastics to transfer chemicals to wildlife and humans.

The ban covers plastic bags, disposable cups and plates, plastic cutlery, non-woven polypropylene bags, plastic pouches and packaging materials, thermocol items etc.

The ban notification also has defined 'Plastic' as material which contains as an essential ingredient a high polymer such as polyethylene terephthalate, high-density polyethylene, vinyl, low density polyethylene, polypropylene, polystyrene resins, polystyrene (thermocol), non-oven polypropylene, multi layered co extruder, poly propylene, poly terephthalate, poly amides, poly methyl methacrylate, plastic micro beads, etc.

Earlier in January 2018, Jammu & Kashmir banned the use of polythene carry bags

India generates 5.6 million tonnes of plastic waste annually, and the country accounts for 60 percent of plastic waste dumped into the world's oceans every year.

INTERNATIONAL

INDIA AND UK LAUNCH JOINT RESEARCH PROJECTS

DATE: 19th February 2018

OBJECTIVE: To deliver mutual benefits and research solutions on clean water and energy

The India and United Kingdom have launched joint research projects on 'Water Quality Research' and 'Energy Demand Reduction in Built Environment'. The research projects on 'Water Quality Research' and 'Energy Demand Reduction in Built Environment were jointly launched in presence of representatives from both countries.

Indian side was represented through, Dr V K Saraswat, Member, National Institution for Transforming India (NITI) Aayog, and Professor Ashutosh Sharma, Secretary, Department of Science and Technology (DST), while Daniel Shah, Director, Research Councils UK (RCUK)-India, represented the UK.

INDIA AS THE GLOBAL HOST FOR WORLD ENVIRONMENT DAY

DATE: 20th February 2018

OBJECTIVE: To act as global host for spreading the awareness and action for environment protection

India will host the World Environment Day in 2018. India will work as the Global host of the event which is celebrated on 5th June across the world every year to encourage worldwide awareness and action for the protection of environment.

Every year World Environment Day has a different global host country, where the official celebrations take place. The focus on the host country helps highlight the environmental challenges it faces, and supports the effort to address them. India also hosted this global event in 2011.

India as the global host for year 2018 was confirmed after the signing of a Letter of Intent between, Erik Solheim, Under-Secretary General, United Nations & Executive Director of UN Environment) and CK Mishra, Secretary, Ministry of Environment, Forest and Climate Change. This was announced by Dr. Harsh Vardhan, Union Minister for Environment, Forest and Climate Change. Mr. Solheim on the occasion said he is very positive about the event and India as a great global host of 2018 Environment Day celebrations.

By hosting World Environment Day 2018, India is accelerating its leadership on an issue of tremendous magnitude. India is emerging as a leader given it has one of the highest recycling rates in the world. It can be instrumental in combating plastic pollution, as the theme of this year celebrations is "Beat Plastic Pollution".

ONLY 13% OF TIGER CONSERVATION AREAS MEET GLOBAL STANDARDS

DATE: 1st March, 2018

In the survey of over a hundred tiger conservation areas by 11 leading conservation organizations and countries with tiger ranges that are part of the Conservation Assured Tiger Standards (CATS) Partnership, It is found that only 13% of tiger conservation areas meet global standards. The surveyed area is home to approximately 70% of the world's wild tigers. At least one-third of these areas are severely at risk of losing their tigers and most of these sites are in south-east Asia. According to survey, despite poaching being one of the greatest threats faced by the big cats, 85% of the areas surveyed do not have the staff capacity to patrol sites effectively and 61% of the areas in Southeast Asia have very limited anti-poaching enforcement. CATS is set of criteria that allow tiger conservation areas to check if their management will lead to successful tiger conservation. It is organized under seven pillars and 17 elements of critical management activity. Its purpose is to secure safe havens for wild tigers. It is important part of Tx2, WWF's global tiger programme that aims to double wild tiger numbers by the year 2022.

14 OF WORLD'S 15 MOST POLLUTED CITIES IN INDIA

DATE: 3rd May

As per the data released by the World Health Organization (WHO), on 2nd May in Geneva, India has 14 out of the 15 most polluted cities in the world in terms of PM 2.5 concentrations, with the worst being Kanpur. While in terms of PM10 levels, 13 cities from India figured among the 20 most-polluted cities of the world in 2016. Delhi's PM2.5 level in 2016 was at 143 micrograms/cubic metre, making it the sixth most polluted city in the world. WHO's database of more than 4,000 cities in 100 countries shows that Delhi's pollution levels improved only marginally between 2010 and 2014 but started deteriorating again in 2015.

However, as per India's Central Pollution Control Board (CPCB) data, Delhi's PM2.5 level was 134 micrograms/cubic meter in 2016 and 125 micrograms/cubic meter in 2017 showing an improvement.

The WHO Global Urban Ambient Air Pollution Database mentions that 9 out of 10 people in the world breathe air containing high levels of pollutants. Around 7 million people die every year from exposure to fine particles in polluted air that break through the lungs and cardiovascular system, causing stroke, heart disease, lung cancer, chronic obstructive pulmonary diseases and respiratory infections. Over 90 % of air pollution-related deaths occur in low and middle income countries, mainly in Asia and Africa regions, followed by Eastern Mediterranean region, Europe and the Americas.

NATIONAL

ARUNACHAL PRADESH DECLARED OPEN DEFECATION-FREE STATE

DATE: 1st January, 2018

OBJECTIVE: To improve cleanliness and sanitary conditions in the country

After Sikkim, Arunachal Pradesh became the second North-east Indian state to be declared as "Open Defecation Free". Arunachal Pradesh attained the feat much before the national deadline of October 2, 2019 which the centre had given to make each Indian state Open Defecation Free.

The initiative was undertaken under the scheme, Swachh Bharat Mission (Gramin). SBM (G) had an extra incentive of Rs 8,000 added per toilet by the State Government in addition to the Centre's support of Rs 12,000, raising the grant for constructing a toilet to Rs 20,000.The Arunachal state government had recently also launched Swachh Arunachal Mission on October 2 last year at Tawang, Arunachal which envisaged the Swachh Protocol (Cleanliness Protocol) aimed at ensuring sustainability of assets created under SBM (Gramin).

INDIAN TYPHOID VACCINE APPROVED FOR GLOBAL USE

Date: 4th January, 2018

OBJECTIVE: to lower the cost of typhoid vaccine

Bharat Biotech, a vaccine company, has received Pre-Qualification tag from the World Health Organisation (WHO) for Typbar TCV or Typhoid Conjugate Vaccine. The WHO tag would allow the firm to access global public vaccination programs. The board of Global Alliance for Vaccines and Immunisation (GAVI) approved funding of $85 million for 2019-2020 to support the administration of the typhoid conjugate vaccine in developing countries. About 12 million cases of typhoid fever were reported in 2016, resulting in the deaths of 1.30 lakh people globally.

The economic costs of typhoid were very high, the known antibiotics have developed resistance, leaving little protection for people. The WHO has recommended the use of typhoid conjugate vaccines on infants between 6 and 23 months of age and for children between 2 and 15 years of age.

FSSAI LAUNCHES PROJECT DHOOP

DATE: 10th April, 2018

OBJECTIVE: To combat Vitamin D deficiencies among youngsters

Food Safety and Standards Authority of India (FSSAI) launches 'Project Dhoop' in association with NCERT, NDMC and North MCD Schools. This initiative urges schools to shift their morning assembly to noon time mainly between 11:00 a.m. to 1:00 p.m. to ensure maximum absorption of Vitamin D in students through natural sunlight.

Micronutrients including vitamins are needed by people in very small amounts, but these are the "magic wands" that enable the body to produce enzymes, hormones and other substances essential for proper growth and development. Fish and fish products are the only real food sources for Vitamin D. For most Indians, Vitamin D is mainly obtained by exposure to sunlight without which deficiency is likely to occur. Sunlight also converts the cholesterol to Vitamin D via additional conversions in the liver and kidneys.

Many factors can contribute to Vitamin 'D' Deficiencies (VDD) such as overuse of sun screen, wearing clothes that cover most of the skin, working inside all day in air-conditioned atmosphere and so on. Studies have found that more than 90% of boys and girls across various Indian cities are deficient in Vitamin D. About 90-97% of school children (aged 6-17 years) in Delhi have VDD and around 10-11% of these children exhibit signs of VDD.

FIRST WELLNESS CENTRE UNDER 'AYUSHMAN BHARAT'

DATE: 15th April

OBJECTIVE: To provide free treatment (up to 5 lakh) for poor families

On the 127th birth anniversary of B R Ambedkar on April 14, Prime Minister Narendra Modi inaugurates the first health centre under Ayushman Bharat Scheme at Bijapur district in Chhattisgarh. This scheme aims to provide medical insurance worth Rs 5 lakh per family per year for secondary and tertiary care hospitalisation to 10 crore poor and vulnerable population based on Socio Economic and Caste Census 2011 (SECC) database.

Under the Scheme, the Govt. is targeting to open 1.5 lakh health and wellness centres by 2022, which will be equipped to provide medical treatment for diseases such as blood pressure, diabetes, cancer, and old age illnesses. It also targets to provide insurance cover to 40 % of India's population, which is deprived of secondary and tertiary care, including instance and hospitalisation costs. Benefits covered under it include pre and post-hospitalisation expenses. It will also cover all pre-existing conditions from beginning of policy. It will also pay defined transport allowance per hospitalization to beneficiary.

'COCHLEAR IMPLANT (CI) AWARENESS PROGRAM' FOR HEARING IMPAIRED CHILDREN

DATE: 6th May

OBJECTIVE: To provide sense of sound to a deaf person

The **Department of Empowerment of Persons with Disabilities (DEPwD)** under Union Ministry of Social Justice and Empowerment organizes a **'Cochlear**

Implant Awareness Programme' at Huda Convention Centre in Faridabad, Haryana. Under the Assistance to Disabled persons (ADIP) scheme of the DEPwD, there is a provision for Cochlear Implant surgeries of hearing impaired children up to the age of 5 years at the cost of Rs 6.00 Lakhs per unit. This programme was organized by DEPwD in association with Indian Red Cross Society and Sarvodaya Hospital & Research Centre.

The cochlear implant is a surgically implanted electronic device that provides a sense of sound to a person who is severely deaf in both ears. With the help of this implant, such children will not only be able to hear normally through one ear but with post surgical rehabilitation, they will be able to speak like normal persons.

The Cochlear Implants are costly and not affordable by the poor people, hence, the Social Justice and Empowerment Ministry has introduced Cochlear Implant program under revised scheme of Assistance to Disabled Persons for purchase/ fitting of aids and appliances (ADIP) for the poor and needy young children.

NIPAH OUTBREAK IN KERALA

DATE: 23rd May 2018

Kerala has been put on high-alert after the reports of outbreak of Nipah virus in the state. At least half a dozen persons were reported dead in Kozhikode.

National Virology Institute (NIV), Pune has confirmed the presence of Nipah virus taken from samples from the infected persons. This is the first time the virus, which has high fatality rate and spreads mainly through bats, pigs and other animals, has been detected in the state.

The Union Health Ministry has rushed a team of experts to assist the state that is struggling to cope with the outbreak. The central team comprises officials from the Department of Animal Husbandry, National Institute of Immunology and Indian Council of Medical Research.

NiV was first identified in Kampung Sungai Nipah, Malaysia in 1998. On that occasion, pigs were the intermediate hosts. However, in subsequent NiV outbreaks, there were no intermediate hosts. In Bangladesh in 2004, humans became infected with NiV as a result of consuming date palm sap that had been contaminated by infected fruit bats.

Earlier Nipah outbreaks were reported in West Bengal (Siliguri, in 2001, with 66 cases and 45 deaths and Nadia, in 2007 with 5 cases with 100% mortality).

Nipah induces flu-like symptoms that often lead to encephalitis and coma. Fruit bats are considered the main carrier of the virus for which there is no vaccination.

AYUSHMAN BHARAT — NATIONAL HEALTH PROTECTION MISSION

DATE: 15th June

Twenty States have signed Memorandum of Understanding (MoU) with Union Ministry of Health and Family Welfare for implementing Ayushman Bharat – National Health Protection Mission. The MoUs were exchanged during Health

Ministers' conclave held in New Delhi. During the conclave, aspects of NHPM, like operational guidelines, model tender document for selection if insurance companies and implementation support agencies for trusts were discussed. The government has launched a web portal to allow states to empanel hospitals under the mission. Training of this empanelment software will be conducted in the next two weeks and states can start using the website by July 1, according to a release by the health ministry.

Key facts

Ayushman Bharat—National Health Protection Mission (AB- NHPM) aims to target over 10 crore families belonging to poor and vulnerable population based on Socio Economic and Caste Census 2011 (SECC) database. It will cover Rs. 5 lakh per family per year, taking care of almost all secondary care and tertiary care procedures. There will be no cap on family size and age in the scheme. The scheme integrates two on-going centrally sponsored schemes viz. Rashtriya Swasthya Bima Yojna and Senior Citizen Health Insurance Scheme.

FSSAI LAUNCHES EAT RIGHT MOVEMENT

DATE: 11th July

OBJECTIVE: To promote safe and healthy food

The Food Safety and Standards Authority of India (FSSAI) launches a national campaign, 'The Eat Right Movement', with health and wellness centres to integrate its existing initiatives 'Safe and Nutritious Food' (SNF) at schools, home and workplace as well as food fortification. FSSAI will provide a training tool kit to health workers at the proposed 1.5 lakh wellness centres under the Ayushman Bharat Scheme for raising public awareness on the issue at the grass root levels. This tool kit would serve as a supplementary engagement resource to be mainstreamed in the national nutrition and public health programmes. It has clear and simple message on eating healthy food and avoiding food with high fat, sugar and salt. It also includes components on eating safe such as maintaining hygiene and sanitation and food adulteration. It aims to train frontline health workers, under the Ayushman Bharat, ASHA and Anganwadi schemes, to deliver these messages effectively to prevent non-communicable diseases like diabetes, obesity and heart ailments, and avoid food borne diseases. Under the Ayushman Bharat Scheme, the government aims to open 1.5 lakh health and wellness centre by 2022, which would be equipped to treat host of diseases, including blood pressure, diabetes, cancer and old-age illness.

INTERNATIONAL

ROTAVAC: FIRST INDIAN VACCINE TO PASS WHO TEST

DATE: 24th January, 2018

OBJECTIVE: To protect against childhood diarrhea caused by the rotavirus

The Rotavac vaccine, developed by the Hyderabad-based Bharat Biotech Limited last year, has been included in India's national immunization program. Rotavac has become first indigenously developed vaccine from India to be pre-qualified by World Health Organization (WHO). It means that vaccine can be sold internationally to several countries in South America and Africa. So far, several vaccines from India have been pre-qualified by WHO. The Rotavac vaccine protects against childhood diarrhea caused by the rotavirus and was built on strain of the virus isolated at the All India Institute of Medical Sciences over 30 years ago.

It is developed under public-private partnership (PPP) model that involved Ministry of Science and Technology, institutions of the US Government and NGOs in India supported by Bill and Melinda Gates Foundation. Rotavirus is responsible for an estimated 36% of hospitalizations for childhood diarrhea around the world and for an estimated 200,000 deaths in low and middle income countries.

SUGAR TAX ON SOFT DRINKS IN UK

DATE: 8th April, 2018

OBJECTIVE: To control obesity and sugar related diseases

UK government launched Soft Drinks Sugar tax to combat obesity and sugar related diseases. This tax is also known as sin tax or sugar tax. With introduction of this tax, UK joins the countries including Mexico, France and Norway that have introduced similar fat taxes. The Soft Drinks Industry Levy was introduced in 2016. This tax is based on levels of sugar in drinks, with most sugary drinks paying highest tax. Drinks containing 5 grams of sugar per 100ml are taxed at 18 pence per liter, and those with more than 5 grams per 100ml taxed at 24 pence per liter. The levy will be applied to manufacturers in Britain and whether they pass it on to consumers or not will be up to them. It will be not applicable to fruit juices as they don't contain added sugar and neither to drinks that have high milk content.

This levy is expected to raise 240 million pounds every year for Treasury. Proceeds from it will be used to directly fund new sports facilities in schools as well as healthy breakfast clubs, ensuring children in UK lead healthier lives.

NEPAL BECOMES TRACHOMA FREE

DATE: 24th May 2018

The Himalayan nation, Nepal becomes the first country in South-East Asia Region to eliminate Trachoma. The World Health Organization (WHO) has validated Nepal for having eliminated trachoma as a public health concern. Trachoma is the leading infectious cause of blindness across the world.

Nepal joins a small number of countries and sixth in the sequence to have eliminated trachoma. Oman, Morocco, Mexico, Cambodia and Laos are other countries.

Trachoma puts more than 190 million people at risk of blindness in 41 countries. It is responsible for the blindness or visual impairment of around 1.9 million people worldwide. It is caused by bacterium *Chlamydia trachomatis*. The infection is transmitted through contact with eye and nose discharge of infected people. Ocular or nasal discharge can be transmitted directly from person to person and also spread through flies which have been in contact with the eyes and noses of infected people.

INDU MALHOTRA FIRST WOMAN LAWYER TO BE DIRECTLY PROMOTED AS SC JUDGE

DATE: 12th January, 2018

The Supreme Court collegium chaired by Deepak Mishra recommends the name of senior advocate Indu Malhotra for the appointment as the Judge of Supreme Court. With this appointment she becomes first woman lawyer from the country to be directly elected for post of judge of the Supreme Court.

Karnataka born Indu Malhotra is reputed senior advocate practicing in SC for the past 30 years.

She came in this profession in 1983 and later secured first position in Advocate-on-Record exam for Supreme Court. She has specialized in law of arbitration and has appeared in various domestic and international commercial arbitrations. She has written Commentary on the Law and Practice of Arbitration in India (2014).

After Leila Seth, she became second woman to be designated as senior advocate by SC in 2007. She is on board of trustees in Save LIFE Foundation and represented NGO in case which resulted in SC passing a slew of laws to protect good Samaritans, who save lives in road accidents.

Since Supreme Court was established 67 years ago, she will be seventh woman judge in SC.

OM PRAKASH RAWAT APPOINTED AS THE NEXT CHIEF ELECTION COMMISSIONER (CEC)

DATE: 21st January 2018

President Ram Nath Kovind appointed Election Commissioner, Om Prakash Rawat as the next chief election commissioner (CEC). Mr. Rawat will take over the post from retiring CEC Achal Kumar Joti.

Senior bureaucrat and former Finance Secretary Ashok Lavasa was appointed as Election Commissioner to fill the vacancy created by Mr Rawat's elevation to the top post in Election Commission.

As newly-elected Chief Election Commissioner Mr. Rawat is expected to oversee elections of Tripura, Nagaland and Meghalaya in next month as one of his first tasks.

The appointments were made by President of India and notified through the Union Law Ministry. The tenure of Om Prakash Rawat will be till December 2018. The normal term of Chief Election Commissioner or Election Commissioner is six years or the age of 65 years, whichever is earlier.

SUBHASH CHANDRA KHUNTIA APPOINTED AS NEW CHAIRMAN OF IRDAI

Subhash Chandra Khuntia has been appointed as new chairman of Insurance Regulatory and Development Authority of India (IRDAI) by The Appointments Committee of Cabinet (ACC). He is appointed for the tenure of three years from the date of joining. He will succeed TS Vijayan whose five-year term ended in February 2018. Subhash Chandra Khuntia is 1981-cadre IAS official from Karnataka.

IRDAI: IRDA is an apex statutory body that regulates and develops insurance industry in India. It was constituted as per provisions of Insurance Regulatory and Development Authority Act, 1999. Its headquarter is in Hyderabad. It protects the rights of insurance policy holders, provide registration certification to life insurance companies, renew, modify, cancel or suspend this registration certificate as and when appropriate; promote efficiency in conduct of insurance business and promote and regulate professional organizations connected with insurance and reinsurance business; regulate investment of funds by insurance companies.

CK PRASAD APPOINTED AS CHAIRMAN OF PRESS COUNCIL OF INDIA (PCI)

Former Supreme Court Judge, CK Prasad has been appointed by Government as Chairman of Press Council of India (PCI) for second term. His nomination was approved by three-member committee headed by Vice President Venkaiah Naidu. He was earlier appointed to post in November 2014 after Justice Markanday Katju stepped down.

Press Council of India (PCI): It is a statutory body with mandate to act as watchdog to oversee conduct of the print media. It derives its mandate from Press Council Act, 1978. It consist of Chairman and 28 other members of whom 20 represent press, five are nominated from two Houses of Parliament and three represent cultural, literary and legal fields.

It adjudicates complaints against and by the press for violation of ethics and for and for violation of the freedom of the press respectively.

SUDHA BALAKRISHNAN APPOINTED AS THE FIRST CHIEF FINANCIAL OFFICER (CFO) BY RBI

Sudha Balakrishnan has been appointed as the first Chief Financial Officer (CFO) by Reserve Bank of India (RBI). She will be the 12th executive director of the RBI and will have tenure of three years.

Balakrishnan is a chartered accountant by profession. Prior to this appointment, she was former executive vice president of National Securities Depository.

The new CFO will be in charge of government and bank account department, which processes government transactions like payments and revenue collections, she will be also the in charge of RBI's balance sheet to ensure accounting policies and procedures comply with regulations. She will also oversee RBI's investments in India and abroad. She will also be in charge of dividend RBI pays to government, which is crucial in final budgetary calculations. Under RBI Act, 1934, RBI is required to pay government its surplus after making provisions for bad and doubtful debts, depreciation in assets and contribution to staff and superannuation fund among others.

JUSTICE RAMALINGAM SUDHAKAR SWORN IN AS CHIEF JUSTICE OF MANIPUR HIGH COURT

Date: 18th May 2018

Senior most judge from the Madras high court Justice Ramalingam Sudhakar was sworn in as the chief justice of the Manipur high court. He was acting as the chief justice of the Jammu and Kashmir high court before his present appointment.

Manipur governor Jagdish Mukhi administered oath to Justice Sudhakar in the Durbar Hall of Raj Bhavan in Imphal.

Justice Sudhakar hails from Panapakkam village in Vellore district, Tamil Nadu. He graduated with a bachelor's degree in life sciences from Loyola College, Chennai, and obtained a law degree from Madras Law College.

He was enrolled as an advocate in 1983 and started practice as an associate of senior advocate Habibullah Badsha, former advocate general of Tamil Nadu.

He was appointed as a judge of the Madras high court in 2005. In 2016, Justice Sudhakar was appointed as a judge of the Jammu and Kashmir high court. He was appointed as the acting chief justice of Jammu and Kashmir high court this year.

KUMMANAM RAJASEKHARAN SWORN IN AS MIZORAM GOVERNOR

Date: 18th May 2018

Kummanam Rajasekharan, who was the BJP's Kerala unit chief for three years, was on May 18 sworn in as the 18th Governor of Mizoram. He replaced Lt. Gen. (retired) Nirbhay Sharma who completed his term on Monday after taking charge in May 2015.

He was state president of Bharatiya Janata Party in Kerala (from 2015–2018). He started his political career as activist of Rashtriya Swayamsevak Sang (RSS) and Sangh Parivar in Kerala in 1970. He was instrumental in spearheading Kerala's Vishva Hindu Parishad (VHP), Balasadanams, Kshetra Samrakshan Samiti and Ekal Vidyalayas. Prior to entering politics, he was working as journalist as sub-editor of Deepika newspaper and other news-dailies.

Ganeshi Lal sworn in as Odisha governor

Ganeshi Lal was sworn in as the new Governor of Odisha at the Raj Bhavan here on May 25. Orissa High Court Chief Justice Vineet Saran administered the oath of the office to him. Mr. Lal is a former Haryana BJP president and also former Haryana Minister.

Bihar Governor Satya Pal Malik was having additional charge of Odisha since March 21 after Governor S.C. Jamir completed his tenure. Lal was a minister in the HVP-BJP government under Chief Minister Bansi Lal from 1996-99.

R K Agrawal appointed President of National Consumer Disputes Redressal Commission.

INTERNATIONAL

NASIRUL MULK NAMED AS PAKISTAN'S CARETAKER PRIME MINISTER

Named as Pakistan's caretaker Prime Minister for two-month period ahead of general elections

Pakistan's former Chief Justice Nasirul Mulk was named as country's caretaker Prime Minister for two-month period ahead of general elections to be held in July 2018. The job of Mulk, as a caretaker Prime Minister is to keep country running between dissolution of parliament and new government being sworn in.

The caretaker government will remain in office until new government is set up through elections. The present ruling government will complete tenure in May 2018. The interim caretaker administration usually does not make any major decisions until new government is elected, though it may act to shore up economy in case of worsening macro-economic outlook.

Nasirul Mulk was born on 17th August, 1950 in Mingora, Swat, in Khyber Pakhtunkhwa province. Before becoming 22nd Chief Justice of Pakistan (from July 2014 to August 2015), He had worked as lawyer and judge for several years. Earlier, he served as acting Chief Election Commissioner of Pakistan from November 2013 to July 2014).

OTHER APPOINTMENTS

January to June 2018

January 2018		
Date	**Name of the Person**	**Designation**
Ist January	Vijay Keshav Gokhale	Foreign secretary
Ist January	Sunny Verghese	Chairman of the World Business Council for Sustainable Development.
2nd January	Rajinder Khanna	Deputy National Security Adviser
2nd January	Salil Parekh	Chief executive officer and managing director of Infosys

Date	Name	Position
8th January	Dilip Asbe	Managing Director and CEO of the National Payments Corporation of India (NPCI)
10th January	K. Sivan	Chairman of the Indian Space Research Organisation (ISRO
10th January	Indu Malhotra	First woman lawyer as judge of the apex court
19th January	IPS officer Sudeep Lakhtakia	Director general of National Security Guard (NSG).
21st January	Om Prakash Rawat	Chief Election Commissioner
22nd January	Ashok Lavasa	Election Commissioner of India
23rd January	Anandiben Patel	Governor of Madhya Pradesh
8th January	AR Rahman	Brand ambassador of Sikkim
22nd January	S Somnath	Director of Vikram Sarabhai Space Centre (VSSC)
23rd January	Jerome Powell	Head of the Federal Reserve
25th January	Usha Ananthasubramanian, MD and CEO of Allahabad Bank	The first woman chairman of Indian Banks' Association (IBA).
25th January	Milos Zeman	Second five-year, Czech Republic's pro-Russia president
28th January	Sauli Niinisto	President of Finland
30th January	Vikram Singh Sisodia	Chef-de-Mission for the upcoming Commonwealth Games
30th January	Lt. Gen Anil Chauhan	Director General of Military Operations (DGMO) of the Indian Army
31st January	Neelam Kapur	Director general (DG) of Sports Authority of India (SAI)

February 2018		
Ist February	John Hennessy	Chairman of Alphabet
4th February	Nicos Anastasiades	President of the Republic of Cyprus.
5th February	Hardayal Prasad	MD & CEO of SBI Card
9th February	Indra Nooyi, chairman and CEO of PepsiCo	First independent female director of the International Cricket Council (ICC) Board
12th February	Chandrashekhara Kambara, Kannada writer and Jnanpith winner	President of Kendra Sahitya Akademi.
15th February	Khadga Prasad Sharma Oli	41st Prime Minister of Nepal.
16th February	Arvind P. Jamkhedhar	Chairman of the Indian Council of Historical Research (ICHR).
19th February	Vice Admiral R B Pandit,	Commandant of Indian Naval Academy
19th February	Murali Ramaswami	Executive directors of Vijaya Bank
20th February	Debashish Mukherjee	Executive directors of Canara Bank
26th February	Michael McCormack	New Deputy Prime Minister of Australia
26th February	Samina Baig , a Pakistani woman	National goodwill ambassador by the United Nations Development Programme (UNDP)
March 2018		
2nd March	Armen Sarkisian	President of Armenia
6th March	Conrad Sangma	Chief Minister of Meghalaya
6th March	Neiphiu Rio	Chief Minister of Nagaland
10th March	Suresh Prabhu	Civil Aviation Minister

10th March	Sitanshu Kar	Director general of the Press Information Bureau
April 2018		
3rd April	Himanta Biswa Sarma	President of Badminton Association of India (BAI)
5th April	Julius Maada Bio	President of Sierra Leone
9th April	Ban Ki-moon	Chairman of Boao Forum
10th April	Rishad Premji	Chairman of Nasscom (2018-19)
11th April	KR Nautiyal	Coast Guard Commander (Eastern seaboard)
12th April	Chandra Shekhar Ghosh	MD & CEO of Bandhan Bank
17th April	Dilip Chenoy	Secretary General of FICCI
25th April	Mario Abdo Benítez	President of Paraguay
26th April	Indu Malhotra	First Woman lawyer to become SC Judge
26th April	Narinder Chauhan	Ambassador of India to the Czech Republic
May 2018		
2nd May	Jagdish Mukhi	Acting Governor, Manipur
4th May	Deepa Ambekar (Indian-American)	Interim Court Judge In New York
7th May	Vladimir Putin	Elected for fourth term President of Russia
8th May	Nikol Pashinyan	Prime Minister of Armenia
8th May	Nitin Bawankule	Country Head For Google Cloud India
16th May	Shashank Manohar	independent chairman of ICC
18th May	Amit Khare	Secretary to the information & broadcasting ministry
18th May	Anil Kumar Jha	CMD of Coal India Limited CIL
19th May	Justice C K Prasad	Chief of Press Council of India for the second time
20th May	Nicolas Maduro	President of Venezuela for a second term

Date	Name	Appointment
22nd May	Pravin L Agrawal	Part-time official Director, BHEL
23rd May	HD Kumaraswamy [JD(S) leader]	Karnataka's chief minister
25th May	Sushil Chandra	chairman of the Central Board of Direct Taxes
26th May	Saad Hariri	Prime Minister of Lebanon for the third time
27th May	Ms. Mia Mottley	First Woman PM of Caribbean Island of Barbados
28th May	Justice R K Agrawal	President of the National Consumer Disputes Redressal Commission (NCDRC).
29th May	Kummanam Rajasekharan	Governor of Mizoram
29th May	Professor Ganeshi Lal	Governor of Odisha

June 2018

Date	Name	Appointment
2nd June	Pedro Sanchez	Spain's new prime minister
2nd June	Abdel Fattah al-Sisi	Egyptian President
5th June	Rudrendra Tandon	Ambassador of India to ASEAN
7th June	Keshari Nath Tripathi	West Bengal Governor to hold additional charge of Tripura
8th June	Sarita Nayyar	World Economic Forum (WEF)'s member to its Managing board
10th June	Arvind Saxena	Acting Chairman of UPSC
10th June	Sharad Kumar	Vigilance Commissioner
11th June	S Ramesh	Chairman of Central Board of Indirect Taxes and Customs
17th June	Omar AI-Razzaz	PM of Jordan
17th June	Ivan Duque	Colombia's new President

SCIENCE & TECHNOLOGY

A WORLD'S FIRST AS CHINESE SCIENTISTS CLONE MONKEY

DATE: 24th January, 2018

OBJECTIVE: To break the technical barrier to copy humans

The two identical long-tailed macaques named as Zhong Zhong and Hua Hua, are the first primates to be cloned from non-embryonic cells. Researchers at the Institute of Neuroscience in Shanghai have cloned monkeys using the same technique that produced Dolly the sheep two decades ago, breaking a technical barrier that could open the door to copying humans.

The macaques were born eight and six weeks ago, making them the first primates — the order of mammals that includes monkeys, apes and humans — to be cloned from a non-embryonic cell.

It was achieved through a process called somatic cell nuclear transfer (SCNT), which involves transferring the nucleus of a cell, which includes its DNA, into an egg which has had its nucleus removed.

Researchers said their work should be a boon to medical research by making it possible to study diseases in populations of genetically uniform monkeys. But it also brings the feasibility of cloning to the doorstep of our own species.

NEW MACHINES FOR MECHANIZED TRACK MAINTENANCE

DATE: 7th April, 2018

OBJECTIVE: To eliminate manual maintenances of tracks

Railway introduces latest integrated track maintenance technology by way of inducting three numbers of 09-3X Dynamic Tamping Express machines. These machines have been manufactured under Prime Minister Narendra Modi's ambitious 'Make in India' initiative. These machines cost about Rs. 27crore each are latest high output integrated tamping machines having multiple functions, so far being carried out by different machines. It can measure pre and post track geometry, correct the track to required geometry, can tamp three sleepers simultaneously, stabilize and measure post tamping track parameters under load to ensure quality of work done. The Railways proposes to induct 42 more such machines over the next three years. This will further improve the safety, reliability and economy in the maintenance of tracks over Indian Railways. Three operations including manual interface are now combined in one machine. For practical hands-on training to operate such advanced track maintenance machines a new 3D state-of-the-art tamping simulator has been installed and commissioned at Indian Railway Track Machine Training Centre Allahabad (IRTMTC) recently. This type of advanced technology simulator is at present available only in five countries including India. The Railways have planned complete mechanization of inspection, monitoring, relaying and maintenance of track by 2024.

INTERNATIONAL

CONTACT LENSES THAT SHADE THE SUN

DATE: 16th April

OBJECTIVE: To help correct the vision of people

The United States Food and Drug Administration have given approval to the Acuvue Oasys Contact Lenses, which are developed by Johnson & Johnson's subsidiary company Vistakon. The product is the first of its kind to use light-adaptive technology. It is designed for daily use to help correct the vision of people who are nearsighted or farsighted. People with certain degrees of astigmatism could also use it.

These lenses have a photo chromic additive that can adapt to the amount of visible light filtered to the eye depending on the amount of ultraviolet light exposure. The effect slightly darkens the lenses in bright sunlight, returning to its regular tint in standard lighting. The findings show that those who wore the lenses had not encountered any vision or driving problems.

WORLD'S FIRST MICRO FACTORY TO HELP TACKLE E-WASTE HAZARD

DATE: 9th April, 2018

OBJECTIVE: To reduce growing problem of electronic waste

An Indian-origin scientist in Australia has launched the world's first micro factory that can transform the components from electronic waste items such as smart phones and laptops into valuable materials for re-use. For example, from e-waste, computer circuit boards can be transformed into valuable metal alloys such as copper and tin while glass and plastic from e-devices can be converted into micro materials used in industrial grade ceramics and plastic filaments for 3D printing.

Using this technology developed after extensive scientific research at the SMaRT Centre, the e-waste micro factory has the potential to reduce the rapidly growing problem of vast amounts of electronic waste that cause environmental harm and go into landfills.

These micro factories can transform the manufacturing landscape, especially in remote locations where typically the logistics of having waste transported or processed are prohibitively expensive. This is especially beneficial for the island markets and the remote and regional regions of the country.

LAUNCHING OF FALCON HEAVY

DATE: 7th February 2018

OBJECTIVE: To test the capability of rockets for advancement in Space Technology.

Falcon Heavy, one of the most powerful rockets was launched successfully from Launch Complex 39A at Kennedy Space Center in Florida, USA. It was launched by the Space flight Company, SpaceX.

It is the most powerful operational rocket in the world by a factor of two; with the ability to lift into orbit nearly 64 metric tons with mass greater than a 737 jetliner loaded with passengers, crew, luggage and fuel. Falcon Heavy's first stage is composed of three Falcon 9 nine-engine cores whose 27 Merlin engines together generate more than 5 million pounds of thrust at liftoff, equal to approximately eighteen 747 aircraft. Only the Saturn V moon rocket, last flown in 1973, delivered more payloads to orbit.

The dummy payload comprised of a mannequin named "Starman" in personal cherry-red Tesla Roadster electric car owned by SpaceX CEO Elon Musk.

HAL DEVELOPS FIRST HAWK-I FLIGHT

DATE: 8th February, 2018

OBJECTIVE: To overcome self dependency and safety in avionics systems in India

The Hindustan Aeronautics Limited (HAL) develops the first flight of Hawk-i with indigenous Real Time Operating System (RTOS). Hawk-i is the first indigenous RTOS developed in India from scratch and certified by Centre for Military Airworthiness and Certification (CEMILAC). The RTOS is the system software which provides a standard run-time environment for real-time applications execution in a safe and reliable manner.

It is a key technology for concurrent execution of multiple applications and optimal use of hardware resources which is of paramount importance for increased complexity of modern avionics software. At present avionics systems in India are developed using commercial RTOS procured from foreign suppliers. The technology imported from abroad is highly costly, provides very limited flexibility in incorporating new features and adaptation to new hardware platforms. The imported RTOS are also vulnerable to cyber-attacks which may compromise the safety and security of the avionics system. To overcome this dependency and achieve self-reliance, the HAL had taken up the onus of designing an indigenous RTOS for safety-critical and mission-critical avionics systems.

ONGC TO INTRODUCE ASIA'S FIRST LARGE SCALE CO_2 INJECTION TECHNIQUE

DATE: 15th February, 2018

OBJECTIVE: To enhance India's energy security

State owned Oil and Natural Gas Corporation (ONGC) is planning to introduce carbon dioxide (CO_2) injection technology in its Gandhar oil field in Gujarat. CO_2 injection technology is a proven concept in the West specially the US and Canada. Under it, CO_2 gas is injected with residual oil in the ageing field in which total oil production has been declining. It reduces its viscosity and makes it easier to displace oil from the rock pores. CO_2 gas also swells oil, thereby pushing it towards the producing well for extraction. Its purpose is to recover extra 20 million barrels of crude oil under enhanced oil recovery (EOR) programme. EOR programme aims at recovering up to 20% of residual oil from ageing oil fields to improve

India's energy security. Under this project, ONGC plans to invest \$75 million in CO_2 capture and another \$200 million in injector producer network to recover an extra 15% of residual oil currently valued at \$1.36 billion. It will be operational in 20 months. ONGC is in talks with National Thermal Power Corporation (NTPC) for utilising nearly 5 million tonnes of emitted gas (CO_2) from the latter's Gandhar plant.

KERALA WILL DEPLOY ROBOTS TO CLEAN UP MANHOLES

DATE: 19th February, 2018

OBJECTIVE: To promote local talent and develop sanitation technology

Kerala Government will soon be utilising the services of Robots to clean sewer holes. A startup company, Genrobotics develops the trial runs of the robot. The product will be launched next week. The robot, equipped with Wi-Fi, Blue Tooth and control panels has four limbs and a bucket system attached to a spider web looking extension to scoop out the waste from sewers. The project is supported by KWA, which has joined hands with Kerala start up mission to transform new ideas into practical technologies for addressing issues relating to pipe leakage and sanitation. Initially, the services of the robot, christened 'Bandicoot' will be utilised in Thiruvananthapuram, which has over 5,000 manholes. The trial run of the robot, developed by the nine-member group of youngsters from varying engineering streams, had been conducted successfully in the state capital recently. The product is being fully funded by the government.

BSNL & NTT AT COLLABORATE FOR 5G TEST

DATE: 20th February 2018

OBJECTIVE: To collaborate in future technologies

The Indian Public sector telecom firm Bharat Sanchar Nigam Limited (BSNL) has entered into a tripartite agreement with NTT Advanced Technology (NTT AT) Corporation of Japan and Virgo Corp for collaboration in futuristic technologies. The MoU was signed to collaborate in futuristic technologies, which include artificial intelligence and Internet of Things (IoT). The firms will also jointly create a 5G test.

The MoU was signed in the presence of Anupam Shrivastava (CMD, BSNL); George Kimura (CEO & President, NTT AT) along with Chairman of Virgo Corp and Board members of the collaborator firms.

NTT Advance Technology Corporation is one of the Telecom leaders in Japan, while Virgo Corps is their Indian partner.

NTT Communications is the wholly-owned subsidiary of Nippon Telegraph and Telephone Corporation, one of the world's largest telecoms with listings on the Tokyo, London and New York stock exchanges. State-owned telecom firm, BSNL is one of the largest & leading public sector units providing comprehensive range of telecom services in India.

SWEDISH RESEARCHERS FIND NEW TOOL TO FIGHT CANCER

DATE: 20th February, 2018

Small molecules that specifically restrain a selenium-containing enzyme in the human body may fight cancer

Swedish scientists found in their new research that Small molecules that specifically restrain a selenium-containing enzyme in the human body may become a tool to fight cancer. The researchers effectively treated over 60 different types of cancer cells under laboratory conditions with these molecules. Selenium is a chemical element that is an essential micronutrient. A selenium-containing enzyme, called TrxR1, can be used to support the growth of various cells and protect them from oxidative stress. Oxidative stress is the imbalance between the production of free radicals, which are highly reactive with other molecules, and the body's ability to counteract or to repair the resulting damage. However, in several forms of cancer, raised levels of TrxR1 could be detected.

After analysing more than 400000 different molecules, researchers found three different types which proved to be active as anti-cancer medicines. This effectiveness against cancer may be a result of cancer cells' seemingly greater sensitivity to oxidative stress when compared to normal cells, which in turn can be utilised in cancer therapy.

DRYPETES KALAMII: NEW PLANT SPECIES FROM WEST BENGAL

DATE: 24th February, 2018

OBJECTIVE: Research on new species of plants

Scientists from the Botanical Survey of India have identified Drypetes kalamii, a new plant species from two protected National Parks in West Bengal. The plant is named after former President Abdul Kalam. It is a small shrub found to be shorter version of its close relative Drypetes ellisii. The researchers have done comparative study of new plant with other *Drypetes* species and found differences in the leaf, flower and fruit structures. There are about 220 species of *Drypetes* identified across the globe of which 20 have been reported from India. The new species is found in wet, shaded areas of subtropical moist semi-evergreen forests, at a height ranging 50-100 metres. It is unisexual 1 meter plant with pale yellow flowers in clusters and bright orange to red fruits, the plant is exclusive to the two national parks. The new species is a close relative of a medicinal plant known in Sanskrit as *Putrajivah.*

UIDAI LAUNCHES BLUE COLOURED BAL AADHAAR

DATE: 26th February, 2018

OBJECTIVE: To stop corruption in availing Government scholarships

The Unique Identification Authority of India (UIDAI) has introduced a blue coloured 'Baal Aadhaar' card for children below the age of five years. This card will be given to children below the age of 5 years. It will be given to the children without any biometric details and will be linked with one of parent's Aadhaar card number and biometric details. When the children turn 5, a mandatory verification process along with biometric update will be required and same will be repeated at the age of 15 years old. The child's school identification card can be used as identity proof for Aadhaar enrolment. Though Aadhaar is not mandatory for children of this age, it is required for those attending educational programmes overseas and availing other government scholarships. Though Aadhaar is not mandatory for children of this age, it is required for those attending educational programmes overseas and availing other government scholarships.

NEW MOBILE APP, EMERGENCY NUMBER FOR HIGHWAY USERS

DATE: 7th March, 2018

OBJECTIVE: To provide highway users with real-time data, expected wait at toll plazas and report any accident to NHAI

Union Govt. launched a mobile app 'Sukhad Yatra' along with a toll free number '1033' for the drivers and travellers of highways in India. Through this app and toll free number drivers will be able to know about the roads and their conditions and can report about any accidents or road trouble in highways. The main objective of launching the app is to facilitate the heavy motor vehicle drivers and light motor vehicle drivers. They will be able to know about the roads and time of travelling. Sukhad Yatra App is developed by the National Highway Authority of India (NHAI) and will be available for the drivers to see the road related information before starting their journey through the Highways. Any sort of information regarding Highways will be available on the app.

Govt. also launches a multi lingual 1033 toll free number for the drivers to make complaints about accidents or any other cases and to register feedbacks on highways experience. One can also call this number for ambulance in case of road accident.

DIU BECOMES INDIA'S FIRST FULLY SOLAR-POWERED UNION TERRITORY

DATE: 9th March, 2018

OBJECTIVE: To become self dependent on electricity

Diu has emerged as the first and only Union Territory to be fully run by solar power. It has made such significant progress in the last three years that now produces more than 100 per cent solar power. Diu has installed solar power plants across 50 acres out of 42 sq km of its total geographical area. Diu, with a population of 56,000, generates about 10.5 MW of electricity daily while it has a peak time demand of 7 MW only. Solar power costs low which reduces monthly expenses of the people.

Three years ago, the people of Diu consumed electricity supplied from the power grid owned by the Gujarat government resulting in huge line losses. Once the local power company started generating electricity from solar energy, the electricity loss was significantly reduced.

CISF LAUNCHES MOBILE APP FOR LOST ITEMS AT AIRPORTS

DATE: 17th March, 2018

OBJECTIVE: To place request to get lost items

The CISF launches a mobile application through which travellers can register complaints to recover items they lost or forgot at various airports. The app called 'Lost and Found' can be downloaded from the website of the Information and Technology Ministry. The main advantage of this mobile app is that the passengers can directly register complaints and get status of their complaint immediately from the airports under security cover. Mobile phone application can also be used to place a request for obtaining technical consultancy provided by the force. The Central Industrial Security Force (CISF) that provides security at 59 airports of the country has finished the trial run of the lost and found mobile application. Passengers can enter details like the date of travel or boarding pass number to trace their belongings, which CISF will deposit with the airport operator.

INNOVATION AND ENTREPRENEURSHIP FESTIVAL

DATE: 19th March 2018

OBJECTIVE: To provide a platform for innovators to build linkages with potential stakeholders whose support can improve their prospects in coming years to develop their ideas into implementable projects for the larger social good

Festival of Innovation and Entrepreneurship (FINE) was inaugurated by President Ram Nath Kovind at Rashtrapati Bhavan. The five day festival is an initiative to recognise, respect, showcase, reward the innovations and to foster a supportive ecosystem for innovators.

The festival is being organised in association with the Department of Science and Technology and the National Innovation Foundation-India. Around 250 innovative exhibits of school students, grassroots innovators, technology students, entrepreneurs, industry representatives and public sector organisations will be on display during the exhibition till March 23 at the Football Ground in the Rashtrapati Bhawan complex.

The broader aim of the festival is to provide platform for innovators for building linkages with potential stakeholders whose support can improve their prospects in coming years to develop their ideas into implementable projects for the larger social good.

The festival will also open doors to creative and innovative solutions for social development through grassroots innovations, students ideas and other technologies for agriculture, rural development, sanitation, health, women and child development, biotechnology and medical innovation for grassroots.

Roundtables will also be a crucial part of the exhibition with themes like S&T-led innovations for societal application, nurturing innovation ecosystem, role of government in scaling up and commercialization of innovations, and innovations for sustainable agriculture with special focus on Bamboo and herbal medicine, aroma, fragrance and flavours.Gandhian Young Technological Innovation (GYTI) Awards will be given on first day of the exhibition

SUCCESSFUL TEST FIRING OF BRAHMOS WITH INDIGENOUS SEEKER

DATE: 22nd March 2018

OBJECTIVE: To check the precision of BrahMos with indigenous seeker

The supersonic cruise missile, BrahMos with indigenous seeker was successfully flight tested at the Pokhran test range in Rajasthan. The supersonic cruise missile and the seeker have been developed jointly by Defence Research and Development Organisation and BrahMos Aerospace Limited.

The precision strike weapon with indigenous seeker flew in its pre-designated trajectory and hit the pre-set target with accuracy. The flight test was conducted by the scientific team from DRDO and BrahMos along with the Indian Army.

The test flight was carried out in the presence of high level team from BrahMos Aerospace and DRDO along with senior officials from Indian Army and Indian Air Force.

Dr Selvin Christopher, Chairman DRDO & Secretary DD R&D, Dr G Satheesh Reddy, Scientific Advisor to Raksha Mantri, Dr Sudhir Mishra, Director General BrahMos were present during the test flight.

BrahMos is a two-stage missile with a solid propellant booster engine as its first stage which brings it to supersonic speed and then gets separated. The liquid ramjet or the second stage then takes the missile closer to 3 Mach speed in cruise phase. The missile has flight range of up to 290-km with supersonic speed all through the flight. It works universally for multiple platforms and works on the principle of 'Fire and Forget'.

FIRST INTERNATIONAL EXHIBITION ON GRAPHIC PRINTS

DATE: 25th March 2018

OBJECTIVE: To discover new artistic trends in graphic printmaking

The Lalit Kala Akademi hosted the first-ever International Exhibition of Graphic Prints in the country. The exhibition 'Print Biennale India 2018' was inaugurated in New Delhi.

A total of 200 original prints created by *artists* of national *and international repute* were put on display during the exhibition. International artists from countries including Italy, Mexico, United States, Israel, Sweden, United Kingdom, etc. had participated in the event. 127 national level prints were selected for display from more than 900 entries received at the entry level. Shakti Burman, the eminent artist-printmaker graced the exhibition as Chief Guest. Addressing on the occasion he expressed his optimism about the regaining the popularity of Lithography with help from Lalit Kala Akademi.

The exhibition was organised keeping in view the search for discovering new artistic trends in printmaking in addition to explore new ideas in the relevant printing arena.

ISRO FORMS TEAM FOR MOON AND MARS MISSION

DATE: 28th March 2018

OBJECTIVE: To expand the scientific knowledge related to Moon and Mars

The Indian Space and Research Administration (ISRO) has started preparing for its future missions. It has formed a study team to formulate plans to explore next Moon and Mars mission.

The Mars Mission, Chandrayaan-2 is based completely on indigenous technique. It is equipped with orbiter, lander and rover configuration to observe and explore the lunar surface.

The orbiter will be placed in 100 km orbit around the Moon, while the lander will be separated from the orbiter after reaching the lunar orbit. The most important part of the lander i.e. soft landing on the lunar surface will be followed by deployment of a rover. The Rover will then move around the landing site. The lander and rover payloads will conduct observations on the elemental composition and study the lunar ionosphere.

The orbiter will continue to orbit around the Moon and will perform remote-sensing observations of surface of moon. It will study the topography of Moon, its elemental and mineralogical distribution and extent of subsurface water ice. Total expenditure on the mission is expected to be around Rs 800 Crore.

The planning for the next Mars Mission is also under progress and other details are likely to be communicated once it is finalised by the team.

GSLV LAUNCHES GSAT-6A SATELLITE

DATE: 29th March 2018

OBJECTIVE: To strengthen the communications capability of country

India's communications Satellite GSAT-6A was launched into its orbit. The launch took place from the Satish Dhawan Space Centre (SDSC) at SHAR, Sriharikota.

GSAT-6A was lifted successfully into Geosynchronous Transfer Orbit (GTO) by Geosynchronous Satellite Launch Vehicle (GSLV-F08). With this launch the GSAT-6A joins a series of satellites for multi-media and mobile applications, hosting a payload comprising five C-by-S and five S-by-C-Band transponders optimized for Satellite Digital Multimedia Broadcasting. The satellite's capacity can also be used for strategic and social applications

This also marked the fifth consecutive success achieved by GSLV carrying indigenously developed Cryogenic Upper Stage.

GSAT-6A is communications satellite which will be used for Government and military purposes. The Satellite will be commissioned into service after the successful completion of orbit raising operations and its positioning in the designated slot in Geostationary Orbit following in-orbit testing of its payloads.

SMART INDIA HACKATHON

DATE: 30th March 2018

OBJECTIVE: To identify new digital technology innovations for solving the challenges faced by country.

World's largest nation-building digital initiative Smart India Hackathon-2018 was organized by Ministry of Human Resource Development, All India Council for Technical Education, Inter Institutional Inclusive Innovation Center (i4C), and Persistent Systems.

Like its last edition Smart India Hackathon-2018 proved to be a unique initiative to identify new and disruptive digital technology innovations for solving the challenges faced by country.

The grand finale of the Smart India Hackathon-2018 (Software Edition) organized at 28 nodal centres across the country.

Altogether participation from 27 Central ministries/departments was received. Additionally 900 problem statements from 17 state governments were also included for the event. Finally 408 problems were finally selected for the Hackathon-2018.

The motive behind organizing Smart India Hackathon is to harness the creativity and energy of bright young students for the development of the nation. The younger generation showed their enthusiasm towards the event as participations crossed more than one lakh.

The HRD Ministry has engaged with Department of Science and Technology to ensure that selected teams could be supported by Technology Business Incubators as Start-ups. At least 27 projects are expected to get implemented and adopted by different departments.

RASHTRIYA SANSKRITI MAHOTSAV

DATE: 15th January 2018

OBJECTIVE: To provide platform and bring together artists from each corner of country.

- Rashtriya Sanskriti Mahotsav under the *Ek Bharat Shreshtha Bharat* programme was held in Bengaluru.

- The 7th edition of Mahotsav was inaugurated by Minister for Parliamentary Affairs Ananth Kumar in the presence of Minister of State for Culture Mahesh Sharma.

- The Rashtriya Sanskriti Mahotsav provided platform to bring together artists from each corner of country.

- Various art forms from classical and folk, music and dance, theatre to literature and visual arts were displayed during the event.

- The aim of celebrating Rashtriya Sanskriti Mahotsav is for national integration and idea of unity in diversity of India along with display of vibrant rich culture and heritage of country.

- *Ek Bharat-Shreshtha Bharat* Programme was launched by Prime Minister Narendra Modi on Ekta Diwas (31st October 2016), on the occasion of birth anniversary of Sardar Vallabhbhai Patel.

- Its objective is to strengthen cultural relations of various parts of country and to embolden mutual connection between people dwelling in different states.

- Under this programme every state/UT is paired with its partner state/UT.

106TH BIHAR DIWAS

DATE: 22nd March 2018

OBJECTIVE: To celebrate the foundation Day events of Bihar

Bihar celebrated its 106th foundation day with vice-president Venkaiah Naidu formally declaring the opening of foundation day celebrations in state capital, Patna. The three-day celebrations started with paying floral tributes to Father of the Nation. The foundation day celebrations are coinciding with closing ceremony of the Champaran Satyagrah centenary celebrations. 'Champaran Satyagrah: Centenary Year' is the theme of the state's Day celebrations. Champaran is synonymous with Satyagrah as it is the first place in India where Gandhiji made his experiments in Satyagrah and then replicated them elsewhere. It is regarded as mother of non-violent experiments of Gandhiji.

Inaugural session witnessed screening of a short documentary which was followed by release of books revolving around Gandhijee and Champaran Satyagrah. The titles of the books were 'Ek Tha Mohan', 'Bapu Ki Chiththi', 'Champaran Ki Kahani' and 'Neel Ke Dhabbe'.

The foundation day celebrations were organized at Gandhi Maidan, Sri Krishna Memorial Hall and Rabindra Bhawan.

Governor Satya Pal Malik, Chief Minister Nitish Kumar, Deputy CM Sushil Kumar Modi and other dignitaries were present at the main event.

The Bihar day celebrations are regularly organized since 2012 to mark the foundation of state. Bihar was carved out from undivided Bengal as an independent state in 1912.

8ᵗʰ THEATRE OLYMPICS

DATE: 8ᵗʰ April 2018

OBJECTIVE: To provide a platform for theatrical exchange

The 8ᵗʰ edition of the Theatre Olympics concluded in Mumbai. It was the biggest international theatre festival held in India for the first time.

The 8ᵗʰ Theatre Olympics was inaugurated in February 2018 in New Delhi. The event was organised by National School of Drama under the aegis of Ministry of Culture, Government of India based on theme "The Flag of Friendship", which brought together around 25,000 artists under the theme.

The event which ran for 51 days across 17 Indian cities witnessed 450 shows from more than 30 countries. Closing event was a display of rich culture as more than 400 artists from different parts of country performed.

The Theatre Olympics was established in 1993 in Delphi (Greece), on the initiative of the famous Greek theatre director, Theodoros Terzopoulos. Delphi hosted the first theatre Olympics in 1995, while at Wrocław (Poland) 7ᵗʰ edition of the event was organised.

NEW ADDITIONS TO UNESCO'S WORLD HERITAGE SITES

DATE: 30ᵗʰ June 2018

OBJECTIVE: To preserve the world's cultural and natural heritage

UNESCO has added new sites to its list of world heritage sites. The announcement was made at ongoing meeting which is scheduled to add more world heritage site as part of its annual meeting in Bahrain.

The new world heritage sites include Aasivissuit-Nipisat (Denmark), Archaeological Border Complex of Hedeby and the Danevirke (Germany) and Victorian Gothic and Art Deco Ensembles of Mumbai (India) among others.

The decision was taken at the 42nd session of the World Heritage Committee of UNESCO, which has been meeting in Manama since June 24. The list also includes eight pre-Islamic sites in Iran, seven ancient Korean mountain Buddhist temples and old Christian sites in Japan.

Victorian and Art Deco Ensembles of Mumbai have been inscribed on UNESCO's World Heritage list from India. The Ensemble comprises of two architectural styles, the 19th century collection of Victorian structures and the 20th century Art Deco buildings along the sea, conjoined by means of the historical open space of the Oval Maidan.

Aasivissuit-Nipisat- The Inuit Hunting Ground between Ice and Sea in Denmark is located inside the Arctic Circle in the central part of West Greenland and contains the remains of 4,200 years of human history.

Archaeological Border Complex of Hedeby and the Danevirke in Germany consists of the remains of a trading town - containing traces of roads, buildings, cemeteries and a harbour dating back to the 1st and early 2nd millennia CE.

VIDARBHA WINS 2017 RANJI TROPHY

DATE: 1st January, 2018

Vidarbha cricket team won 2017 Ranji Trophy tournament. It is Vidarbha's first Ranji Trophy title. Until 2017, Vidarbha had never won a single Ranji Trophy in the 84-year long history of the tournament. But come the first day of 2018, that record changed for good as Vidarbha won the title after beating Delhi by nine wickets at Indore's Holkar stadium. Last year, it was Gujarat which won their maiden Ranji title and now it is Vidarbha that continue this exceptional trend of first time winners. En route their title-winning campaign, Vidarbha blew away seasoned former Ranji champions like Punjab (1 title), Bengal (2 titles), Delhi (7 titles) and Karnataka (8 titles).

Quick Facts about Ranji Trophy:
* Format – First Class Cricket
* First tournament held in – 1934
* Administrator – Board of Control for Cricket in India (BCCI)

ICC UNDER-19 WORLD CUP

DATE: 13th January, 2018

The ICC Under-19 world cup cricket tournament will begin on 13th January in New Zealand. Altogether 16 teams representing different countries including defending champion West Indies and last year runner-up India will participate in the event. The first Under-19 world cup was played in 1988 in Australia and then discontinued for 10 years. This biennial event is held since 1998 on a regular basis.

Three time U-19 champions, India will try to aim for their record 4th world cup under the captaincy of Prithvi Shaw and Coach Rahul Dravid.

This 22-day cricket extravaganza will be played across seven venues in the cities of Christchurch, Queenstown, Tauranga and Whangarei and the final will be played in Bay Oval, Mount Maunganui on 3rd February 2018.

AUSTRALIAN OPEN TOURNAMENT

DATE: 14th January 2018

AGENDA/ISSUE: To declare Champions in different events at the tournament

Target/ Application: The first grand slam of the 2018 session will start from 15th January at Melbourne. It will be played at Melbourne Park during 15-28 January 2018. It marks the 106th edition of the Australian Open of all-time, 50th edition of the tournament in the Open Era and the 200th overall Grand Slam event of the Open Era. The tournament consists of events for professional players in singles, doubles and mixed doubles play. Junior and wheelchair players compete in singles and doubles tournaments.

Serena Williams and Roger Federer are the defending champion in the women's and Men's singles event respectively.

 India's Yuki Bhambri will be India's sole representative in Single's event. While in Double's event Veteran Leander Pae will play with his partner Purav Raja, while Rohan Bopanna will team up with É. Roger-Vasselin.

ICC MEN'S CRICKET AWARDS

DATE: 18th January 2018

Virat Kohli declared as the winner of the Sir Garfield Sobers Trophy at the 2017 ICC Awards for the overall World Cricketer (Men's) of the Year. It was a double bonus for the Indian Captain as he also named as ICC ODI Player of the Year.

Steve Smith (Australia) was named Test Cricketer of the Year, while Yuzvendra Chahal (India) bagged the award for T20I Performance of the Year. Anya Shrubsole (England) won the ICC Spirit of Cricket award. David Shepherd Trophy for ICC Umpire of the year won by Marais Erasmus (South Africa).

Kohli dominated the awards as he was selected as captain in both Test and ODI teams of the year by ICC. In the qualification period from 21 September 2016 to the end of 2017, Kohli scored 2,203 Test runs (avg. 77.8) including 8 centuries, 1,818 ODI runs (avg. 82.6) including 7 centuries and 299 T-20I runs at a strike rate of 153.

The performance of David Warner (Australia) and Quinton de Kock (South Africa) in both the older formats of game was recognized and they were selected in ICC Test as well as ODI team. The ICC Test team also comprises Cheteshwar Pujara and R. Ashwin while Rohit Sharma and Jasprit Bumrah found a place in ODI team. Last year's winner of Sir Garfield Sobers Trophy was Ravichandran Ashwin.

INDIA LIFTS BLIND CRICKET WORLD CUP

DATE: 21st January 2018

OBJECTIVE: To promote cricket among visually impaired

India declared winner of the 5th Blind Cricket World cup in Sharjah (UAE). Defending champions India defeated arch-rivals and co-host Pakistan by 2 wickets in a thrilling final to retain the Blind Cricket World Cup.

It was like a replica of 4th Blind World Cup final played in Cape Town (South Africa, 2014), in which Pakistan faced defeat by India.

The World cup was jointly organized by Pakistan and United Arab Emirates. India, Pakistan, Sri Lanka, Bangladesh, Australia and Nepal were qualified to play in the tournament. Earlier Blind World Cups were held in Cape Town (2014), Islamabad (2006), Chennai (2002) and New Delhi (1998). South Africa (1998), Pakistan (2002 & 2006) and India (2014) are the previous world champions.

KHELO INDIA SCHOOL GAMES

DATE: 31st January 2018

OBJECTIVE: To provide a platform for budding sportspersons to showcase their best talent.

Prime Minister Narendra Modi declared the first edition of the Khelo India School Games (KISG) open, at the Indira Gandhi Indoor Stadium in New Delhi.

PM gave emphasis on importance of sports in the lives of youth and sports as means of personality development.

The KISG is being held across 16 disciplines in the U-17 category and 5,000 school children from 29 states and 7 UTs are participating in the event. It will conclude on 8th Feb. 2018. The best talent selected through the competition will be amongst the 1000 budding athletes eligible for a scholarship worth 5 lakhs each per year for a period of 8 years. Every year, new athletes will be added under the Khelo India scheme. Thus, over the period of the scheme, the country will have a solid bench-strength for all sports.

The games are being conducted at par with international level competitions so as to give the best experience to players and other stakeholders. The format of the game is providing an opportunity for the State/UTs to compete against each other. It also provided a platform to showcase their best budding sporting talent.

Anu Kumar of Uttarakhand grabbed the 1st gold medal of the Games, as Tamil Nadu won 2 of 6 gold medals on offer on the first day of the athletics extravaganza.

AUSTRALIAN OPEN

DATE: 29th January 2018

Roger Federer defeated Marin Cilic to win the Men's single at Australian Open Tennis Tournament. In womens' single, Caroline Wozniacki became the first Danish player to win a Grand Slam singles title, defeating Simona Halep in the final.

This was Roger Federer's record 20th grand slam title. He overcame the Croatian 6-2 6-7 6-3 3-6 6-1 and defended his title at Melbourne Park. The Maestro became the oldest Australian Open winner (at age 36) since Ken Rosewall (age 37) in 1972.

Federer is the first man in history to break the teen barrier and win 20 majors, doing so in his 30th grand slam final. He also equalled the record for most Australian Open crowns with six, sitting alongside Novak Djokovic and Roy Emerson.

Rohan Bopanna of India could not increase his number of Grand Slam Mixed Doubles titles as he was defeated in a thrilling final by Gabriela Dabrowski (Canada) and Mate Pavic (Croatia). His teammate was Timea Babos of Hungary. The Pair of Oliver Marach (Austria) and Mate Pavic (Croatia) won the Men's Doubles title while Kristina Mladenovic (France) Timea Babos (Hungary) clinched the Women's Doubles title.

KERALA LIFTS SANTOSH TROPHY

DATE: 1ˢᵗ April 2018

Kerala beat West Bengal in the final of Santosh Trophy Football Tournament. The winning team claimed its sixth Santosh Trophy title at the Salt Lake Stadium, Kolkata.

32 times champion and defending champion West Bengal could not score enough to beat Kerala in the keenly-contested final which resulted in a tie-breaker as match remain undecided after extra time. In the penalty shoot-out Kerala scored perfectly to keep their score to 4 while Bengal strikers could not get past keeper V. Midhun on two occasions and can score only twice.

The Satheevan Balan, head coach of Kerala team tasted the santosh title victory after a gap of 14 years. Kerala lifted their earlier Santosh Trophy title in October 2004 beating Punjab.

Santosh Trophy is an Indian football tournament. In this annual domestic tournament different Indian states and some government institutions participate. In the inaugural year in 1941, Bengal was declared as the winner.

XXI COMMONWEALTH GAMES

DATE: 4ᵗʰ April 2018

The XXI Commonwealth Games inaugurated in Gold Coast, Australia. The Venue of the Opening Ceremony was Carrara Stadium. The Opening Ceremony began with musical final countdown followed by the official sports protocol and the finale which witnessed a mixture of musical and dance performances.

Around 35,000 spectators in the stadium and around 1.5 billion television viewers worldwide witnessed the ceremony which displayed the rich Australian tradition and culture.

P.V. Sindhu led the Indian contingent during the Opening Ceremony.

Going on with the tradition of Commonwealth Games the event began with the arrival of Head of Commonwealth which was represented with Prince Charles, Prince of Wales along with his wife Camilla, Duchess of Cornwall arrive during the Opening Ceremony

Gold Coast 2018 is unique in the history of a major multi-sport Games as it is the first time there will be an equal number of medal events for men and women.

'Borobi' is officially named as the mascot of the 2018 Commonwealth Games which will formally conclude on 15ᵗʰ April.

Gold coast is the fifth Australian city to host the Commonwealth Games following Sydney (1938), Perth (1962), Brisbane (1982) and Melbourne (2006).

The Commonwealth is a collective of diverse nations spread across every continent and ocean and makes up to 30% of the world's population.

The Commonwealth Games have been conducted by the Commonwealth Games Federation and held at an interval of every four years. Since the first British Empire Games were held in Hamilton (Canada, 1930) the Games have grown from an event featuring 11 countries and 400 athletes to a sporting extravaganza with 71 nations and territories and over 6,600 athletes and team officials.

SENIOR NATIONAL TT CHAMPIONSHIP

DATE: 1st February 2018

OBJECTIVE: To declare winners of different categories in the tournament

Suthirta Mukehrjee and Achanta Sharath Kamal win the National Singles Table Tennis title in Women's and Men's category respectively. A. Sharath Kamal (PSPB) beat top-seeded Anthony Amalraj (PSPB) to win the National Men's Singles title for the record eighth time. He equaled the feat of Kamlesh Mehta in the 79th edition of the Senior Nationals at the Mega Sports Complex in Ranchi.

Suthirta Mukehrjee from West Bengal emerged the new women champion, beating last year winner Manika Batra (PSPB).

In women's doubles final, the West Bengal duo of Krittwika Sinha Roy and Mousumi Paul defeated the PSPB combine of Mouma Das and Archana Kamath, while in Men's Doubles final Soumyajit Ghosh and Jubin Kumar of Haryana beat Mohit Verma and Sourav Saha (Haryana). In the Mixed Doubles final, RBI's Raj Mondal and Akula Sreeja beat North Bengal's Akaash Nath and Ankita Das to claim the Gold.

Sharath Kamal also led PSPB to the Men's team title Championship, while Manika Batra contributed immensely for the PSPB to grab Women's team Championship.

INDIAN OPEN INTERNATIONAL BOXING TOURNAMENT

DATE: 1st February 2018

OBJECTIVE: To promote Boxing and declare winners at each category

Mary Kom, Pwilao Basumatary and Manish Kaushik won Gold Medals in the inaugural India Open International Boxing Tournament. The tournament for senior men and women was held in New Delhi from January 28 to February 1, 2018.

Mary Kom won against Filipino Josie in the 48kg class among women, while Pwilao Basumatary defeated Sudaporn Seesondee of Thailand in 64kg category. National champion Manish Kaushik (60kg) was given a walkover by his Mongolian rival Battumur Misheelt. Other Indian Gold Medalists were Lovlina Borgohain (69kg) and Sanjeet (91kg).

Asian Games bronze-medalist Satish Kumar (+91kg), lost to Uzbekistan's Bakhodir and won silver Medal. Dinesh Dagar (69kg), Devanshu Jaiswal (81kg), Pooja (69kg), L. Sarita Devi (60kg) and Saweety Boora (75kg), all settled with silver.

The India Open acted as the perfect stage for the Commonwealth Games preparation as Indian pugilists competed against world class boxers from more than 20 countries including Cuba, Uzbekistan, Kazakhstan and Russia.

In this USD 100,000 event, every Gold-medalist received USD 2500, while the Silver and Bronze medalists bagged USD 1000 and USD 500 respectively.

INDIA LIFTS U-19 CRICKET WORLD CUP

DATE: 3rd February 2018

OBJECTIVE: To promote cricket among youngsters & declare the winner of the tournament

Last year runner-up India defeated Australia in the final and emerged as winner of ICC Under-19 Cricket World Cup. Indian team chased Australia's 217 comfortably as Manjot Kalra contributed to the team's victory with an unbeaten century.

Manjot was named Man of the Match while other Indian Shubman Gill was declared Man of the Tournament.

This was record 4th world cup title for the Indian Team and they become the first team to win the trophy maximum time. Indian team played under the captaincy of Prithvi Shaw and Coach Rahul Dravid.

One of the semifinalists of the tournament, Pakistan finished at third position.

This 22-day cricket championship was played across seven venues in the cities of Christchurch, Queenstown, Tauranga and Whangarei with the final at Bay Oval, Mount Maunganui in New Zealand.

Total 16 teams participated in the tournament, including defending champion West Indies. The first Under-19 world cup was played in 1988 in Australia and then discontinued for 10 years. This biennial event is held since 1998 on a regular basis. South Africa will host the next edition of the world cup.

KHELO INDIA SCHOOL GAMES

DATE: 8th February 2018

OBJECTIVE: To provide a platform for budding sportspersons to showcase their best talent.

The first edition of the Khelo India School Games (KISG) was concluded in New Delhi. This National level multidisciplinary grassroots games were started with the aim to prepare children under-17 age group for the future international sporting events.

In the first edition of KISG, Haryana topped the Medal Rally with 108 medals including 38 Golds, 26 Silver and 38 Bronze. Maharashtra (110 Medals including 36 Golds) and Delhi (94 Medals including 25 Golds) bagged the second and third position respectively.

The KISG was held across 16 disciplines in the U-17 category and more than 3000 school children from 29 states and 7 Union Territories participated in this mega event. The best talent selected through the competition will be amongst the 1000 budding athletes eligible for a scholarship worth 5 lakhs each per year for a period of 8 years. Among these 1000 athletes, 562 will be selected from the Games themselves with 438 to be picked from various centres and sporting hotbeds across the country. It is anticipated that the entire scholarship amount would not be transferred to the athlete directly and only Rs. 1.5 lakh is being directly transferred and the rest will be available for reimbursement or expenses on gear, training etc.

Every year, new athletes will be added under the Khelo India scheme. Thus, over the period of the scheme, the country will have a solid bench-strength for all sports.

XXIII OLYMPIC WINTER GAMES

DATE: 9th February 2018

OBJECTIVE: To promote winter sports and encourage competition amongst sportspersons

The XXIII Olympic Winter Games inaugurated in Pyeongchang, South Korea. The Opening Ceremony was held at the PyeongChang Olympic Plaza. The Musical Ceremony titled "Peace in Motion" was delivered to the spectators. The honour of lighting of the Olympic Cauldron was given to Yuna Kim, the Gold Medalist from the 2010 Vancouver Olympics.

Shiva Kesavan and Jagdish Singh are Indian representatives at the Game. They will compete in Cross country Skiing and Luge respectively.

The mascot of the event, Soohorang, evolved from his cute and loveable self and transformed into a magnificent white tiger, taking centre stage at the stadium. The traditional Parade of Athletes started with Greece with other delegations, following in alphabetical order according to the Korean alphabet. The name of each country, written in Hangeul, flashed around the LED screens on the stadium, accompanied by each NOC's flag. This was truly a special moment for the athletes marching.

Around 35,000 people braved the cold to watch the ceremony, which also witnessed North and South Korean athletes marching together under the same flag for the first time. The cost of the Winter Olympics is set to reach over $10 billion, and it looks like it might be one of the coldest Games ever, with below-freezing temperatures and 35mph winds.

BID ADIEU TO THE PYEONGCHANG 2018

DATE: 25th February 2018

OBJECTIVE: To promote winter sports and encourage competition amongst Sportspersons

The XXIII Olympic Winter Games concluded in Pyeongchang, South Korea. It marked the musical culmination of the wonderful celebration of sports and community that has been part of PyeongChang Winter Games for last 17 days.

The closing Ceremony showcased not only the contemporary and traditional arts of Korea but also witnessed 'performances' by drones. The Intel drones made a welcome appearance during the ceremony, displaying shape of a giant 'Soohorang' to a love heart. Athletes and spectators also enjoyed LED shell of aerial shots of the 'Sashindo'; 'mighty towers of the Pagoda'.

The main attraction of opening ceremony- the storytellers -'children of Gangneung' returned to show the way to the future in saying goodbye to PyeongChang 2018. The crowd stepped into the party mood when CL and EXO performed. K-Pop sensation performed her biggest hits such as "The Baddest Female" and 2NE1's "I Am The Best" while EXO sang and danced on mega-hits "Growl" and "Power".

Norway, Germany and Canada emerged as the top three countries in the Medal tally. Johannes Hoesflot Klaebo, Martin Fourcade and Marit Bjoergen became the top rankers in the multi medallist category.

Thomas Bach, IOC President awarded the Olympic Order in Gold to PyeongChang 2018 Organising Committee (POCOG) President Hee-beom Lee.

Olympic flame was extinguished as "snow" fell on the cauldron and finally the Olympic flag was officially lowered and replaced with that of the next Winter Olympics host China (Beijing).

KARNATAKA LIFTS VIJAY HAZARE TROPHY

DATE: 27th February 2018

OBJECTIVE: To promote the domestic cricket in India

Karnataka beat Saurashtra to win the Vijay Hazare Trophy title at the Ferozeshah Kotla in Delhi. Brilliant performances by Karnataka Opener Mayank Agarwal, batsman Pavan Deshpande and off spinner Krishnappa Gowtham paved the way for Karnataka to clinch the Vijay Hazare Trophy for the third time. Karnataka emerged as the winner of Vijay Hazare in 2013-14 and 2014-15.

The Karun Nair-led side beat the Cheteshwar Pujara-led Saurashtra by 41 runs in the final thanks to the overall team performance. The captain of the losing side waged a lone battle of 94 runs as compared to null by the winning captain. Kamlesh Makvana of the Saurashtra clinched four wickets.

The Vijay Hazare Trophy was started in 2002–03 as 50-overs, domestic cricket tournament involving zonal teams from the Ranji Trophy plates. It is named after Former Indian Captain Vijay Samuel Hazare. He was among the first cricketers to be honoured with Padma Shri and also led India to its first ever Test cricket win against England.

SULTAN AZLAN SHAH CUP HOCKEY TOURNAMENT 2018

Date: 3rd March 2018

OBJECTIVE: To encourage international hockey and to train young hockey players

The Sultan Azlan Shah Cup is the 27th edition of the hockey tournament which will be held in Ipoh, Perak, Malaysia from 3 to 10 March 2018.

The number of teams will be the same as the last year equalling to six. However, Japan and New Zealand which were a part of tournament last year are replaced by Argentina and Ireland.

The six participating countries are World No. 1 Australia, Rio Olympics champions Argentina, defending champions England, Ireland and hosts Malaysia, besides India.

The match can be seen live on Star Sports 1 channel or using live streaming on www.Hotstar.com.

The tournament will be played in the round-robin format where each team plays the other once and the top two at the end of the league stage will qualify for the final.

The tournament is considered to be one of the best international grooming grounds for youngsters. The match will have its finals on 10th March with the winning team lifting the prestigious trophy.

SANGEET NATAK AKADEMI AWARDS

DATE: 17th January 2018

OBJECTIVE: To recognize sustained individual work and contribution in the field of performing arts

- Sangeet Natak Akademi Fellowships and Awards for year 2016 were presented by President Ram Nath Kovind to eminent artists and scholars of performing arts in a function held at the Rashtrapati Bhavan.
- Arvind Parikh, R Vedavalli, Ram Gopal Bajaj and Sunil Kothari were conferred with fellowships (*Akademi Ratna*) of the Sangeet Natak Akademi. Additionally, 43 more artists received the Akademi Awards (*Akademi Puraskar*).
- Some of the notable awardees include-

  Padma Talwalkar (Hindustani Vocal Music), Geeta Chandran (Bharatanatyam), Kusum Kumar (Playwriting), Braj Kishor Dubey and Yogesh Gadhavi (Folk Music), Prabhitangsu Das and Dattatreya Aralikatte (Puppetry), Mohan Joshi (Acting), Avinash Pasricha and Pappu Venugopal Rao (Overall Contribution/ Scholarship in the Performing Arts).
- The Akademi fellowship is the most prestigious and rare honour which is restricted to 40 numbers at any given period of time.
- The honour of Akademi Awards and Fellowship has been conferred since 1952 and 1954 respectively.
- These honours not only symbolise the highest standard of excellence and achievement, but also recognise sustained individual work and contribution.

FILMFARE AWARDS

DATE: 22nd January 2018

OBJECTIVE: To honour artistic and technical excellence of professionals of Indian film Industry

Veteran Bollywood actress Mala Sinha and music composer Bappi Lahiri received the Lifetime Achievement Award at the 63rd Filmfare Awards.

Hindi Medium and Newton were declared as the Best Film and Critics' Award for Best Film respectively. Vidya Balan (Tumhari Sulu) and Irrfan Khan received the award for Best Actor in a Leading Role Female/Male respectively. Best Actor in a Supporting Role was bagged by Meher Vij (Female-Secret Superstar) and Rajkummar Rao (Male-Bareilly Ki Barfi). Ashwiny Iyer Tiwari (Bareilly Ki Barfi) and Konkona Sensharma (A Death in the Gunj) received the award for Best Director and Best Debut Director respectively. Amit Masurkar was declared the winner of Best Original Story award for the movie Newton. Pritam was declared the winner of best background score as well as Best Music Album both for Jagga Jasoos. Best Playback Singer in Female/Male category was received by Meghna Mishra (Nachdi phira- Secret Superstar) and Arijit Singh (Roke na ruke naina - Badrinath Ki Dulhania) respectively. Amitabh Bhattacharya declared as best lyricist (Galti se mistake- Jagga Jasoos). Critics' Award for Best Actor (Male) was received by Rajkummar Rao for 'Trapped' while Zaira Wasim declared winner in Female category for Secret Superstar.

NATIONAL BRAVERY AWARDS

DATE: 24th January 2018

OBJECTIVE: To honour children with exemplary courage under highly adverse circumstances

Prime Minister Narendra Modi presented the National Bravery Awards to 18 children including three posthumously

Kumari Nazia (Uttar Pradesh) was awarded the Bharat Award, Kumari Netravati M Chavan (posthumously) from Karnataka, Loukrakpam Rajeshwori Chanu (posthumous) of Manipur and Lalchhandama (posthumous) of Mizoram awarded with Geeta Chopra Award. Sanjay Chopra Award was awarded to Karanbeer Singh (Punjab). Mamata Dalai (Odisha), Betshwajohn Peinlang (Meghalaya) and Sebastian Vincent (Kerala) has won the Bapu Gaidhani award.

The other recipients are Mansha N, N. Shangpon Konyak, Yoaknei, Chingai Wangsa (all from Nagaland), Zonuntluanga (Mizoram), Laxmi Yadav (Chattisgarh), Samridhi Sushil Sharma (Gujarat), Pankaj Semwal (Uttarakhand), Nadaf Ejaj Abdul Rauf (Maharashtra), Pankaj Kumar Mahanta (Odisha).

 First announced in 1957, the Bravery Awards have so far been given to 680 boys and 283 girls. The awards carry a medal, a certificate and a cash prize. Eligible awardees are also granted financial assistance until they finish school. The awards are divided into five categories - Bharat Award, Geeta Chopra Award, Sanjay Chopra Award, Bapu Gaidhani Award, and General National Bravery Awards.

PADMA AWARDS

DATE: 25th January 2018

OBJECTIVE: To recognize distinguished personalities in various disciplines

President of India has approved conferment of 85 Padma Awards for this year. The list comprises 3 Padma Vibhushan, 9 Padma Bhushan and 73 Padma Shri Awards. The list also includes 16 persons from NRI/PIO/OCI/foreigners category, 14 women and 3 posthumous awardees.

India's second most civilian award Padma Vibhushan will be awarded to music maestro Ilaiyaraaja, noted musician Ghulam Mustafa Khan and Scholar Parameswaran Parameswaran. Padma Bhusan awadees are Mahendra Singh Dhoni, Sharda Sinha, Pankaj Advani, Philipose Mar Chrysostom, Alexander Kadakin (Posthumous), Ramachandran Nagaswamy, Ved Prakash Nanda, Laxman Pai and Arvind Parikh.

Some of Padma shri awardees are Prafulla Govinda Baruah, Saikhom Mirabai Chanu, Somdev Devvarman, Anwar Jalalpuri (Posthumous), Manoj Joshi, Manas Bihari Verma, Doddarange Gowda, Digamber Hansda, Ramli Bin Ibrahim , Jose Ma Joey Concepcion III , Nouf Marwaa.

The Awards are given in various disciplines activities like art, social work, public affairs, science and engineering, trade and industry, medicine, literature and education, sports, civil service, etc. 'Padma Vibhushan' is awarded for exceptional and distinguished service; 'Padma Bhushan' for distinguished service of high order and 'Padma Shri' for distinguished service in any field. The awards are announced on the occasion of Republic Day.

These awards are conferred by the President at ceremonial functions at Rashtrapati Bhawan around March/ April every year.

GALLANTRY AWARDS

DATE: 25th January 2018

OBJECTIVE: To honour heroes of the armed and Paramilitary forces of the country

President approved 390 gallantry awards and other Defence decorations for the Armed Forces personnel and others on the 69th Republic Day.

The awards include 1 Ashok Chakra, 1 Kirti Chakra, 14 Shaurya Chakras and 28 Param Vishisht Seva Medals among others.

Corporal Jyoti Prakash Nirala of Indian Air Force has been conferred the Ashok Chakra posthumously. Corporal Nirala, a Garud commando of the Air Force martyred fighting terrorists in Bandipora of Jammu and Kashmir in November.

Kirti Chakra has been awarded to Major Vijayant Bisht of the Army, while Sergeant Milind Kishor Khairnar and Corporal Nilesh Nayan have been posthumously conferred the Shaurya Chakra for their supreme sacrifice in fighting against terrorists.

The Ashok Chakra is the highest peacetime military decoration followed by Kirti Chakra and the Shaurya Chakra.

Government also announced winners of the 19 Param Vashishtha Seva medal, 4 Uttam Yudh seva medals, 49 Ati Vishisht Seva Medals, 10 Yudh Seva Medals, two Bar to Sena Medals (Gallantry), 86 Sena Medals (Gallantry), one Nao Sena Medal (Gallantry), three Vayu Sena Medals (Gallantry), two Bar to Sena Medals (Devotion to Duty), 38 Sena Medals (Devotion to Duty), 13 Nao Sena Medals (Devotion to Duty), 14 Vayu Sena Medals (Devotion to Duty), one Bar to Vishisht Seva Medal and 121 Vishisht Seva Medals in addition to numerous other decorations to honour heroes of the armed and paramilitary forces of the country.

PRIME MINISTER SHRAM AWARDS

DATE: 26th January 2018

OBJECTIVE: To recognize workers for their distinguished performances, innovative abilities in the field of productivity

Prime Minister Shram Awards for the year 2016 have been announced. Total 50 workers have been selected for the awards including 34 workers from PSUs and 16 workers from Private Sectors. As per announcement by the Ministry of Labour & Employment 12 workers from SAIL, BHEL and TATA Steel Ltd. were selected for the Shram Bhushan Awards, while 18 workers from Naval Dockyard, Ordnance Factory, Rashtriya Ispat Nigam, TATA Steel, Engine Factory, Hindalco Industries, Brahmos Aerospace, Paradeep Phosphates Ltd. and SAIL were selected for Shram Vir/Shram Veerangana Award. 20 workers from Cement Corporation of India, Naval Ship Repair Yard, TATA Steel, TATA Motors, Surat Lignite Power Plant, L & T Ltd., BHEL, SAIL, BEML Ltd., Rashtriya Ispat Nigam and Hindalco Industries were selected for Shram Shree/Shram Devi Awards.

 Prime Minister Shram Awards were instituted in 1985. These awards are given to workers in PSUs, Departmental Undertakings of Central/State Governments and Private Sector units employing 500 or more workers. These awards are announced every year by Ministry of Labour and Employment and awarded to workers for recognition of their distinguished performances, innovative abilities, outstanding contribution in the field of productivity and exhibition of exceptional courage and presence of mind.

Shram Ratna: ₹ 2 lakhs and a 'Sanad'. Shram Bhushan Awards carries a cash award of ₹ 1 lakh and a 'Sanad'. Shram Vir/Shram Veerangana Awards carries a cash award of ₹ 60,000 and a 'Sanad', while shram shree/shram Devi Awards carries a cash award of ₹ 40,000 and a 'sanad'.

PROF. ROBERT LANGLANDS RECEIVES THE ABEL PRIZE

DATE: 26th March 2018

Professor Robert Phelan Langlands has been awarded the Prestigious Abel Prize for his contributions in the field of Mathematics. The American-Canadian Prof. Langlands suggested deep links between theories which had previously been considered as unrelated- the number theory and harmonic analysis.

His proposed mechanism is studied as Langlands program and it has enlisted hundreds of the world's best mathematicians over the last five decades.

He will receive the Prize from King Harald V at an award ceremony in Oslo on 22 May.

The Abel Prize is one of the most recognized awards in the field of Mathematics and popularly known as Mathematics Nobel. It was established by the Norwegian Government on the occasion of the 200th anniversary of Niels Henrik Abel's birth in 2002. The Abel Prize recognizes contributions to the field of mathematics that are of extraordinary depth and influence.

The Norwegian Academy of Science and Letters awards the Abel Prize based on a recommendation from the Abel committee. The prize carries a cash award of 6 million Norwegian Krone and has been awarded annually since 2003. The Abel Prize Laureates list includes all the great Mathematicians like Yves Miller, John Nash, Endre Szemeredi and S R Srinivasa Varadhan to name a few.

65TH NATIONAL FILM AWARDS

DATE: 13th April 2018

OBJECTIVE: To honour artistic and technical excellence of Indian film Industry

The jury headed by renowned filmmaker Shekhar Kapur announced the 65th National Film Awards. Veteran Bollywood actor Vinod Khanna is chosen for Prestigious Dada Saheb Phalke Award (posthumous)

Village Rockstars (Assamese) and Baahubali-The conclusion were declared as the Best Film and Best Popular Film respectively. The Nargis Dutt Award for Best Feature Film on National Integration went to the Marathi film Dhappa, while the Malayalam film Aalorukkam was recognised as the Best Film on Social Issues. Jayaraj (Bhayanakam) and Pampally (Sinjar) received the award for Best Director and Indira Gandhi Award for Best Debut film of a Director respectively.

Late film actor Sridevi (Mom) and Bengali artist Ridhhi Sen (Nagar Kirtan) awarded in the category of Best Actress and Best Actor respectively. Best Actress award in a Supporting Role is bagged by Divya Dutta (Irada). Fahad Faazil is honoured with Best Actor in a Supporting Role (Thondimuthalum Driksakshiyum).

K. J. Yesudas was recognised as the Best Male Singer for his song 'Poy Maranja Kalam' in the Malayalam film Viswasapoorvam Mansoor, while the award for Best Female Singer went to Shashaa Tirupati for the song 'Vaan' in Tamil film Kaatru Veliyidai.

Rima Das's Assamese film Village Rockstars also received the awards for Best Location, Sound Recordist, Editing, and Best Child Artiste (Bhanita Das).

 Malayalam film Bhayanakam also secured award for Best Screenplay (adapted) for Jayaraj and Best Cinematography for Nikhil S. Praveen.

Oscar Awardee AR Rahman bagged the Best Music Director award for Kaatru Veliyidai and also won the Best Background Score award for the film 'Mom.'

The 10-member panel for film awards comprises Imtiaz Hussain, Mehboob, Gautami Tadimalla, P Sheshadri, Aniruddha Roy Chowdhury, Ranjit Das, Rajesh Mapuskar, Tripurari Sharma and Rumi Jaffrey.

MANAGING INDIA AWARD

DATE: 19th April, 2018

Indu Jain receives annual Managing India Award

AIMA, which recognises achievers who have made a fundamental difference to society through its annual Managing India Awards, conferred on Indu Jain the award for managing the Times Group. The Times Foundation had been doing a lot of work towards implementation of government schemes.

BACKGROUND: Indu Jain is Chairperson of The Times Group. The Times Foundation runs Community Services, Research Foundation and Times Relief Fund for disaster reliefs like floods, cyclones, earthquakes and epidemics.

Indu Jain is also founder President of the Ladies wing of FICCI (FLO (March 2017). She is also the Chairperson of the Bharatiya Jnanpith Trust which awards India's most prestigious and highest literary award, the Jnanpith award and supports endeavours.

MITHALI RAJ CONFERRED WITH THE 'SPORTSPERSON OF THE YEAR' AWARD

Indian women's cricket team captain Mithali Raj was adjudged 'Sportsperson of the Year' while ace shuttlers Kidambi Srikanth and P V Sindhu bagged the best senior male and female athletes at the Telangana Sports Journalists Association annual awards for 2017.

Former BCCI president N Shivlal Yadav gave away the 'best senior male athlete' award to Srikanth while tennis star Sania Mirza presented the 'best senior female athlete' award to Sindhu.

Former Indian cricketer V V S Laxman presented 'best coach of the year' award to Gopichand, who received this award for second time in a row. Triple Olympian and former national hockey player N Mukesh Kumar was honoured with the Lifetime Achievement award at the event.

MS DHONI CONFERRED WITH PADMA BHUSHAN AWARD

MS Dhoni added yet another jewel to his crown after being conferred with the prestigious Padma Bhushan Award at the Rashtrapati Bhawan. Dhoni, who is the most successful Indian captain, is the only skipper to win all the ICC trophies- ICC Cricket World Cup, World Twenty20 and the Champions Trophy. In Test cricket, he helped India achieve numero uno status in 2009. MS Dhoni announced his retirement from Test cricket in 2014. Later in 2017, he relinquished his captaincy in ODI cricket. Dhoni has won numerous accolades in his career. He was awarded the Rajiv Gandhi Khel Ratna award in 2007. He also holds the distinction of being the first player to win the ICC ODI Player of the Year award twice (2008, 2009).

Along with MS Dhoni, cueist Pankaj Advani was also awarded the Padma Bhushan. As many as 85 recipients were selected for the prestigious awards this year. The government announced names of the recipients on the eve of the 69th Republic Day.

VINOD KHANNA (POSTHUMOUSLY) HONOURED WITH THE DADASAHEB PHALKE AWARD

At the 65th National Film Awards, late actor Vinod Khanna was posthumously honoured with the Dadasaheb Phalke Award. This award is considered as the highest honour in Indian cinema and is presented annually by the Ministry of Information and Broadcasting. The award is given for a personality's "outstanding contribution to the growth and development of Indian cinema".

Vinod Khanna is the 49th recipient of the Dadasaheb Phalke Award. In a career spanning over four decades, Khanna was primarily known for his work in Hindi films during the 1970s. Amar Akbar Anthony, Mere Apne, Hera Pheri, Muqaddar Ka Sikander and Qurbani are just some of the popular films that he has appeared in. After taking a short break from the movies in the 1980s, Khanna returned and gained acclaim for his performances in films like Chandni and Dayavan.In his later years, Vinod Khanna appeared in many popular films like Wanted, Dabangg and Dilwale among many others.

MISS INDIA 2018

Miss Anukreethy Vas from Tamil Nadu won the 55th edition of Femina Miss India 2018 pageant

GLOBAL ENERGY PRIZE

Australia's "father of PV," Martin Green, awarded the 2018 Global Energy Prize, for revolutionizing the efficiency and cost of solar photovoltaics and making it the lowest cost option for bulk electricity supply.

SARASWATI SAMMAN 2017

Renowned Gujarati poet Sitanshu Yashaschandra was on April 28, 2018 chosen for the 2017 Saraswati Samman for his collection of verses (poetry) titled 'Vakhar', published in 2009.

NATIONAL INTELLECTUAL PROPERTY AWARD 2018

The Council of Scientific and Industrial Research (CSIR) was on April 26, 2018 awarded the National Intellectual Property Award, 2018 for being the top research and development organisation for patents and commercialisation.

PULITZER PRIZE 2018

List of 2018 Pulitzer Prize winners in Journalism Category

Category	Winners	Field
Public Service	The New York Times for reporting by Jodi Kantor and Megan Twohey and The New Yorker for reporting by Ronan Farrow	Exposed powerful and wealthy sexual predators like Harvey Weinstein
Breaking News Reporting	Staff of The Press Democrat, Santa Rosa, California	For coverage of historic wildfires that devastated Santa Rosa and Sonoma County
Investigative Reporting	Staff of The Washington Post	For revealing a candidate's alleged past sexual harassment of teenage girls that changed the course of a Senate race in Alabama
Explanatory Reporting	Staff of The Arizona Republic and USA Today Network	For reporting the difficulties and consequences of fulfilling President Trump's pledge to construct a wall along the US border with Mexico through text, video, podcasts and virtual reality.

Local Reporting	Staff of The Cincinnati Enquirer	For a story and a video that documented seven days of Cincinnati's drug epidemic that ruined families and communities.
National Reporting	Staff of The New York Times and The Washington Post	For a reporting that deepened the nation's understanding of Russian interference in the 2016 presidential election and its connections to the Trump campaign
International Reporting	Reuters staff - Clare Baldwin, Andrew R.C. Marshall and Manuel Mogato	For exposing brutal killing campaign behind Philippines President Rodrigo Duterte's war on drugs.
Feature Writing	Rachel Kaadzi Ghansah, freelance reporter, GQ	For portrayal of murderer Dylann Roof who killed nine people inside Emanuel AME Church in Charleston, S.C.
Commentary	John Archibald of Alabama Media Group, Birmingham	For a commentary rooted in Alabama that exposed corrupt politicians, championing the rights of women and calling out hypocrisy.
Criticism	Jerry Saltz of New York magazine	For conveying a daring perspective on visual art in America
Editorial Writing	Andie Dominick of The Des Moines Register	For examining the harmful consequences for poor Iowa residents of privatising the administration of Medicaid.
Editorial Cartooning	Jake Halpern, freelance writer, and Michael Sloan, freelance cartoonist at The New York Times	For accounting the daily struggles of a real-life family of refugees and its fear of exile

Breaking News Photography	Ryan Kelly of The Daily Progress, Charlottesville	For a frightening image that captured the moment of impact of a car attack during a racially charged protest in Charlottesville
Feature Photography	Photography Staff of Reuters	For photographs that exposed violence faced by Rohingya refugees in fleeing Myanmar.

List of 2018 Pulitzer Prize winners in Arts Category

Category	Works	Artists
Fiction	Less	Andrew Sean Greer
Drama	Cost of Living	Martyna Majok
History	The Gulf: The Making of an American Sea	Jack E. Davis
Biography	Prairie Fires: The American Dreams of Laura Ingalls Wilder	Caroline Fraser
Poetry	Half-light: Collected Poems 1965-2016	Frank Bidart
General Nonfiction	Locking Up Our Own: Crime and Punishment in Black America	James Forman Jr.
Music	DAMN	Kendrick Lamar

UNESCO Press Freedom Prize

Jailed Egyptian photographer Mahmoud Abu Zeid, popularly known as Shawkan, on April 23, 2018 won the 2018 Guillermo Cano World Press Freedom Prize of the United Nations Educational, Scientific and Cultural Organization's (UNESCO).

65TH NATIONAL FILM AWARDS

President Ram Nath Kovind on May 3, 2018 presented the 65th National Film Awards at Vigyan Bhavan, New Delhi.

List of awardees

Category	Winners
Best Feature Film	Village Rockstar (Assamese)
Indira Gandhi Award for Best Debut Film of a Director	Sinjar
Best Film on social issue	Aalorukkam

Best Children's Film	Mhorkya
Best Popular Film Providing Wholesome Entertainment	Baahubali 2: The Conclusion
Best Director	Jayaraj for Bhayanakam
Best Actor	Riddhi Sen for Nagarkirtan
Best Actress	Sridevi for Mom
Best Supporting Actor	Fahad Faasil for Thondimuthalum Driksakshiyum
Best Supporting Actress	Divya Dutta for Irada
Best Child Artist	Neeta Das for Village Rockstar
Best Male Playback Singer	Yesudas
Best Regional Film	Ladhakh
Best Jasari Film	Sinjar
Best Tulu Film	Paddayi
Best Tamil Film	To Let
Best Gujarati Film	Dhh
Best Telugu Film	Ghazi
Best Marathi Film	Kaccha Limbu
Best Malayalam Film	Thondimuthalum Driksakshiyum
Best Kannada Film	Hebbettu Ramakka
Best Hindi Film	Newton
Best Bengali Film	Mayurakshi
Best Assamese Film	Ishu
Best Special Effects	Baahubali 2: The Conclusion
Best Music Direction	AR Rahman for Kaatru Veliyidai
Best Film on Environment Conservation/ Preservation	Irada
Nargis Dutt Award for Best Feature Film on National Integration	Dhappa
Dada Saheb Phalke Award	Vinod Khanna
Special Mentions	Pankaj Tripathi (Newton), Parvathy (Take Off), Prakruti Mishra (Hello Arsi), Yasharaj Karhade (Mhorkya)

Man Booker International prize 2018
Polish author Olga Tokarczuk on May 23, 2018 won the Man Booker International Prize 2018 for her novel 'Flights', becoming Poland's first ever writer to win the award.

Nari Shakti Puraskar 2017
The Union Minister for Women and Child Development, Maneka Gandhi presented the prestigious Nari Shakti Puraskar 2017 to the members of the INSV Tarini team in New Delhi on May 24, 2018.

National Biodiversity Award
Arunachal Pradesh's Singchung Bugun Village Community Reserve, a non-governmental organisation, on May 24, 2018 won the National Biodiversity Award 2018 for conserving a bird species 'Bugun Liocichla', a rare wildlife resources found in the area.

Santokbaa Humanitarian Award
President Ram Nath Kovind on May 30, 2018 presented the 'Santokbaa Humanitarian Award' to Child rights activist and Noble Laureate Kailash Satyarthi and to space scientist A S Kiran Kumar, former Chairman of Indian Space Research Organisation (ISRO).

Japan's prestigious Nikkei Asia Prize
Bindeshwar Pathak, noted social reformer and founder of Sulabh International, was on June 13, 2018 honoured with Japan's prestigious Nikkei Asia Prize. The award was conferred to Pathak under the 'Culture and Community' category for his significant work in tackling poor hygiene and discrimination.

BOOKS & AUTHORS

Books	Authors
Daughters of the Sun	Ira Mulchoty
Eleven Gods and a Billion Indians	Boria Majumdar, Simon & Schuster
She Goes to War, Women Militants of India	Rashmi Saksena
Courting the People	Anuj Bhuwania
Triple Talaq : Examining Faith	Salman Khurshid
The Making of Early Kashmir	Shonaleeka Kaul
Who We Are And How We Got Here	David Reich
Kashmir : Exposing the Myth Behind the Narrative	Khalid Bashir Ahmad
Mothering a Muslim—The Dark Secret in Our Schools and Playgrounds	Naria Erum
We That Are Young	Preti Taneja
Reporting Pakistan	Meena Menon
Sell; The Art, The Science; the Witchcraft	Subroto Bagchi
Moong over Microchips: Adventures of a Techie-Turned-Farmer	Venkat Iyer
Indian Instincts: Essays on Freedom and Equality in India	Miniya Chatterji

OBITUARIES

PANDIT BUDDHADEV DAS GUPTA

DIED: 15th January, 2018

Sarod maestro Pandit Buddhadev Dasgupta died of cardiac arrest at his residence in south Kolkata. He was 84. The Padma Bhushan awardee was suffering from respiratory problems. He is survived by wife and two sons. Dasgupta's body was kept at the Peace Haven morgue for people to pay their last respects.

Background: Padmabhushan Buddhadev Dasgupta was an Indian classical musician who played the sarod. He used to reside in Kolkata. He was one of the artists featured in Nimbus Records' The Raga Guide'. The musician, born in 1933 at his maternal home in Bhagalpur, Bihar, learnt sarod under the tutelage of Pt Radhikamohan Moitra. His father, Prafulla Mohan Dasgupta, was a district magistrate and a music aficionado. At a very early age, Buddhadev started taking Sarod lessons from the sarod maestro Radhika Mohan Maitra. His first program on the All India Radio was as a guest artist. He eventually performed more than 17 national programs on All India Radio. He was conferred Sangeet Mahasamman and Bangabibhusan in 2015.

HONSEN LYNGDOH

DIED : 23rd Jan, 2018

Noted entrepreneur Honsen Lyngdoh passed away at the age of 82 years. He is survived by his wife, six children and six grandchildren. With enormous understanding of machinery along with hard dedication became one of the most respected businessmen of Shillong. He was also 1st Class Contractor with Public Works Department (Roads), government of Meghalaya, Meghalaya Energy Corporation Ltd. CPWD, IOC, MES.

Achievements: He had participated and won many vintage car rallies (from 1975 till date) and was awarded 1st prize from DUNLOP, GOOD YEAR, MRF and State Bank of India for the same. As for construction of roads, he had constructed many roads in remotest rural areas, to connect the villages with PWD roads and National Highways. Among his achievements, he was a recipient of "The National Citizens Award 1991" on September 14, 1992 for the contribution to the Development of the North Eastern States of India. He was also awarded the 'Life Time Achievement Award' on January 30, 2015, by 5th North-East Consumer Awards for Social Entrepreneurship. Lyngdoh also bagged the Recipient of 'Silver Elephant Award' on the February 16, 2015 for his contribution to Scouts & Guides movement. He was a Lifetime Member and Member of the Managing Body Committee of the Indian Red Cross Society, Meghalaya State Branch, Executive Member of the YMCA, Shillong.

SUPRIYA DEVI

DIED: 25th January, 2018

Veteran Bengali film actress and Padmashri awardee, Supriya Devi (Supriya Chowdhury), passed away at her residence in Kolkata, following a severe cardiac arrest. She was 83.

Supriya Devi made her debut in the Uttam Kumar-starrer *Basu Parivar* in 1952. During her over five-decade career in the Bengali film industry she delivered hits and classics like *Sonar Harin, Chowringhee, Bagh Bandi Khela, Meghe Dhaka Tara,* among others. Some of her other contemporaries and co-stars include Soumitra Chatterjee and Sabitri Chattopadhyay.

She was also awarded the Banga Vibushan - the highest-ever civilian award given by the Bengal Government, and a Life Time Achievement Award by filmfare during their eastern India version of the award show.

SHRIVALLABH VYAS

DIED: 7th January, 2018

Career: Shrivallabh Vyas, known for his work in films like Lagaan and Sarfarosh, passed away on January 7, 2018 in Jaipur. Shrivallabh Vyas had appeared in over 60 Hindi films, with occasional stints in regional cinema, television and theatre. He had to take a break from acting in 2008 after he collapsed in his hotel room in Gujarat.

 Vyas was known for his impactful characters. The actor is survived by his wife Shobha Vyas and two daughters.

JOHN YOUNG

DIED: 5 January 2018

Legendary astronaut John Young, who walked on the Moon and later commanded the first space shuttle flight, died on 5th January, 2018 in Texas, US. Young was 87.

NASA called Young one of its pioneers—the only agency astronaut to go into space as part of the Gemini, Apollo and space shuttle programs, and the first to fly into space six times. He was the ninth man to walk on the Moon.

Counting his takeoff from the Moon in 1972 as commander of Apollo 16, his blastoff tally stood at seven, for decades a world record. Young remained an active astronaut into his early 70s, long after all his peers had left, and held on to his role as NASA's conscience until his retirement in 2004.

BHIMSAIN KHURANA

DIED: 19th April, 2018

Animation pioneer and multiple Indian National Award winner Bhimsain Khurana died at the age of 82. Khurana is known for films like *Gharonda* and for iconic animation shorts like *Ek Anek Ekta.*

Background: Khurana obtained his diploma in Fine Arts and Classical Music from Lucknow University. In 1970, he made his debut with his first animation short *The Climb*, which earned him the Silver Hugo Award in the Chicago Film Festival. Soon after, he directed and produced several animation and advertisements. He further established his repute as a director and producer with his landmark animation short *Ek Anek Ekta*, which won him an Indian National Award. Khurana also tried his hand at TV show production. His first tryst was in 1985 with popular sitcom *Choti Badi Baatein*, based on superstitions. He also made several documentaries. Khurana was also a writer and penned at least six books. His banner Climb Films has been running over the last 31 years.

OTHER OBITUARIES		
Name	**Profession**	**Country**
C.V. Rajendran	Film director	India
Efrain Rios Montt	Military Dictator	Guatemala
Surendra Nihal Singh	Veteran Journalist	India
Barbara Bush	Former US President	United States
PP Lakshaman	Former AIFF Secretary	India
Keyur Bhushan	Freedom fighter and Writer	India
Dave Michener	Animator	United States
Anne V. Coates	Oscar-winning film editor	United States
Balkavi Bairagi	Poet-politician	India
Torn Wolfe	Author of 'The Right Stuff'	United States
Yarnunabai Waikar	Lavani singer	India
Balakumaran	Tamil writer	India
Alan Bean	4th man of Appollo 12 mission	United States

INDIA SLIPS 10 RANKS TO 42 ON DEMOCRACY INDEX

DATE: 1st February, 2018

Global Democracy Index amid "rise of conservative religious ideologies" and increase in vigilantism and violence against minorities as well as other dissenting voices. While Norway has again topped the list, followed by Iceland and Sweden, compiled by the Economist Intelligence Unit (EIU), India has moved down from 32nd place last year and remains classified among "flawed democracies". India's overall score dropped by 0.58 points from 7.81 to 7.23. The EIU is the research and analysis division of the UK-based media behemoth 'The Economist Group'. The index ranks 165 independent states and two territories on the basis of five categories: electoral process and pluralism, civil liberties, the functioning of government, political participation and political culture. The list has been divided into four broad categories—full democracy, flawed democracy, hybrid regime and authoritarian regime.

This year's report which also measured the state of media freedom around the world noted that in India, media is "partially free". Moreover, journalists are at risk from government, military and non-state actors and radical groups, and the threat of violence has a chilling effect on media coverage.

INDIA RANKS 81 IN GLOBAL CORRUPTION PERCEPTION INDEX

DATE: 22nd February, 2018

Transparency International released 'The 2017 corruption perception index.' In its index, India is at 81 among 180 countries and territories. This report has, in fact, named India among the worst offenders in terms of graft and press freedom in the Asia Pacific region. The index is based on perceived levels of public sector corruption according to experts and business people, using a scale of 0 to 100, where 0 is highly corrupt and 100 is very clean. India has a little better than neighbours Sri Lanka (ranked 91), Pakistan (117), Myanmar (130) and Bangladesh (143), but is behind Bhutan (26) and China (77). The current report of Transparency International shows that corruption in many countries is still strong and when individuals dare to challenge the status quo, they are met with threats and bodily harm, including death. Transparency International further said, "In some countries across the region (Asia Pacific), journalists, activists, opposition leaders and even staff of law enforcement or watchdog agencies are threatened, and in the worst cases, even murdered".

INDIASIZE-SIZING SURVEY FOR INDIAN POPULATION

DATE: 28th February 2018

Objective: To prepare a comprehensive size chart for the Indian population.

Ministry of Textiles, Government of India will begin a National Sizing Survey –INDIA size. The aim of the survey is to develop a comprehensive size chart for ready-to-wear industry based on the body measurements of the Indian population. The survey will be conducted through National Institute of Fashion Technology (NIFT), New Delhi.

The sampling will involve around 25,000 people (equal number of men and women) in the age group of 15-65 years, across six regions in the country – Kolkata (east), Mumbai (west), New Delhi (north), Hyderabad (centre), Bengaluru (south) and Shillong (north east). The measurements will be done using high-tech 3D whole body scanners which are part of a non-contact method of taking body measurements and analyzing the collected data to create size charts.

The data will help cater the need of Indian textile Industry which is still relying on tweaked versions of size charts of other countries in the absence of standardized size chart and is resulted in 20% to 40% returns of garments. The data created as part of this project will be confidential and secure. The duration of the project will take around two to three years from the date of actual commencement.

INDIA RANKS 133RD IN WORLD HAPPINESS INDEX 2018

DATE: 15th March, 2018

The World Happiness Index 2018 placed India in the 133rd position

India is ranked 133rd in a global list of the happiest countries, according to an UN-based report. The World Happiness Index 2018, which measures 156 countries in terms of happiness, has placed India in the 133rd position, a drop of 11 places from last year's 122nd rank. The country was ranked 118th in 2016. India's ranking was far behind from other neighbouring countries such as Pakistan, Nepal and China. Among the South Asian Association for Regional Cooperation (SAARC) countries, Pakistan was ranked 75th, while Nepal was ranked at 101st. Bhutan has been placed at 97th rank and Sri Lanka at 116th position. Bangladesh is ranked at 115th in the happiness index. Finland, in this index is at top. The places of United States and United Kingdom in this index are at 18 & 20 respectively. The African countries - Tanzania (153rd), South Sudan (154th), Central African Republic (155th) and Burundi (156th) occupied the bottom positions in the happiness index. The UN Sustainable Development Solutions Network's (SDSN) 2018 World Happiness Report ranks 156 countries in GDP per capita, social support, healthy life expectancy, social freedom, generosity and absence of corruption.

INDIA'S PLACE IN DIFFERENT INDEXES-2018

Index	Index released by	India's Rank	1st Rank	Lowest Rank
Worst New-born Mortality Rate	UNICEF	12th	Pakistan	
Hurun Global Rich List 2018 – Highest Number of Billionaires	Hurun Research Institute	3rd	China	
Global Climate Risk Index	German watch	6th	Haiti	
World Happiness report	UN Sustainable Development Solutions Network	133rd	Finland	Burundi (156th)
Ease of Doing Business	World Bank	100th	New Zealand	Somalia (190th)
Inclusive Development Index	World Economic Forum	62nd	Norway (Advanced) Lithuania (Emerging)	
Global Hunger Index GHI	IFPRI (International Food Policy Research Institute)	100th		Central Africa Republic (119th)
Global Gender Gap Index 2017	World Economic Forum	108th	Iceland	Yemen (144th)
Passport Index	Arton Capital	75th	Singapore	Afghanistan (94th)
Global Wealth Migration Review 2018	AfrAsia Bank Global Wealth Migration	6th	United States	
India Solar Market Leader board 2018	Mercom Communications	3rd	China	

Index	Index released by	India's Rank	1st Rank	Lowest Rank
World press freedom index	Reporters Without Borders	136	Norway, Sweden and Finland	
Renewable energy attractiveness index		4	China	
Global milk production Index		1	India	
Global Economic Freedom Index	American think-tank	130th	Hong Kong	North Korea
Environmental Performance Index 2018	World Economic Forum	177th	Switzerland	Burundi (180th)
List of Wealthiest countries	New World Wealth	6th	USA	
Global Democracy Index	EIU (Economist Intelligence Unit)	42nd	Norway	North Korea (167th)
Asia Pacific on Power Index	Lowy Institute and Australian think tank	4th	US	Nepal
Worldwide military spending	Stockholm International Peace Research Institute (SIPRI)	5th	US	
Global Urban Air Pollution database	World Health Organization (WHO)	14 Indian cities	India	
Inclusive Development Index	World Economic Forum's	62	Lithuania	
Global talent competitiveness index	World Economic Forum	81	Switzerland	

FIRST NEPAL-INDIA BROAD GAUGE RAILWAY LIKELY IN DECEMBER

Nepal plans to operate its first ever broad-gauge passenger railway service from Janakpur town to Indian border town Jayanagar in Bihar starting December. This is a section of 69 km Nepal-India cross border railway line from Jayanagar to Nepal's southeastern region. The other five cross-border railway lines between the two neighbours are either being constructed or are on the drawing board.

RAILWAYS TO SEEK RS 2,500 CRORE LOAN THROUGH IRFC FOR CCTV PROJECT

Indian Railways is exploring the loan route to raise Rs 2,500 crore to install CCTVs at all stations and coaches to ensure state-of-the-art surveillance systems in the entire rail network across the country.

The loan is to be raised through Indian Railways Finance Corporation (IRFC), the finance arm of the national transporter. It raises financial resources for expansion and running from the capital markets and other avenues.

RAILWAYS TO FILL UP OVER 1 LAKH VACANCIES BY MARCH-APRIL 2019: ASHWANI LOHANI

Indian Railways will fill up over one lakh vacant posts by March-April next year, according to Railway Board chairman Ashwani Lohani. The railways has received around 2.27 crore applications for about 1.10 lakh vacancies it had advertised earlier this year. The examination for the posts, including those in the Railway Protection Force, will be conducted in the months of September, October and November this year.

INDIAN RAILWAYS TO REPAINT 30,000 MAIL, EXPRESS COACHES IN BEIGE AND BROWN

Indian Railways would be repainting all Mail and Express trains, except Rajdhani, Shatabdi, Duronto and newly launched Tejas, Gatimaan and Humsafar Express, with a new colour scheme - beige and brown. The new colour scheme will replace the dark blue colour, which was introduced in 1990s replacing the brick red colour introduced earlier.

INDIAN RAILWAYS TO BUILD ANOTHER BRIDGE OVER YAMUNA TO EASE GHAZIABAD-NEW DELHI CONGESTION

Indian Railways has proposed an additional rail bridge over the river in the capital. While the old Yamuna rail bridge—also known as Loha Pul—will give way to a new double-line rail bridge by March next year, another bridge is set to come up near the existing Nizamuddin rail bridge to ensure faster and seamless movement of about 150 outbound and inbound passenger and freight services.

INDIA'S FIRST BULLET TRAIN MANAGES TO DRIVE THROUGH LAND ACQUISITION DEADLOCK

India's ambitious Japan-backed Mumbai-Ahmedabad bullet train project costing $17 billion, expected to be constructed by August 2022, was likely to be delayed due to problems in land acquisition. It faced stiff resistance from farmers and tribal villages, especially in the Palghar district of Maharashtra. The Indian Railways is acquiring around 1,400 hectares of linear land in Maharashtra and Gujarat at a cost of ₹10,000 crore.

GOOGLE'S FREE WIFI NOW AVAILABLE AT 400 INDIAN RAILWAYS STATIONS

Google has announced the completion of the free service at 400 railway stations across India in collaboration with RailTel, the telecom arm of Indian Railways. Dibrugarh in Assam has become the 400th railway station to get the free WiFi service from Google.

RAILWAYS TO BECOME 'NET ZERO CARBON EMITTER' BY 2030: PIYUSH GOYAL

Indian Railways will become a "net zero" carbon emitter by 2030, according to Railways Minister Piyush Goyal. With the current action plans on anvil for 100 per cent electrification, coupled with renewable strategies, Indian Railways will become a net zero carbon emitter by 2030.

RAILWAYS NOW OFFERS FREE WIFI AT OVER 700 STATIONS, COVERS 8 MILLION PEOPLE A MONTH

Indian Railways now offers free public WiFi service at more than 700 stations across India and it covers around 8 million people every month. The service is being offered in collaboration with tech giant Google.

'RAIL MADAD' TO EXPEDITE PASSENGER GRIEVANCES REDRESSAL

Objective: To expedite and streamline passenger grievance redressal

The Union Ministry of Railways has launched Rail MADAD (Mobile Application for Desired Assistance During travel) Application to expedite and streamline passenger grievance redressal. The application was launched in line with Union Government's Digital India Initiative.

The app registers complaint of passengers with minimum inputs. It also has option and issues unique ID instantly. It relays complaint online to relevant field officials for immediate action. The action taken on complaint is also relayed to passenger through SMS. It also displays various helpline numbers like Child and Security helpline etc. and provides direct calling facility for immediate assistance in one easy step. It integrates all modes of filing complaints including offline and online modes on single platform. It presents holistic picture of weak and deficient areas and enable focused corrective action by officials concerned. It also aids in data analysis of reports to generate trends on various performance parameters of selected train and stations like cleanliness and amenities etc. to make managerial process more precise and effective.

RAIL PROJECTS WORTH ₹ 18,790 CR UNDER IMPLEMENTATION: GOVERNMENT

Objective: To bring down logistics costs by providing rail connectivity to ports

In order to bring down logistics costs by providing rail connectivity to ports, Indian Port Rail Corporation along with other agencies is implementing projects worth ₹18,795 crore.

IPRCL, a joint venture between major ports and Rail Vikas Nigam Ltd (RVNL), as a dedicated SPV is developing railways as a mode of transport in the port sector under the government's ambitious initiative Sagarmala – a flagship programme for port led-development in the country.

More than 50 per cent of the rail connectivity projects identified under Sagarmala are under implementation through various agencies such as IPRCL.

SOME FACTS & FIGURES ABOUT INDIAN RAILWAYS

- It operates the fourth-largest railway network in the world by size, with 121,407 kilometres (75,439 mi) of total track over a 67,368-kilometre (41,861 mi) route.
- Net income 64.25 billion (US$960 million) (2017–18)
- Number of employees 1.308 million (March 2016)
- 49% of the routes are electrified with 25 KV AC electric traction
- 33% of them are double or multi-tracked.
- Runs more than 13,000 passenger trains daily, on both long-distance and suburban routes, from 7,349 stations across India.
- In the fiscal year 2017-18, have earnings of ₹ 1.874 trillion (US$28 billion), consisting of ₹ 1.175 trillion (US$18 billion) in freight revenue and ₹ 501.25 billion (US$7.5 billion) in passenger revenue, with an operating ratio of 96.0 percent.
- The Mumbai-Ahmedabad bullet train project (₹1.08-lakh-crore) with an 80% loan from Japan is to meet the August 2022 deadline for starting operations.
- The total land is over 1,400 hectares, with 353 hectares in Maharashtra and the rest in Gujarat.

MODEL AGRICULTURAL PRODUCE AND LIVESTOCK CONTRACT FARMING ACT, 2018

As Union Finance Minister in the budget for 2017-18 announced, Agriculture Produce and Livestock Contract Farming and Services (Promotion & Facilitation) Act, 2018 was unveiled by Union Agriculture Minister Radha Mohan Singh to ensure better price of the produces to farmers. The act lays special emphasis on protecting the interests of the farmers including pre-production, production and post-production services. Under the act, Farmer's producer organizations (FPO's) shall have a major role in promoting Contract Farming and Services Contract. On behalf of farmers they can enter into an agreement with the sponsor.

Apart from this, Contracted produce will be covered under crop and livestock insurance in this act and no any permanent structure can be developed on farmers' land and premises. This act will not only cover contract farming in agriculture crops but also in livestock, dairy and poultry products.

PRADHAN MANTRI KRISHI SINCHAYEE YOJANA

The Union Government has approved initial corpus of Rs.5,000 crore for setting up of dedicated Micro Irrigation Fund (MIF) with the help of NABARD under Pradhan Mantri Krishi Sinchayee Yojana (PMKSY) at the very low rate of 3%. Of allocated money, 2,000 crore rupees will be utilized during 2018-19 and rest money during 2019-20.

NABARD will also extend this loan amount to State Governments during this period. And this money shall be paid back to NABARD in 7 years including the grace period of two years.

By this effort the dedicated Micro Irrigation Fund would help "Per Drop More Crop Component (PDMC)" of Pradhan Mantri Krishi Sinchayee Yojana in an effective and timely manner.

GREEN REVOLUTION-KRISHONNATI YOJANA

The Cabinet Committee on Economic Affairs, chaired by the Prime Minister Shri Narendra Modi has given its approval on 2nd May, 2018 for the Umbrella Scheme, "Green Revolution – Krishonnati Yojana" in agriculture sector beyond 12th Five Year Plan for the period from 2017-18 to 2019-20 with the Central Share of Rs. 33,269.976 crore. This scheme comprises of 11 Schemes/Missions that look to develop the agriculture and allied sectors in a holistic and scientific manner to increase the income of farmers by enhancing production, productivity and better returns on produce.

The Committee primarily focus on creating and strengthening of infrastructure of production, reducing production cost and marketing of agriculture and allied produce. These schemes will be now continued for three financial years, i.e., 2017-18, 2018-19 and 2019-20 with an expenditure of ₹ 33,269 crore.

FINANCIAL ASSISTANCE TO SUGAR MILLS FOR CLEARING CANE DUES

The Cabinet Committee on Economic Affairs (CCEA), has given its approval on 2nd May, 2018 to provide financial assistance @ of Rs. 5.50 per quintal of sugarcane crushed in sugar season 2017-18 to sugar mills to offset the cost of sugar cane, in order to help sugar mills to clear sugar cane dues of farmers. The assistance shall be paid directly to the farmers on behalf of the mills. It will be adjusted against the cane price payable due to the farmers against Fair and Remunerative Price (FRP) including arrears relating to previous years. Subsequent balance if any shall be credited into the mill's account. Assistance shall be provided to those mills which will fulfil the eligibility conditions as decided by the Government.

ITC & NITI AAYOG TO TRAIN FARMERS TO INCREASE THEIR INCOME

ITC has joined hands with NITI Aayog on 27th April, to train 2 lakh farmers to increase their income and raise productivity of major crops in 25 "aspirational districts" across seven states in the country by 2022. These 25 aspirational districts are in Assam, Bihar, Jharkhand, Madhya Pradesh, Maharashtra, Rajasthan and Uttar Pradesh and partnership is for a period of four years, i.e. up to April 2022.

Its prime objective is to increase net returns from farming through reduction in costs of production and increasing productivity of major crops in each of the identified districts. The trainers will disseminate sustainable agricultural practices and templates for seasonal planning at gram panchayat level, while the baseline and end line data will be collected by ITC for impact documentation, mapping of government schemes and programmes for improving efficiency of delivery. In order to ensure implementation, performance review and problem-solving will be undertaken by a specially constituted Project Management Committee (PMC) at the district level. PMC will work as a team under the concerned District Magistrates looking after the Aspirational District programme.

NATIONAL BAMBOO MISSION

The Cabinet Committee on Economic Affairs chaired by the Prime Minister, Shri Narendra Modi today has approved National Bamboo Mission (NBM) under National Mission for Sustainable Agriculture (NMSA). An outlay of Rs.1290 crore (with Rs. 950 crore as Central share) is provisioned for implementation of the Mission during the remaining period of 14th Finance Commission (2018-19 and 2019-20).

The scheme will benefit directly and indirectly the farmers as well as local artisans and associated people engaged in bamboo sector including associated industries.

It is proposed to bring about one lakh ha area under plantation and about one lakh farmers would be directly benefitted in terms of plantation. Bamboo plantation will contribute to optimizing farm productivity and income thereby enhancing livelihood opportunities of small & marginal farmers.

KRISHI UNNATI MELA 2018

The three-day annual Krishi Unnati Mela was held in New Delhi with focus on doubling farmers' income. The objective of fair was to create awareness among farmers about latest agriculture-related technological developments. In it, Prime Minister Narendra Modi laid foundation stone for 25 Krishi Vigyan Kendras and unveil a portal on organic farming. PM Modi also conferred Krishi Karman Award and Pandit Deen Dayal Upadhaya Krishi Vigyan Protsahan Puruskar to progressive farmers and states on the occasion.

The Krishi Mela this year will be significant owing to the interests of farmers and those involved in allied sectors. More than 900 stalls have been set up. The theme pavilions were on doubling of farmers income, organic farming, cooperatives, farm inputs to assist farmers with latest developments in farming technique and popularize dairy, animal husbandry, fisheries and horticulture.

PUNJAB GOVT BANS SALE OF 20 INSECTICIDES

Punjab government has issued a notification to ban the distribution and sale of 20 insecticides that are considered harmful for human beings and also cause damage to the environment. The ban will be applicable till March 30 because the Centre is likely to bring the Pesticide (insecticide) Management Bill in the ongoing Parliament session. A draft of the Bill has already been prepared by the Union government. Presently, state governments do not have the final power to permanently disallow the use of toxic pesticides.

NANAJI DESHMUKH KRISHI SANJIVANI YOJNA

The Maharashtra government approved ₹ 4, 000-crore project aimed at promoting climate-resilient agriculture, to be partially funded by the World Bank. The project, named Nanaji Deshmukh Krishi Sanjivani Yojna, will be implemented in 5, 142 villages across 15 districts. The total cost of the project is ₹ 4, 000 crore, 70 per cent of which will be borne by the World Bank while the state will contribute 30 per cent over six years. The scheme would cover small- and medium- scale farmers, who are more vulnerable to the impact of climate change. Seven-member panel, headed by principal secretary, agriculture, will select drought-prone villages for the implementation of this project.

CURRENT AFFAIRS MCQ's

1. Which State Government has published first draft of Supreme Court monitored National Register of Citizens (NRC)?
   (a) Manipur   (b) Mizoram
   (c) Assam   (d) Nagaland

2. Which state government had launched 'Saubhagya Yojana', aimed at providing electricity to all the villages across the state?
   (a) Bihar   (b) Gujarat
   (c) Assam   (d) Jharkhand

3. After Sikkim, Which state was declared as the second state in the Northeast to be declared Open Defecation Free (ODF)?
   (a) Manipur   (b) Mizoram
   (c) Nagaland (d) Arunachal Pradesh

4. To which Profession does Ananta Ojha belong to?
   (a) Singer   (b) Dancer
   (c) Actor   (d) Musician

5. Which state government launched a special police force to safeguard tourists?
   (a) Karnataka (b) Andaman Nicobar
   (c) Puducherry (d) Goa

6. In which state GAIL India Ltd it has commissioned India's second largest rooftop solar power plant?
   (a) Gujarat   (b) Karnataka
   (c) Bihar   (d) Uttar Pradesh

7. Soumeylou Boubeye Maiga was appointed the new Prime Minister of which country?
   (a) Mali   (b) Maldives
   (c) Liberia   (d) Libya

8. What is NARI?
   (a) Submarine (b) Online Portal
   (c) Navy Ship (d) Satellite

9. Which state launched 'Chah Bagichar Dhan Puraskar Mela 2017-18'?
   (a) Assam   (b) Manipur
   (c) Mizoram   (d) Nagaland

10. How many member countries are there in United Nations Security Council?
    (a) 10   (b) 13
    (c) 15   (d) 20

11. Which International Bank is providing technical and financial assistance for the Jal Marg Vikas Project at a cost of Rs 5369 crore?
    (a) Ally Bank (b) World Bank
    (c) Bank of America
    (d) Bank5 Connect

12. Which of the following is the world's largest cleanliness survey carried out by Union Ministry of Housing and Urban Affairs ?
    (a) Swachh Abhiyan - 2018

    (b) Swachh Bharat - 2018

    (c) Swachh Survekshan - 2018

    (d) Swachh Sankalp - 2018

13. Name the platform launched by the Government, to get suggestions from citizens of India from all walks of life?

    (a) MySuggestions

    (b) MyGov

    (c) MyGovernment

    (d) MyIndia

14. Who became the first batsman to score three hundreds in T20 internationals?

    (a) Virat Kohli

    (b) Colin Munro

    (c) Kylle Mills

    (d) Aaron Finch

15. When is the "World Braille Day" observed all over the world?

    (a) 4 January (b) 5 January

    (c) 6 January (d) 7 January

16. Lok Sabha passed a bill to hike the salaries of judges of Supreme Court and 24 high courts. The bill proposes to raise the monthly salary of Chief Justice of India from the present Rs. one lakh per month to __________ per month?

    (a) ₹2.40 lakh

    (b) ₹2.55 lakh

    (c) ₹2. 60 lakh

    (d) ₹2. 80 lakh

17. What is the base colour of the new Rs.10 note issued by RBI?

    (a) Burnt umber

    (b) Sulphate Blue

    (c) Chocolate Brown

    (d) Dark pink

18. Which state announced the setting up of 24X7 'Gudiya helpline' for reporting crimes against women?

    (a) Himachal Pradesh

    (b) Gujarat

    (c) Kerala

    (d) Karnataka

19. In which state, The International Kite Festival was celebrated?

    (a) Gujarat

    (b) Rajasthan

    (c) Maharashra

    (d) Uttar Pradesh

20. Who has sworn in as the first woman advocate to directly become a Judge of the Supreme Court?

    (a) Anita Barnwa

    (b) Vinita Grover

    (c) Ranjita Bisht

    (d) Indu Malhotra

21. What is India's rank on the World Press Freedom Index, released by Reporters Without Borders (RSF)?

    (a) 126   (b) 138

    (c) 115   (d) 108

22. Union Cabinet has given its approval for declaration of Scheduled Areas under the Fifth Schedule in which state?

    (a) Gujarat

    (b) Rajasthan

    (c) Odisha

    (d) Madhya Pradesh

23. Who has sworn in as the 70th Secretary of State of USA?

    (a) John Cornyn

    (b) Dick Durbin

    (c) Mike Pompeo

    (d) Bob Corker

24. Which of the following Indian entreprenuers has been named in the 2018 TIME magazine's 100 most influential people in the world?

    (a) Ritesh Agarwal

    (b) Bhavish Aggarwal

    (c) Vijay Shekhar Sharma

    (d) Sachin Bansal

25. Which team won the 3rd edition of National Blind Football Tournament, held in Kochi?

    (a) Mumbai   (b) Bengal

    (c) Kochi   (d) Hyderabad

26. Which company has partnered with Ministry of Tourism to bring a series of 360-degree virtual reality videos for the Incredible India Tourism campaign?

    (a) Microsoft (b) Google

    (c) Facebook (d) Tripadvisor

27. India is conducting a joint military exercise named 'Harimau Shakti', in collaboration with which country?

    (a) Malaysia (b) Thailand

    (c) Singapore (d) Indonesia

28. Which Nobel Prize for 2018 has been postponed by the Swedish Academy?

    (a) Literature (b) Chemistry

    (c) Medicine (d) Physics

29. What is the name of the mineral recently found by scientists, which could point to the abundant hidden reserves of water ice under the surface of the Moon?

    (a) Kuiper   (b) Mafalda

    (c) Iggiteor (d) Moganite

30. Government has approved a new type of license plates for e-vehicles. The license plates will follow which colour code?

    (a) Orange   (b) Purple

    (c) Gold   (d) Green

31. Which of the following has become India's first railway station fully powered by solar power?

    (a) Puri   (b) Nagpur

    (c) Guwahati (d) Surat

32. Which country has agreed to give India economic and military access to Sabang port?

    (a) Madagascar

    (b) Indonesia

    (c) Nauru

    (d) Fiji

33. Which country has launched world's first floating nuclear power plant, named 'Akademik Lomonosov'?

    (a) Japan   (b) China

    (c) Georgia (d) Russia

34. Which city hosted the first informal Summit between India and Russia?
    (a) Hyderabad
    (b) St. Petersburg
    (c) India
    (d) Sochi

35. Finance Ministry has announced to release a commemorative coin of _______ denomination to mark 350th birth anniversary of Guru Gobind Singh?
    (a) ₹ 100   (b) ₹ 500
    (c) ₹ 350   (d) ₹ 350

36. Which football team has won Santosh Trophy title at the Salt Lake Stadium, Kolkata?
    (a) Kerala   (b) Punjab
    (c) Bengal   (d) Maharashtra

37. Which satellite did China recently launch aboard its Long March-3B rocket for its satellite navigation system?
    (a) Tiangong-2
    (b) BeiDou-3
    (c) Ziyuan-III
    (d) Chang'e 2

38. Who has been appointed as the new President of Nasscom?
    (a) Aruna Kotecha
    (b) Shobhana Khulbe
    (c) Bharati Sinha
    (d) Debjani Ghosh

39. V. Sriharsha, who recently passed away, was a?
    (a) Journalist   (b) Politician
    (c) Jurist   (d) Diplomat

40. Which sports federation has launched a mobile app 'Scout-Me' to find talent?
    (a) BCCI   (b) AIFF
    (c) IBF   (d) SAI

41. Who was adjudged 'Sportsperson of the Year - Female' at the ESPN Multi-Sport Awards?
    (a) Mithali Raj
    (b) Sakshi Malik
    (c) Saina Nehwal
    (d) PV Sindhu

42. Which state government has prepared a Water ATM Policy to provide clean drinking water?
    (a) Haryana
    (b) Madhya Pradesh
    (c) Gujarat
    (d) Maharashtra

43 What was India's rank on the Commonwealth Innovation Index?
    (a) 15th   (b) 10th
    (c) 20th   (d) 25th

44. International Tennis Federation has proposed to transform which of the following tournaments into a 18-nation World Cup of Tennis?
    (a) Davis Cup
    (b) Grand Slam
    (c) Hopman Cup
    (d) Fed Cup

45. As per the data released by National Payments Corporation of India (NPCI), which company accounted for almost 40% of the total UPI transactions?

    (a) PhonepPe

    (b) Paytm

    (c) Google Tez

    (d) BHIM

46. RBI has recently imposed a penalty of Rs 5 crore on which payments bank?

    (a) Aditya Birla Idea Payments Bank

    (b) Paytm Payments Bank

    (c) Airtel Payments Bank

    (d) Fino Payments Bank

47. Which of the following organizations has approved India's membership as its 69th member?

    (a) European Bank for Reconstruction and Development (EBRD)

    (b) East African Development Bank (EADB)

    (c) Economic Cooperation Organization Trade and Development Bank (ETDB)

    (d) International Investment Bank (IIB)

48. President Ram Nath Kovind inaugurated the World Hindi Secretariat building in______.

    (a) Sri Lanka (b) Mauritius

    (c) Nepal   (d) Thailand

49. Who has written the book 'Framed as a terrorist'?

    (a) Kartar Lalvani

    (b) Anita Nair

    (c) Md. Aamir Khan

    (d) Scott Kelly

50. PM Narendra Modi recently inaugurated the 105th Indian Science Congress, on the focal theme "Reaching the Unreached through Science and Technology", in ______.

    (a) Itanagar   (b) Dispur

    (c) Shillong   (d) Imphal

51. Which team won the 4th edition of Hero Indian Super League (ISL) title?

    (a) FC Goa

    (b) Bengaluru FC

    (c) Aizwal FC

    (d) Chennaiyin FC

52. FIFA has lifted its three-decade ban on hosting international football from which country ?

    (a) Iraq   (b) Nigeria

    (c) Pakistan (d) Sudan

53. Mar 20 was observed by the UN to celebrate which language?

    (a) English   (b) Russian

    (c) Arabic   (d) French

54. Who has sworn in as the president of Peru?

    (a) Mario Vargas

    (b) Pedro Pablo Kuczynski

    (c) Ollanta Humala

    (d) Martin Vizcarra

55. Which indigenously built frigate of the Indian Navy has been decommissioned in Mumbai recently?

    (a) INS Gomati

    (b) INS Beas

   (c) INS Betwa

   (d) INS Ganga

56. Which state government has imposed a permanent ban on hookah bars?
   (a) Punjab   (b) Uttar Pradesh
   (c) Goa   (d) Telangana

57. Which airline flew the first commercial flight to Israel through Saudi Arabia's airspace?
   (a) Jet Airways
   (b) IndiGo
   (c) Air India
   (d) SpiceJet

58. Which of the following has been declared as Kerala's official fruit?
   (a) Coconut   (b) Jackfruit
   (c) Banana   (d) Tapioca

59. Union Cabinet has approved the extension of the term of the Commission set up to examine Subcategorization of OBC in the Central List, upto June 2018. The Commission is headed by?
   (a) G. Rohini
   (b) Sobhana Mohapatra
   (c) Bharti Sinha
   (d) Aruna Srinivas

60. What is the name of world's largest cruise ship which is going to make its maiden voyage from Barcelona?
   (a) Symphony of the Seas
   (b) Allure of the Seas
   (c) Oasis of the Seas
   (d) Anthem of the Seas

61. As per the Economic Affairs Secretary Subhash Chandra Garg, India will become a $5 trillion economy by ____.
   (a) 2025   (b) 2022
   (c) 2030   (d) 2020

62. Which of the following has become the first district in India to have 100% solar powered Primary Health Centers (PHC)?
   (a) Kannur   (b) Surat
   (c) Nagpur   (d) Kannauj

63. Asia's largest tulip garden has been opened for tourists in ___.
   (a) Srinagar   (b) Darjeeling
   (c) Gangtok   (d) Manali

64. Indian Coast Guard has commissioned a patrol vessel named 'Charlie-435', at_____.
   (a) Porbandar   (b) Kavaratti
   (c) Diglipur   (d) Karaikal

65. Which city has become the first in India to have a common mobility card for bus and metro rides?
   (a) Mumbai   (b) Delhi
   (c) Lucknow   (d) Bangalore

66. Which ministry has launched Smart Freight Operation Optimisation & Real Time Information (SFOORTI) App for Freight Managers?
   (a) Road Transport & Highways
   (b) Railways
   (c) Shipping
   (d) Commerce & Industry

67. On 5th June 2018, Ministry of AYUSH and which ministry signed an MoU in New Delhi, to create synergies through institutions and schemes of both ministries for development of AYUSH enterprises in India?

    (a) Ministry of Commerce and Industry
    (b) Ministry of Science and Technology
    (c) Ministry of MSME
    (d) Ministry of Urban Development

68. Name the four-year old boy of North Lakhimpur district, Assam who was honoured with the 'Youngest Author of India' title by The India Book of Records?

    (a) Krish Kalyan
    (b) Ayan Gogoi Gohain
    (c) Avan Desai
    (d) Madhukar Roy

69. The government is planning merger of 4 banks : Bank of Baroda, Central Bank , IDBI bank, and which other bank?

    (a) Oriental Bank of Commerce
    (b) Indian Bank
    (c) Indian Overseas Bank
    (d) Canara Bank

70. As a part of Indian Prime Minister Narendra Modi's 3 nation Visit to Indonesia , Malaysia and Singapore, how many MoUs were signed between India and Indonesia?

    (a) 14   (b) 15
    (c) 12   (d) 5

71. On June 1,2018, PM Modi gave Padma Shri award to former Singaporean Diplomat ____.

    (a) Tommy koh
    (b) Yuan Chong
    (c) Min Chuah (d) Adil Rahman

72. Which state government has recently launched a health insurance scheme for journalists?

    (a) Punjab
    (b) Maharashtra
    (c) Madhya Pradesh
    (d) Odisha

73. What is the name of the virtual assistant launched by SIDBI on its foundation day?

    (a) Pragati   (b) Samridhi
    (c) Unnati   (d) Vriddhi

74. Minister of State for Power, RK Singh, laid the foundation stone of the 60 MW Naitwar Mori Hydro Electric Project (NMHEP) in_____.

    (a) Himachal Pradesh
    (b) Jammu & Kashmir
    (c) Uttarakhand
    (d) Sikkim

75. What is the name of the 'new organ' discovered by researchers recently?

    (a) Gallarium
    (b) Photophore
    (c) Interstitium
    (d) Irisin

76. Which state's Chief Minister has announced raising the retirement age of State government

employees from 60 years to 62 years?

(a) West Bengal

(b) Telangana

(c) Madhya Pradesh

(d) Rajasthan

77. Which space agency has announced to launch 'Gravity Recovery and Climate Experiment FollowOn' (GRACE-FO)?

(a) ISRO   (b) CNSA

(c) NASA   (d) ESA

78. Kotak Mahindra Bank has launched India's first artificial intelligence-powered voicebot in the banking sector, named ________.

(a) Cara   (b) Tara

(c) Nell   (d) Keya

79. Who has won the men's singles title in the Miami Open, held in Florida, USA?

(a) Grigor Dimitrov

(b) Alexander Zverev

(c) John Isner

(d) Bob Bryan

80. Which Indian player with his 43rd win has become the most successful doubles player in the history of Davis Cup?

(a) Rohan Bopanna

(b) Leander Paes

(c) Ramkumar Ramanathan

(d) Mahesh Bhupathi

81. Which airline has launched operations from Delhi to Pathankot under the Ude Desh ka Aam Naagrik (UDAN) scheme?

(a) Turbo Megha

(b) Alliance Air

(c) Air Deccan

(d) SpiceJet

82. What was the theme of 8th Theatre Olympics which concluded in Mumbai?

(a) Together in Joy

(b) Flag of Friendship

(c) March for Peace

(d) Celebration of Unity

83. In a first, which state government is going to launch a 'community radio' to connect with the farming community?

(a) Maharashtra

(b) Haryana

(c) Madhya Pradesh

(d) Kerala

84. Ministry of Tribal Affairs has approved establishment of the first "Van Dhan Vikas Kendra" on the pilot basis in ________.

(a) Jharkhand (b) Chhattisgarh

(c) Bihar   (d) Odisha

85. India has overtaken which country to become the world's second largest producer of crude steel?

(a) Vietnam

(b) USA

(c) Philippines

(d) Japan

86. The Transport department of which state has received the highest award 'Skoch Platinum Award' of Skoch Group for the year 2017?
    (a) Madhya Pradesh
    (b) Andhra Pradesh
    (c) Karnataka
    (d) Goa

87. Who has become the most expensive wrestler in the history of Pro Wrestling League after being acquired by Delhi Sultans for Rs 55 lakh?
    (a) Geeta Phogat
    (b) Sakshi Malik
    (c) Vinesh Phogat
    (d) Sushil Kumar

88. Who led the Indian Air Force team which has successfully completed 'Mission Seven Summits' by scaling Mt Vinson in Antarctica recently?
    (a) VK Gohil (b) RC Tripathi
    (c) L Punia   (d) M Ranade

89. Which state has become the first in India to offer its residents email ids in Hindi?
    (a) Uttar Pradesh
    (b) Haryana
    (c) Rajasthan
    (d) Madhya Pradesh

90. Which state government has developed a mobile application, named 'Urban Genie', to help citizens in urban areas find trained and certified technicians and workers?
    (a) Karnataka
    (b) Madhya Pradesh
    (c) Telangana
    (d) Rajasthan

91. How much amount of loan has been sanctioned by World Bank to India for skill development programme SANKALP?
    (a) $125 million
    (b) $300 million
    (c) $250 million
    (d) $100 million

92. The first-ever Electronic Manufacturing Cluster (EM (c) in India is going to come up in___.
    (a) Andhra Pradesh
    (b) Gujarat
    (c) Maharashtra
    (d) Odisha

93. Who has become the first Indian to win gold at the World Para Swimming Championship, which was held in Mexico?
    (a) Ashish Kumar
    (b) Ayush Uppal
    (c) Kanchanmala Pande
    (d) Prasanth Panda

94. In a first, which state has launched a 'Food Safety on Wheel' mobile laboratory?
    (a) Andhra Pradesh
    (b) Rajasthan
    (c) Punjab
    (d) Goa

95. Prime Minister Narendra Modi has inaugurated the B R Ambedkar International Centre in ___.

    (a) Bhopal

    (b) Lucknow

    (c) New Delhi

    (d) Pune

96. Who has been chosen for 2017 Vyas Samman for her novel "Dukkham Sukkham"?

    (a) Dhanya Bhaumik

    (b) Renu Tripathy

    (c) Mamta Kalia

    (d) Padmini Awasthi

97. President Ram Nath Kovind recently inaugurated the Naval Maritime Aircraft Museum in___.

    (a) Coimbatore

    (b) Visakhapatnam

    (c) Trichy

    (d) Mangalore

98. Which of the following is going to deploy drone cameras (UAV/NETR (a) to monitor projects and activities of relief and rescue operations?

    (a) NHAI   (b) BRO

    (c) Railways   (d) NDRF

99. Union Cabinet has fixed the term of the chairman and members of the board of National Trust at ______.

    (a) 6 years   (b) 3 years

    (c) 5 years   (d) 4 years

100. What is the name of India's fastest and first "multipetaflops" supercomputer, recently inaugurated by Minister of S&T Dr. Harsh Vardhan?

    (a) Pratyush   (b) Ravi

    (c) Surya   (d) Aditya

101. HD Kumaraswamy sworn in as the ____ CM of Karnataka.

    (a) 23rd   (b) 22nd

    (c) 21st   (d) 24th

102. Which state is on high alert due to a deadly Nipah viral infection

    (a) Maharashtra

    (b) Uttar Pradesh

    (c) Arunachal Pradesh

    (d) Kerala

103. US retailer Walmart acquired ____ stake in Indian e-commerce Flipkart.

    (a) 77   (b) 87

    (c) 67   (d) 97

104. What is the current repo rate in the second bi-monthly monetary policy review of RBI for FY19?

    (a) 6.25%   (b) 6.50%

    (c) 6.00%   (d) 6.75%

105. Narayan Prasad Singh, who passed away recently, was the renowned lyricist of which state?

    (a) Jharkhand

    (b) Bihar

    (c) West Bengal

    (d) Odisha

106. Who has been appointed a new Deputy Governor of the Reserve Bank of India (RBI)?

    (a) B. Shriram

    (b) M.K Jain

    (c) Kishor Piraji Kharat

    (d) Basant Seth

107. The World Bank has approved how much amount for Atal Bhujal

Yojana (ABHY) of Government of India (GoI)?

(a) ₹ 8000 crore

(b) ₹ 5000 crore

(c) ₹ 7000 crore

(d) ₹ 6000 crore

108. Which country hosted the 2018 IBSA Foreign Ministers' Meeting?

(a) India

(b) Brazil

(c) South Africa

(d) Argentina

109. Who has been appointed as the new Prime Minister of Jordan?

(a) Kamel Mahadin

(b) Omar Razzaz

(c) Abdullah Ensour

(d) Faisal Al-Fayez

110. Which union ministry has launched 'Krishi Kalyan Abhiyaan' to help farmers in raising their income?

(a) Ministry of Rural Development

(b) Ministry of Agriculture and farmers welfare

(c) Ministry of Panchayati Raj

(d) Ministry of Food Processing Industries

111. Which country is the global host nation for the 43rd edition of World Environment Day (WED -2018) event?

(a) Belgium

(b) Norway

(c) South Korea

(d) India

112. Who has been appointed as the new chairperson of British Academy of Film and Television Arts (BAFTA)?

(a) Pippa Harris

(b) Jane Lush

(c) Caro Newling

(d) Sam Mendes

113. Which country is hosting the 2018 BRICS Foreign Ministers' meeting?

(a) Brazil   (b) South Africa

(c) India   (d) China

114. Who is the newly elected President of Egypt?

(a) Sami Anan

(b) Shadi Ghazali Harb

(c) Sherif Ismail

(d) Abdel Fattah al-Sisi

115. Which state government has launched the scheme "Gopabandhu Sambadika Swasthya Bima Yojana" for journalists?

(a) Punjab   (b) Odisha

(c) Jharkhand (d) Assam

116. Kendrick Lamar has been honoured with the 2018 Pulitzer Prize for music. He belongs to which country?

(a) South Africa

(b) United States

(c) Russia

(d) Egypt

117. Who of the following has been conferred with the 'Santokbaa Humanitarian' award 2018?

(a) Dalai Lama and Sudha Murthy

(b) Narayan Desai and Gautam Navlakha

(c) Kailash Satyarthi and A S Kiran Kumar

(d) Parvez Imroz and Akshay Kumar

118. What is the theme of the 2018 World Milk Day (WMD) in India?

(a) Drink Move Be Strong

(b) Milk: A Healthy Drink

(c) Natural Drink for Health

(d) Be Strong Be Healthy

119. The first biannual Indian Air Force Commanders' Conference 2018 was held in which city?

(a) Pune

(b) Guwahati

(c) New Delhi

(d) Mumbai

120. Which union ministry has launched an online Analytical tool to monitor foreign contributions by various organisations under FCRA?

(a) Ministry of Finance

(b) Ministry of Home Affairs

(c) Ministry of External Affairs

(d) Ministry of Corporate Affairs

121. Which state government has recently declared official symbols for the state?

(a) Telangana (b) Mizoram

(c) Tripura

(d) Andhra Pradesh

122. What is the theme of the 2018 World No Tobacco Day (WNTD)?

(a) Get Ready for Plain Packaging

(b) Tobacco and Heart Disease

(c) Tobacco - a threat to development

(d) Stop Illicit Trade of Tobacco Products

123. Patanjali has tied up with which telecom company to launch Swadeshi Samriddhi SIM cards?

(a) BSNL

(b) Reliance Jio

(c) Vodafone

(d) Airtel

124. Who has been appointed as the new Deputy National Security Advisor (NSA)?

(a) Geeta Shrivastav

(b) Manoj Malhotra

(c) Pankaj Saran

(d) Nikunj Khanna

125. Which country will become the first Latin American 'Gobal Partner' of North Atlantic Treaty Organization (NATO)?

(a) Argentina (b) Brazil

(c) Peru (d) Colombia

126. Who has won the International Cricketer of the Year at the CEAT Cricket Ratings awards?

(a) Trent Boult

(b) Shikhar Dhawan

(c) Virat Kohli

(d) Rashid Khan

127. Who has won the Formula 1 Monaco Grand Prix 2018?

(a) Lewis Hamilton

(b) Sebastian Vettel

(c) Sebastian Vettel

(d) Daniel Ricciardo

128. The Talakona waterfall is located in which state?

(a) Himachal Pradesh

(b) Andhra Pradesh

(c) Kerala

(d) Assam

129. Who has been appointed as the new Governor of Odisha?

(a) Satya Pal Malik

(b) Kummanam Rajasekharan

(c) Nirbhay Sharma

(d) Ganeshi Lal

130. The 9th edition of 'Rashtriya Sanskriti Mahotsav' has started in which state?

(a) Karnataka

(b) Gujarat

(c) Uttarakhand

(d) Madhya Pradesh

131. The Wanakbori Thermal Power Station (WTPS) is located on the bank of which river in Gujarat?

(a) Narmada River

(b) Luni River

(c) Sabarmati River

(d) Mahi River

132. Which city is hosting the ASEAN India Film Festival 2018?

(a) Pune   (b) New Delhi

(c) Kochi   (d) Mumbai

133. Name the Tiger Reserve in Indian Wildlife Sanctuary has highest number of clouded leopards in South East Asia.

(a) Rajaji Tiger Reserve, Uttarakhand

(b) Amrabad Tiger Reserve, Telangana

(c) Sunderbans Tiger Reserve, West Bengal

(d) Dampa Tiger Reserve , Mizoram

134. IBBI has amended the rules for information utilities. Expand IBBI.

(a) Insolvency and Bankruptcy Board

(b) Inconsistency and Bankruptcy Board

(c) Improvement and Bankruptcy Board

(d) Irregularity and Bankruptcy Board

135. Name the Adobe investment on integration of Aadhaar-based authentication in its e-signature solution.

(a) "Adobe e- Sign"

(b) "Adobe Sign"

(c) "Adobe e-solution"

(d) "Adobe Aadhar e-sign"

136. World Animal Day is observed on ______________ every year.

(a) 1st Oct.   (b) 2nd Oct.

(c) 3rd Oct.   (d) 4th Oct.

137. Ken Youngstein's book ,'The Singing Tree' launched to spread awareness on preventing child __________.

(a) Labour   (b) Cancer

(c) Begger   (d) Blindness

138. Name the state government has launched 'Mukhyamantri Samoohik Vivaah Yojana'.

(a) Madhya Pradesh

(b) Rajasthan

(c) Haryana

(d) Uttar Pradesh

139. For whom the Karnataka government launched 'Mathru Purna' scheme?

(a) Children

(b) New born babies

(c) old aged persons

(d) Pregnant Women

140. Where was the Mahatma Gandhi's statue unveiled?

(a) Northern Ireland

(b) Scotland

(c) Wales

(d) California

141. Which temple was awarded the best 'Swachh Iconic Place' (Cleanest Iconic Place) in India?

(a) Brihadeeswara temple , Tamilnadu

(b) Amarnath Temple, Jammu and Kashmir

(c) Khajuraho Temple, Tamilnadu, Kerala

(d) Meenakshi Sundareswarar Temple, Tamilnadu

142. The Melkote Temple Wildlife Sanctuary (MTWS) is located in which state?

(a) Karnataka (b) Chhattisgarh

(c) Kerala   (d) Odisha

143. Which committee has drafted the 3rd National Wildlife Action Plan (NWAP) for 2017-2031?

(a) Krishna Murthy committee

(b) JC Kala committee

(c) Prabhakar Reddy committee

(d) K C Patan committee

144. Which bank has launched 'Project Nishchay' to improve financial performance?

(a) PNB

(b) SBI

(c) ICICI Bank

(d) IDBI Bank

145. Which state government has launched 'Solar Briefcase' to provide electricity in remote areas?

(a) Jharkhand

(b) Uttarakhand

(c) Uttar Pradesh

(d) Madhya Pradesh

146. The Aralam Wildlife Sanctuary (AWS) is located in which state?

(a) Odisha   (b) Punjab

(c) Kerala   (d) Manipur

147. Which state has become the India's first state to incorporate skill development programme in higher education?
    (a) Himachal Pradesh
    (b) Chattisgarh
    (c) Punjab
    (d) Rajasthan

148. Which country becomes smallest nation ever to enter FIFA World Cup ?
    (a) India
    (b) Iceland
    (c) Bulgaria
    (d) Ethiopia

149. The Pratham-Shyok bridge is located in _________ .
    (a) Jammu and Kashmir
    (b) Himachal Pradesh
    (c) Punjab
    (d) Sikkim

150. The International Dussehra festival has started in which state of India?
    (a) Karnataka
    (b) Rajasthan
    (c) Uttarakhand
    (d) Himachal Pradesh

151. The government has announced the issue of Sovereign Gold Bonds 2017-18 series-III. As per the scheme a discount of ₹ _____ would be exclusively offered to online/ digital investors.
    (a) 60
    (b) 70
    (c) 80
    (d) 50

152. The RBI opened its branch in _____, Uttarakhand.
    (a) Dehradun
    (b) Haridwar
    (c) Roorkee
    (d) Kashipur

153. The Central government sanctioned a Cash Credit Limit (CCL) of ₹ 28,262.84 crore for procurement of paddy for_____ in the Kharif marketing season 2017-18.
    (a) Haryana
    (b) Rajasthan
    (c) Maharashtra
    (d) Punjab

154. The Ratapani Tiger Reserve (RTS) is located in which state?
    (a) Madhya Pradesh
    (b) Sikkim
    (c) Rajasthan
    (d) Karnataka

155. The National Police Commemoration Day (NPCD) is observed on which date in India?
    (a) October 21
    (b) October 22
    (c) October 20
    (d) October 23

156. Which of the following commodity exchange has launched India's first commodity options in gold?
    (a) Indian Commodity Exchange Limited (ICEX)
    (b) National Spot Exchange Limited (NSEL)
    (c) Multi-Commodity Exchange of India Ltd (MCX)
    (d) National Commodity & Derivatives Exchange Limited (NCDEX)

157. The Chhilchhila Wildlife Sanctuary (CWS) is located in which state?

(a) Sikkim   (b) Mizoram

(c) Haryana   (d) Nagaland

158. The Karera Wildlife Sanctuary (KWS) is located in which state?

(a) Madhya Pradesh

(b) Tamil Nadu

(c) Uttar Pradesh

(d) Punjab

159. Who is the author of the book "Beyond the Dream Girl"?

(a) Bhavna Somaiya

(b) Ram Kamal Mukherjee

(c) Ramesh Sippy

(d) Bala Krishna

160. According to a save the children "End of Childhood index 2018", what is the raking of India among 175 countries?

(a) 145th   (b) 106th

(c) 113th   (d) 135th

161. Read the following statements about International Solar Alliance (ISA).

I.   The Alliance is jointly led by India, France and USA.

II. The main aim of the ISA is to make available solar energy at an affordable price.

Choose the correct option.

(a) I only   (b) II only

(c) Both I and II (d) None of the above

162. Read the following statements about Olympic Winter Games, 2018?

I.   It was held in Pyeongchang.

II. Norway and Canada emerged as the top two countries in the Medal tally.

III. Next Olympic Games will be held in Shanghai.

Choose the incorrect statements.

(a) I and II   (b) II and III

(c) I and III   (d) None of the above

163. Read the following statements about Vijay Hazare Trophy and answer the following

I.   It is organised as limited over domestic cricket tournament.

II. Karnataka is the current winner of Vijay Hazare Trophy.

Choose the correct option

(a) I only

(b) II only

(c) Both I and II

(d) None of the above

164. In which of the following states the growth rate was highest in the country during 2016-17 as per state economic survey?

(a) Punjab

(b) Himachal Pradesh

(c) Bihar

(d) Gujarat

165. Ministry of Textiles planned a National Sizing Survey to develop a comprehensive size chart for ready-to-wear industry based on the body measurements of the Indian population under which name ?

(a) bodyINDIA

(b) chartINDIA

(c) INDIAmeasure

(d) INDIAsize

166. What is the colour of Bal Aadhaar Card?

(a) Red   (b) Blue

(c) Pink   (d) Orange

167. Which is the nodal agency to issue Aadhar Card?

(a) Unilateral Identification Authority of India

(b) Unified Identification Authority of India

(c) United Identification Authority of India

(d) Unique Identification Authority of India

168. Under which of the following does Unique Identification Authority of India function?

(a) National Statistical Commission

(b) National Human Rights Commission of India

(c) Planning Commission of India

(d) Election Commission of India

169. Civil Aviation Minister inaugurated the first-of-its-kind Aviation Multi Skill Development Centre in which city?

(a) Chandigarh

(b) Chennai

(c) Kolkata

(d) Bengaluru

170. Consider the following statements about Petro?

I. It is a Crypto Currency launched by Venezuela.

II. It is a physical Currency accepted in all American Countries.

Which of the statements given above is/are correct?

(a) I Only

(b) II Only

(c) Both I and II

(d) Neither I nor II

171. Gandhi Nagar railway station was recently in news. Consider the following statements about this station?

I. Gandhi Nagar railway station located at the capital of Gujarat becomes 1st fully women operated Station in the country.

II. Gandhi Nagar Railway Station in Jaipur, Rajasthan becomes India's first non-suburban station fully operated 24x7 by women staff.

Which of the statements given above is/are correct?

(a) I Only

(b) II Only

(c) Both I and II

(d) Neither I nor II

172. Consider the following statements about Drypetes kalamii?

I. It is a shorter version of its close relative Drypetes ellisii.

II. Drypetes kalamii is a close relative of a medicinal plant known in Sanskrit as Putrajivah.

Which of the statements given above is/are correct?

(a) I Only

(b) II Only

(c) Both I and II

(d) Neither I nor II

173. Which Muslim Country recently has permitted its women to enlist in army?

(a) K.S.A.   (b) U.A.E.

(c) Iran   (d) Iraq

174. Which Country recently has scraped term limit for president?

(a) North Korea

(b) U.S.A.

(c) China

(d) Russia

175. What is the rank of India in global corruption perception index, 2017 released recently by Transparency International?

(a) 40   (b) 91

(c) 117   (d) 81

176. Which of the following companies has recently introduced Asia's first large scale CO2 injection technique?

(a) ONGC

(b) HPCL

(c) Reliance Industries

(d) GAIL India

177. Consider the following statements about CO2 injection technique?

I. It reduces its viscosity and makes it easier to displace oil from the rock pores.

II. Its purpose is to recover extra 20 million barrels of crude oil

under enhanced oil recovery (EOR) programme.

Which of the statements given above is/are correct?

(a) I Only

(b) II Only

(c) Both I and II

(d) Neither I nor II

178. What is the name of antibiotics discovered from soil recently?

(a) Neo-Fradin

(b) Malacidins

(c) Kanamycin

(d) Amikacin

179. Which state of India deploys robots to clean up manholes ?

(a) Kerela   (b) Tamil

(c) Karnataka (d) Assam

180. Consider the following statements about 'Bandicoot'?

I. It is a name of Robot to clean sewer holes.

II. It is the Robot which has been deployed in army.

Which of the statements given above is/are correct?

(a) I Only

(b) II Only

(c) Both I and II

(d) Neither I nor II

181. Consider the following statements about 'Asmita Yojana?'

I. It is launched to provide affordable sanitary pads to school girls.

II. Maharastra Govt. has launched this Yojana.

Which of the statements given above is/are correct?

(a) I Only

(b) II Only

(c) Both I and II

(d) Neither I nor II

182. Consider the following statements about 'Modicare Scheme?'

I.   It is the dubbed name of Ayushman Bharat Scheme.

II. Its purpose is to provide health insurance to poor and vulnerable households.

Which of the statements given above is/are correct?

(a) I Only

(b) II Only

(c) Both I and II

(d) Neither I nor II

183. Which state has become the first state to opt out of the National Health Protection Scheme (NHPS) -"Modi Care"?

(a) Karnataka (b) West Bengal

(c) Punjab   (d) Kerela

184. Which of the following states are involved in the dispute of water share of river Cauvery?

(a) Karnataka & Tamilnadu

(b) Karnataka & Maharashtra

(c) Tamilnadu & Maharashtra

(d) Tamilnadu & Andhra Pradesh

185. Which committee has been constituted by Union Government to expedite capital acquisition for Armed Forces modernization?

(a) Vinay   Sheel   Oberoi committee

(b) Rabindra Thapa committee

(c) Vijayan Kumar committee

(d) Narendra Singh committee

186. Which country has become the world's first country to repeal same-sex marriage?

(a) Greece

(b) Portugal

(c) South Africa

(d) Bermuda

187. Which country recently has withdrawn itself from UN refugee programme?

(a) Tanzania   (b) USA

(c) Myanmar (d) India

188. Consider the following statements about Vinay Sheel Oberoi Committee?

I.   This committee is constituted to expedite capital acquisition for armed forces.

II. The committee will have tenure until end of this year.

Which of the statements given above is/are correct?

(a) I Only

(b) II Only

(c) Both I and II

(d) Neither I nor II

189. Scientists from which country/ countries recently grew the human eggs in laboratory.

(a) Britain

(b) U.S.

(c) (a) & (b) both are correct

(d) None of the above are correct

190. NHAI has launched ranking system for toll plazas with an aim to

(a) address issues that affect highway users.

    (b) create a competitive atmosphere and provide best services to highway users.

    (c) (a) & (b) both are correct

    (d) None of the above are correct

191. Consider the following statements about 'Indo-HCM'?

    I. It is High Way Capacity Manual.

    II. It has been developed by CSIR & CRRI.

    Which of the statements given above is/are correct?

    (a) I Only

    (b) II Only

    (c) Both I and II

    (d) Neither I nor II

192. Read the following statements about Bhasa Samman.

    I. Bhasa Samman is awarded to encourage writers and scholars in languages not formally recognised by the Akademi.

    II. Recently Magadhi (Magahi) Author Shesh Anand Madhukar was honoured with the award.

    III. Bhojpuri writer Dharikshan Mishra is one of the previous awardee.

    Choose the correct option.

    (a) I and II   (b) II and III

    (c) I and III   (d) All of the above

193. Read the following statements about U-19 Cricket World Cup?

    I. Recently it was held in Australia.

    II. India defeated Australia in the final.

    III. Manjot Kalra was declared Man of the Tournament.

    Choose the incorrect statements.

    (a) I and II   (b) II and III

    (c) I and III   (d) All of the above

194. Read the following statements about World Cancer Day and answer the following

    I. It is observed across the globe on 4th February

    II. The theme for this year is "We will. I will".

    Choose the correct option.

    (a) I only   (b) II only

    (c) Both I and II   (d) None of the above

195. Who is the winner of National Singles Table Tennis title in Men's Category, 2018?

    (a) Kamlesh Mehta

    (b) A. Sharath Kamal

    (c) Soumyajit Ghosh

    (d) Anthony Amalraj

196. Who is the author of book "Exam Warriors"?

    (a) Ram Nath Kovind

    (b) Narendra Modi

    (c) Shashi Tharoor

    (d) Sushma Swaraj

197. Which city has launched India's first helitaxi service?

    (a) Bengaluru   (b) Hyderabad

    (c) Mumbai   (d) Ahmadabad

198. A multilingual toll free number launched by Govt. for highways

users to report an accident or any emergency conditions is

(a) 1092   (b) 1033

(c) 1035   (d) 1039

199. Which aviation company has launched an app for Helitaxi service in Bengaluru?

(a) Air Charter Services Pvt Ltd

(b) Thumby Aviation Pvt Ltd

(c) Haveus Aerospace

(d) Taneja Aerospace

200. Consider the following statements about Sukhad Yatra App?

I. It is a mobile app for the drivers and travellers of highways in India.

II. Sukhad Yatra App is developed by the National Highway Authority of India (NHAI).

Which of the statements given above is/are correct?

(a) I Only

(b) II Only

(c) Both I and II

(d) Neither I nor II

ANSWERS KEY

No.	Ans	No.	Ans	No.	Ans	No.	Ans	No.	Ans	No.	Ans	No.	Ans
1	(c)	31	(c)	61	(a)	91	(c)	121	(d)	151	(d)	181	(c)
2	(d)	32	(b)	62	(b)	92	(a)	122	(b)	152	(a)	182	(c)
3	(d)	33	(d)	63	(a)	93	(c)	123	(a)	153	(d)	183	(b)
4	(c)	34	(d)	64	(d)	94	(d)	124	(c)	154	(a)	184	(a)
5	(c)	35	(d)	65	(b)	95	(c)	125	(d)	155	(a)	185	(a)
6	(d)	36	(a)	66	(b)	96	(c)	126	(c)	156	(c)	186	(d)
7	(a)	37	(b)	67	(c)	97	(b)	127	(d)	157	(c)	187	(a)
8	(b)	38	(d)	68	(b)	98	(c)	128	(b)	158	(a)	188	(a)
9	(a)	39	(a)	69	(a)	99	(b)	129	(d)	159	(b)	189	(c)
10	(c)	40	(b)	70	(b)	100	(a)	130	(c)	160	(d)	190	(c)
11	(b)	41	(d)	71	(a)	101	(a)	131	(d)	161.	(b)	191	(c)
12	(c)	42	(a)	72	(d)	102	(d)	132	(b)	162.	(b)	192	(d)
13	(b)	43	(b)	73	(b)	103	(a)	133	(d)	163.	(c)	193	(c)
14	(b)	44	(a)	74	(c)	104	(a)	134	(a)	164.	(c)	194	(a)
15	(a)	45	(b)	75	(c)	105	(d)	135	(b)	165	(d)	195	(b)
16	(d)	46	(c)	76	(c)	106	(b)	136	(d)	166	(b)	196	(b)
17	(c)	47	(a)	77	(c)	107	(d)	137	(d)	167	(d)	197	(a)
18	(a)	48	(b)	78	(d)	108	(c)	138	(d)	168	(c)	198	(b)
19	(a)	49	(c)	79	(c)	109	(b)	139	(d)	169	(a)	199	(b)
20	(d)	50	(d)	80	(b)	110	(b)	140	(c)	170	(a)	200	(c)
21	(b	51	(d)	81	(b)	111	(d)	141	(d)	171	(b)		
22	(b)	52	(a)	82	(b)	112	(a)	142	(a)	172	(c)		
23	(c)	53	(d)	83	(d)	113	(b)	143	(b)	173	(a)		
24	(b	54	(d)	84	(b)	114	(d)	144	(d)	174	(c)		
25	(c)	55	(d)	85	(d)	115	(b)	145	(b)	175	(d)		
26	(b)	56	(a)	86	(a)	116	(b)	146	(c)	176	(a)		
27	(a)	57	(c)	87	(d)	117	(c)	147	(d)	177	(c)		
28	(a)	58	(d)	88	(b)	118	(a)	148	(a)	178	(b)		
29	(d)	59	(a)	89	(c)	119	(c)	149	(a)	179	(a)		
30	(d)	60	(a)	90	(c)	120	(b)	150	(d)	180	(a)		

WHAT ARE SOVEREIGN GOLD BONDS (SGBS)?

Sovereign Gold Bonds are government securities denominated in grams of gold issued by the Reserve Bank of India on behalf of the Government of India. They offer the same benefits as of physical gold. The value of gold bond increases with the increase in the market rate of gold. The aim of this scheme is to reduce the demand for physical gold thereby keeping a tab on imports of gold in India and utilising resources effectively. These Bonds are sold through banks, Stock Holding Corporation of India Limited (SHCIL), designated post offices and recognised stock exchange viz. National Stock Exchange and Bombay Stock Exchange. These Bonds are interest-bearing instruments and pay interest to the buyer. These are also available in the digital and Demat form and can be used as collateral for loans. **The tenor of the Bond will be for a period of 8 years with exit option in 5th, 6th and 7th year, to be exercised on the interest payment dates.**

WHAT IS FIAT DIGITAL CURRENCY?

Fiat digital currency is the digital form of flat money which is a currency established as money by government regulation or law. Fiat digital currency is part of the base money supply, together with other forms of the currency. This blockchain technology based currency will be issued by central bank. They will be legal tender as compared to virtual currencies that raise concerns of consumer protection, market integrity and money laundering, among others. Blockchain technology behind it has potential benefit for financial inclusion and enhancing efficiency of financial system. Digital fiat currency is secure, transparent, and efficient. The digital payment instrument issued by the Central Bank infuses trust in all digital transactions. Digital fiat currency is currently being studied and tested by governments and central banks in order to realize the many positive implications it contributes to financial inclusion, economic growth, technology innovation and increased transaction efficiencies.

WHAT IS INTRA-STATE E-WAY BILL?

E-way Bill is the short form of Electronic Way Bill. It is a unique document/bill, which is electronically generated for the specific consignment/movement of goods from one place to another, either inter-state or intra-state and of value more than INR 50,000, required under the current GST regime. This has been mandated by the government in terms of Section 68 of the Goods and Services Tax (GST) Act. An E-Way bill is generated through the GST Common Portal for e-Way bill system by registered users or transporters who cause movement of goods of consignment. The implementation of E-way bill kicked in from 15th April 2018 in a phased manner wherein all the states are divided into 4 lots to execute the phased rollout. The e-Way Bill has replaced the Way Bill, which was a physical document and existed during the VAT regime for the movement of goods.

WHAT IS NIPAH VIRUS?

Nipah virus (NiV) infection is a newly emerging zoonosis that causes severe disease in both animals and humans. The southern Indian state of Kerala has been put on "all-time alert" after at least 17 people infected with Nipah virus died in the past weeks. The virus can be transferred through infected bats, pigs or humans who have been infected. Symptoms from infection vary from none to fever, cough, headache, shortness of breath, and confusion. This may worsen into a coma over a day or two. The Nipah virus is a type of RNA virus in the genus Henipavirus. It can both spread between people and from other animals to people. Spread typically requires direct contact with an infected source. The virus normally circulates among specific types of fruit bats. Till now, there is no vaccine for either humans or animals. The primary treatment for human cases is intensive supportive care.

WHAT IS TRACHOMA?

Trachoma is a contagious bacterial infection which affects the conjunctival covering of the eye, the cornea, and the eyelids. It is the leading infectious cause of blindness in the world. Infection spreads from person to person, particularly from child to child and from child to mother to child. The disease thrives especially in crowded living conditions where there are shortages of water, inadequate sanitation and where numerous eye-seeking flies are present. The bacteria that cause the disease can be spread by both direct and indirect contact with an affected person's eyes or nose. The affected individual develops redness and irritation of the eyes with tearing, which can progress through repeated new infection to scaring and vision loss. Children spread the disease more often than adults. Globally, about 80 million people have an active infection. Efforts to prevent the disease include improving access to clean water and treatment with antibiotics to decrease the number of people infected with the bacterium.

WHAT IS 2-STATE SOLUTION?

The two-state solution refers to the idea that the most practical solution to the Palestinian-Israeli conflict is one that divides the land historically called Palestine between a Jewish and a Palestinian Arab state. Since Israelis and Palestinians want to run their countries differently i.e. Israelis want a Jewish state, and Palestinians want a Palestinian one and neither side can get what it wants in a joined state, the only possible solution that satisfies everyone involves separating Palestinians and Israelis. The two-state solution envisages an independent State of Palestine alongside the State of Israel, west of the Jordan River. The framework of the solution is set out in UN resolutions on the "Peaceful settlement of the question of Palestine". Such an arrangement could effectively end the state of war that has existed between Israel and its Arab neighbours since Israel's establishment and bring a degree of stability in the region.

WHAT IS BS-VI FUEL?

BS which stands for Bharat Stage signifies the emission regulation standards set by the central government to keep a check on the pollutant levels emitted by vehicles that use combustion engines. The BS norms are based on European emission norms that are followed largely by all automakers across the globe. BS-VI is the latest emission norms adopted by India to help bring down the pollution emitted from the vehicles. Indian cities like New Delhi, Mumbai and Bangaluru etc. are among the top polluted cities of the world where the air quality index has degraded to extreme condition. The high level of smog and fog has caused the government to take preventive measures and therefore, the Indian government has recently announced that India would skip BS-V norms altogether and adopt BS-VI norms by 2020. The BS-VI fuel has been made available in the NCR (National Capital Region) from April 1, 2018.

INDIA'S E-WASTE GENERATION

Electronic waste or e-waste is a term for electronic products that have become unwanted, non-working or obsolete, and have essentially reached the end of their useful life. Despite the government's emphasis on Swachh Bharat Abhiyaan and Smart Cities project, India continues to be generating highest e-waste vis-à-vis China, USA, Japan and Germany. In India, the electronic waste management assumes greater significance not only due to the generation of our own waste but also dumping of e-waste particularly computer waste from the developed countries. With extensively using computers and electronic equipment's and people dumping old electronic goods for new ones, the amount of E-Waste generated has been steadily increasing. With India's e-waste generation estimated to reach 52 lakh tonnes in 2020, the future doesn't look too bright, unless stringent recycling procedures are followed. India needs to bring the unorganised sector (shops and industries which engage contract labourers and are dealers of electronic equipment) under proper supervision and monitoring, so that majority of the e-waste generated could be recycled properly.

EXAM UPDATES

Name of the Exam	Important Dates
RBI Grade B 2018	Preliminary Exam: 16th August 2018 Mains Exam (General): 7th September 2018 (Tentative)
IBPS RRB	Preliminary Examination: Officer Scale-I & Office Assistants 11th, 12th, 18th, 19th, 25th August Mains Exam office Scale-I: 30th September 2018 Mains Exam Office Assistant: 7th October 2018
NIACL	Preliminary Exam : 8th, 9th September 2018 (Tentative) Mains Exam : 6th October 2018 (Tentative)
SBI PO	Preliminary Examination: 1st, 7th & 8th July 2018 Main Examination: 4th August 2018
IBPS PO	Preliminary Examination: 13th, 14th, 20th & 21th October 2018 Main Examination: 18th November 2018
IBPS Clerk	Preliminary Examination: 8th, 9th, 15th & 16th December 2018 Main Examination: 20th January 2019
IBPS Specialist Officer	Preliminary Examination: 29th, 30th, December 2018 Main Examination: 27th January 2019
Joint Entrance Examination (JEE) Main	6th – 20th January 2019
JEE Advanced	3rd week of May 2019
VIT University Engineering Entrance Exam (VITEEE)	1st & 2nd week of April 2019

www.ingramcontent.com/pod-product-compliance
Lightning Source LLC
LaVergne TN
LVHW051139200726
843495LV00022B/1730